T3-BWG-219

DAILY LIFE
IN LATER LIFE

SOME OTHER VOLUMES IN THE
SAGE FOCUS EDITIONS

DAILY LIFE IN LATER LIFE

Comparative Perspectives

Edited by
Karen Altergott

SAGE PUBLICATIONS
The Publishers of Professional Social Science
Newbury Park   Beverly Hills   London   New Delhi

Copyright © 1988 by Sage Publications, Inc.

All rights reserved. No part of this book may be reproduced or utilized in any form or by any means, electronic or mechanical, including photocopying, recording, or by any information storage and retrieval system, without permission in writing from the publisher.

For information address:

SAGE Publications, Inc.
2111 West Hillcrest Drive
Newbury Park, California 91320

SAGE Publications Inc.
275 South Beverly Drive
Beverly Hills
California 90212

SAGE Publications Ltd.
28 Banner Street
London EC1Y 8QE
England

SAGE PUBLICATIONS India Pvt. Ltd.
M-32 Market
Greater Kailash I
New Delhi 110 048 India

Printed in the United States of America

Library of Congress Cataloging-in-Publication Data

Altergott, Karen.
    Daily life in later life.

    (Sage focus editions ; v. 99)
    Bibliography: p.
    1. Aged—Time management—Cross-cultural studies.
2. Aging—Social aspects—Cross-cultural aspects.
3. Aged—Government policy—Cross-cultural studies.
I. Title.
HQ1061.A546   1988   305.2′6   88-3245
ISBN 0-8039-2897-1
ISBN 0-8039-2898-X (pbk.)

FIRST PRINTING 1988

Contents

To Reuben Hill,

Virginia C. Little,

and

Donald O. Cowgill

Preface

The path traveled by comparative researchers is narrow and winding, not well marked, and leads us through the woods wherein confusion reigns. Comparativists are those who see in this confusion both a potential for understanding and a challenge to understanding that is greater than working more settled and familiar territories. This is really a brief history of a small group of social gerontologists from seven different countries who are committed to walking together on the long, arduous route toward greater understanding of social aging through cross-national, comparative, and cooperative inquiry. We didn't run out of energy or experience any of the other fates of explorers who neither reach their goal nor return home. This book is one product of our ongoing collaboration across national boundaries.

First, let me tell you why we packed for this particular journey and how we came to be fellow travelers.

A serious commitment to cross-national inquiry is essential to furthering our knowledge in social gerontology. Existing knowledge shows clearly that large-scale societal and cultural conditions influence the course of an individual's life. While sociologists from Mannheim to C. W. Mills have encouraged us to focus on this intersection of individual and societal processes, scholars in aging have moved quite far in the conceptualization and study of this intersection. Theoretical work, research findings, and writings of kindred spirits have provided social gerontologists with both encouragement and courage to take the comparative approach and, furthermore, to treat it as essential. Phenomena such as demographic aging of populations, policies of the labor force and income maintenance of the nonlabor force, cultural variance in ways of living (and therefore ways of aging), and the institutional/organizational arrangements of society are all powerful determinants, we know, of conditions of life in old age. But further work is required to understand how these societal and cultural forces influence the older individual. Even among modern industrial/post-industrial nations, a great deal of variation exists in macrosocial and microsocial aspects of aging. The challenge to be met is to understand how particular macro-conditions influence aging individuals. How has this challenge been met in gerontology?

In the past, some scholars started from their separate sides of the forest and walked toward the center, carrying their research findings and theoretical conclusions with them. They met in a temporary clearing to share their separately constructed knowledge of aging in their own nations. Our group of scholars chose to meet at the edge of the forest and we tried to walk together through the many steps of research.

The group of scholars who began working together on a comparative research plan first met when I acted as convener for a roundtable, "Daily Life in Late Life: Time Use and Social Activities," at the 1981 International Congress of Gerontology in Hamburg. This allowed about 15 scholars from eight countries to discuss (1) cross-national comparative gerontological inquiry in general and (2) study of time use or daily life in particular. Individual interests, qualms about the feasibility of a cooperative project, and models of international comparison in social science were shared. We even moved further to establish three main areas of inquiry. These areas were *activities of daily life* (e.g., market and nonmarket productivity, leisure in retirement for women and men), *personal relationships* and integration, and the *relationship between policy and personal condition*. The older person acting and interacting in society was our common focus. We had the advantage of a common research design that informed each of our research projects.

After the group's first meeting, we recognized the need for continued communication as we planned our journey. I established a newsletter and sent it to the 15 who attended the roundtable in Hamburg, and also to a wider group of scholars whose interests combined aging and daily life. A snowball strategy, with members of the original group suggesting colleagues to the newsletter editor, was very helpful. The newsletter served to recruit several more committed researchers, to stimulate general interest in our effort, and to connect members of the active core. Virginia Little was instrumental in discussing this project with her many European colleagues while I focused on discussing participation with other time-use researchers. Further meetings were planned and accomplished with varying membership at each meeting due to exigencies of

travel schedules and budgets. A meeting in Toronto during the joint
U.S./Canadian Gerontology meetings in 1981, a meeting in Mexico
City during the International Congress of Sociology in 1982, a meeting
at the ICG in New York in 1985, as well as additional editions of a
newsletter resulted in a core group of scholars who contributed chapters
to this project and a group of interested others who supported the
project.

The larger group of interested others played a very important role.
First, they sustained our belief that it is indeed possible and important to
conduct international projects. Second, they contributed intellectual as
well as emotional support simply by sharing suggestions and calling
attention to relevant work they have done or that they know of. These
interested scholars may work with us to develop new national teams that
will broaden the scope of our inquiry.

The contributions to be made by our writing and research efforts will
be judged by others. We believe that there is a contribution to be made
by the very act of cooperating across national boundaries in the social
sciences. On behalf of each author, I hope you find value in our project.

Finally, I would like to express appreciation to the many people who
made contributions to this project. First and foremost of the contributors is Virginia Little, whose presence in the research group, from its first
meeting until the last opportunity she had to meet with us, provided true
nurturance for the very idea of international cooperation in the study of
aging. She and I also prepared various proposals and applications to
gain funding for various aspects of this project. Though none of the
proposals was successful, the project succeeded, in large part due to the
constant encouragement and internationalism Virginia provided. Don
Cowgill, whose colleagueship I valued at the University of Missouri, had
agreed to write the preface to this volume. Given his outstanding
contributions to the worldwide view of aging, his preface would have
illuminated the issues as his keen intelligence was always able to do. Of
course, Reuben Hill deserves appreciation. It was his course in
comparative family and his introduction to the work of the time-budget
scholars that facilitated the first steps in the development of this project.
These three contributors are greatly appreciated and deeply missed.

Mentors to the project were many and varied. M. Powell Lawton,
Max Kaplan, Miriam Ross, and Regula Herzog stand out as people who
were always ready to share a podium, provide an insight, or help us
formulate a portion of our project. In addition to the contributors, other
colleagues either considered contributing chapters or provided intel-

lectual support for the development of this volume. And many other sociologists and gerontologists participated in the roundtables, seminars, and working groups that were organized around the basic research issue at professional meetings around the world and over the years. They too should be thanked for their interest and insight. It is hoped that the project will further the memory of those who insisted on looking at the world as a whole, encourage the scholars who would like to pursue international inquiry, and inform those interested in the daily lives of ordinary older people in the developed nations.

Finally, I would like to thank the staff members at Purdue University for producing the manuscript for this book. Robert Thayer, Becky Harshman, and Phoebe Herr have spent many hours preparing the chapters of this volume. Their patience, perfectionism, and goodwill are greatly appreciated.

—Karen Altergott

1

Daily Life in Late Life

Concepts and Methods for Inquiry

KAREN ALTERGOTT

The first purpose of this volume is to document, with accuracy and comparability, the activities and interactions of daily life for older people in a set of developed societies. *Daily life* is a central concept throughout this volume. It is in the domain of daily life, through self-organized activities ranging from self-care to production of goods for others, that older people create independence. It is in the domain of daily life that integration into public and private social worlds is achieved or isolation from others is experienced. In practice, daily life is the domain for intervention as well.

The authors of this volume expect the daily life perspective to help us understand the well-being of older people in society. Learning more about behavior patterns, the conditions that affect them, and the outcomes in terms of personal condition could help us define constructive measures for enhancing quality of life in later life. Whether loneliness, fear of public places, or inactivity is perceived as a problem, the only way to solve it is to modify daily life. Whether interdependence, integration, or productivity is seen as a social value, the only way to achieve it is in daily life.

The second purpose of this book is to discover some of the policies that produce differences in the daily lives of older citizens in developed

AUTHOR'S NOTE: Virginia Little contributed to early drafts of this chapter.

nations. Developed nations were selected for attention because it is in these nations that the "self-conscious analysis of old age" and concern "with the problems and conditions of aging" (Cowgill, in Palmore, 1980, p. 501) have progressed the furthest. The knowledge base, the availability of comparable studies, and the number of active researchers enable comparative inquiry. Conceptually, the importance of studying developed nations lies in analyzing differences in the daily lives of older people within most similar systems. The structural and demographic characteristics vary little from one nation to the next. Cultural variation is more obvious. Historical events and transformations cannot be ignored. But the greatest attention will be paid to the explicit and implicit policies that differentiate the nations considered. Policies intervene between structure, culture, and population characteristics in shaping the nature of everyday life. By examining the daily life of ordinary people in different national contexts, we can begin to draw links between policy and individual ways of living.

The issues that more highly developed nations face may be instructive for the less developed nations as well, because most of the world's older people will soon be in the less developed rather than the most developed nations. In particular, policy directions chosen by the more developed nations may or may not produce desirable life patterns. Exploring the consequences of policies can provide developing nations with an advantage in age-related policy, design, and implementation.

Concepts for Inquiry

Theories of Aging and Daily Life

What is significant about the daily lives of older people in developed societies? First, explaining how older people use their time is central to social theories of aging. Many of the theories developed in sociology of aging concern the impact of society on the aging individual. The structural component of that often discredited theory, disengagement, postulates a process of exclusion from society. To prevent the disruption of organized activities, the "system" pushes older individuals, who are more likely to die, out and away from vital functions. The resulting privatization of the individual in domestic activities, peripheral social activities, and personal relationships of little public consequence is labeled disengagement. The well-adjusted individual does more than accept this fate. He or she cooperates and furthermore feels satisfied with the results. Most authors condemn the overly simplified version of disengagement theory because of assumptions of universality and functionality (Hochschild, 1975; Maddox, 1969). But do conditions in society discourage or prevent, enhance or permit, the full participation of older citizens? How involved are older people in private and public spheres of action? We need to answer these descriptive questions in a variety of social contexts in order to provide a base for more adequate theories of society and old age.

The age stratification model builds on the common assumption that all societies have role structures and populations differentiated by age (Riley, 1976). People are allowed to or prevented from taking roles and are socialized to enter or exit from roles based on their age. Unequal access to roles and resources is an essential feature of this model. The model itself, however, provides no specific predictions about what type of society will have what type of roles open for older people. The model draws attention to the descriptive question: Within a society, what is the structure of social action and relations for people of varying ages?

Sociological models have also summarized possible sources of differences between premodern and modern societies. An adequate theory of aging must deal with variations in the social experiences of old age, because anthropological and sociological work has clearly shown that dramatic differences exist (Keith, 1982; Cowgill and Holmes, 1972; Sokolovsky, 1983; Cowgill, 1986). the most notable of the existing theories, the modernization model (Cowgill, 1974) specifies the changes in society that are likely to reduce the status of older people. Improved health and increased longevity, new technologies in the labor force, elaborated educational systems, and urbanization leave older people alive, underemployed, untrained in the latest technologies, and separated from family/community webs of relationships (Shanas et al., 1968; Havighurst et al., 1969; Palmore, 1980; Sokolovsky, 1983). Historians have argued over the salience of cultural and structural explanations for the differences (Fischer, 1977; Achenbaum, 1978; Cherry and Magnuson-Martinson, 1981), but most research on modernization and aging encompasses both hypotheses (Bengtson et al., 1975).

Based on the concepts in the modernization model, older people in the most modern societies would be similar in their life chances and life-styles. One basic thesis of this book is that national characteristics, other than level of modernity, affect the personal conditions of older people. Why would the daily life experience of an older person in

Sweden differ from that of someone in the Netherlands or in the United States, given similar, though not identical, levels of modernization?

Policy, Aging, and Daily Life

How open are the options for older people in a society? First, each national context represents a set of cultural, and subcultural in some cases, values and beliefs. These define the age structure, the status of the aged, and the desirable activities, places, and companions of later life. Second, the institutional arrangements—including family and household structure and labor force, medical, and service sector characteristics—shape the context for daily life. Third, historical events—such as population changes, wars, and economic transformations—modify the experiences of old age. Fourth, explicit and implicit policies influence the options and opportunity structures older people live within. Resources and activities are influenced by policies.

Although sociological models contain concepts of social structure (labor force, household and family structure, and technological development), demography (aging of the population and migration), and culture (status of older people, definitions of age strata and age-graded roles, and beliefs about achievement, individualism, efficiency), policy remains a critical concept for the explanation of differences in old age experiences among highly developed countries. We know a great deal about policies in the nations included in this study. The final chapter summarizes and compares these policies. But linking policies to personal condition and daily life experiences is a task not yet undertaken.

Older people in highly developed societies are uniquely dependent on policy initiatives that shape their life chances and personal conditions directly and profoundly. For example, policy affects the economic resources of an elderly woman in Sweden. The daily life experience available to a pension recipient with a rent subsidy and living in the state-supported service environment of Stockholm is different than the experience of an elderly resident of age-segregated housing in the urban environment of Philadelphia or an aging Asian immigrant in Toronto or an elderly woman in Amsterdam. The activities, locales, and interactions that constitute the daily life experiences of older people are shaped by the structure, culture, population characteristics, *and* policies of modern nations.

In addition to these societal characteristics, there are variations among people based on gender, age, health, marital status, living arrangements, work status, income maintenance, education, and subjective state. These personal characteristics and conditions modify the choices people make and the opportunities they face. We will seek national and intranational patterns of daily life based on structural and individual constraint.

Methods for Inquiry

The general question: How do the daily lives of older people in modern societies vary? A group of researchers from seven countries planned a comparative analysis of daily life among older people. Interest in cross-national inquiry, access to time-use data sets that contained sizable numbers of older people, and collaborative working relationships enabled the research design underlying this volume to be carried out.

The elements of the research design included a common framework for inquiry within nations and a single concluding chapter that contained the comparative analysis.

The research design for the within-nation analysis reflects our attempt to maximize comparability. First, the problem is to describe and compare the daily lives of older people within nations. At a minimum, age and gender differences among people 55 and older were to be documented. If possible, researchers were also asked to examine differences in daily life due to marital status and type of community (urban/rural). Sampling design varied somewhat from nation to nation. Each author describes the sample used for his or her chapter. Data collection provides a strong common chord that holds the volume together. Each author relies on time-budget data, the optimal data for large-scale inquiry into daily life.

Time Budgets of Daily Life

The potential of time budgets to capture essential qualities of daily life is great. The ideal method may be to observe activities in daily life directly. Having observers record the details of daily life has been done in studies of daily lives of children and older people in a midwestern community (Barker and Wright, 1955; Barker and Barker, 1968) and in studies of spatial and temporal patterns within the family-household (Kantor and Lehr, 1975). The rewards of directly observing daily life as it occurs are great indeed. Each of these studies balanced the rewards of direct observation of daily life (rich and detailed information, sequences of action in a natural setting) against the costs (data collection cost and effort, small and usually nonrepresentative samples, data-reduction and analysis tasks, and observer error and bias).

While the direct observation method has led to invaluable and fresh theoretical insights and careful description, *time-budget methods* obtain optimal behavioral data for many research problems regarding daily life.

This method of data collection can be considered indirect observation. Time budgets are best considered "quasi-observational" given that relatively untrained observers, who are also the research subjects, are relied on to reconstruct their behaviors through an interview or to record them in a diary. This leads to similarities between time budgets and surveys as well as between time budgets and observational methods.

This time-budget tradition has many advocates and analysts (e.g., Aas, 1982; Altergott, 1982; Little, 1984). The advantages of time budgets include the following: the ability to collect records of activity that can be either brief and abstract or detailed and lengthy; the ability to use large and representative samples of individuals; the flexibility in data analysis; and, important for the present study, an international tradition that allows comparability.

In an analysis of the time-budget tradition, Altergott (1982) identified the multinational study coordinated by Szalai (1972) as the exemplar of the method. The elements of the research design tradition include a pattern of strengths and flaws. The general approach highlights the significance of daily behavior that constitutes social life. A great deal of thought has gone into the conceptualization of time and the relevance of daily life to culture and social structure (Moore, 1963; Lefevre, 1968). Descriptive research is predominant, rather than theory testing or theory generation. Because of the conceptual orientation toward time use and social activities, authors in this tradition often link their work only to other time-use research (e.g., Chapin, 1974; Robinson, 1977). This has limited the integration of time-use research with other bodies of knowledge.

Data collection is the most outstandingly different aspect of the time-budget research design. Diaries are kept by the respondent or interviews are conducted in person or over the phone. In either case, a central feature of the time-budget tradition is the sequential record of events for a 24-hour period. The questions to elicit information on the events of daily life are simple and straightforward. The typical range of events over a 24-hour period is from 20 to 80.

Events, as defined in the time-use tradition, comprise social activities, locations, companions, and secondary activities. Duration of time spent in a place, at an activity, or in a social interaction context are considered central indicators of the investment in or salience of that place, activity, or context. The most well-known method of, and the international standard for, classifying primary and secondary activities is that found in the Szalai volume. One hundred activities are collapsed into ten general types of activity: work related, domestic work, care to children, purchasing of goods and service, adult education and training, civic and collective participation, entertainment and social leisure, sports and active leisure, and passive leisure. Likewise, ten types of social companions are defined: with spouse (or fiancée), children, other adults in the household, relatives and friends outside of the household, co-workers or fellow students, members of an organization, neighbors or their children, administrative personnel or clients, others, or solitude. Locations considered are in or outside one's own house, at the workplace, at someone else's home, outdoors in public space, inside service buildings, inside leisure establishments, eating and drinking locales, and others (Szalai, 1972). Most of the authors in this volume used a detailed coding scheme similar to this international standard. They then combined information about human behavior into larger categories similar also to this international standard.

Robinson, Juster, and others assessed the reliability and accuracy of measures of behavior based on the time budget, with highly satisfying results (Juster and Stafford, 1985). Analysis of time-budget data offers many unique but underutilized options. The data produced in time-budget studies are rich and elaborate.

Major comparisons that have predominated in the time-use literature are based on middle-aged adult role sets. It is common to compare employed men, employed women, and housewives (Szalai, 1972; Robinson, 1977). In many time-use studies, only people of working ages (18-65, for example) are included. A unique contribution of this volume is the examination of time use of older people.

Most often, the comparisons that are made in the time-budget tradition are not based on hypotheses, but are general descriptive comparisons. The basic information that is typically presented in a time-budget research report consists of mean amounts of time allocated to particular activities and perhaps the proportion of people spending any time at all in that activity. Explicit tests of the magnitude of the differences are not always reported.

In an extensive review of the application of time-use methods to the study of aging, Virginia Little (1984) considers the history of the method and the central concepts and techniques of time-use research. One of the significant differences among time-use researchers, according to Little, is the conceptualization that leads to particular analysis strategy. In the traditional form of analysis, the time-budget researcher selects socially meaningful subgroups and presents aggregate analyses. These are compared and contrasted. The present volume uses this approach in all chapters. This is an appropriate strategy to answer the basic research question. The newer trend, however, is to conduct individual-level analyses, such as Lawton's (1985), and assess the affects of individual characteristics and conditions on time spent in various activities. This approach is also used by some of the contributors to this volume.

Several aspects of daily life receive a great deal of attention in this volume: work, retirement, and productive activities; gender differences in time use; family interaction and other social involvements; and leisure activities. These topics are drawn from the literature in social gerontology and reflect basic issues regarding aging in developed nations.

Central Topics

The chapters present information on the age strata most likely to be retired. The study of adjustment to *retirement* of men in three countries and two occupations was a ground-breaking piece of comparative research. Although they did not have precise time-use data, Havighurst and colleagues (1969) were able to document distinct differences, based on class and nation, in the daily lives of these retired men. Other studies of work and retirement in later life published since then have tended to be single-nation studies (Abrams, 1978, 1980). The analyses here can address the question: What do the retired do? Are they the new "leisure class" (Michelon, 1954)? If older people gain temporal resources in retirement, in what forms of social activity do they engage? Do they continue in productive activities?

Research, theoretical, and political attention has focused on *unpaid productive activities* in recent years. This form of productivity is especially salient for older people; it represents a continuing contribution to the social economy and community. Women, through their housework and caring activities, constitute an invisible welfare system (Wariness, 1978). Older people are both providers and recipients of benefits from this system, as is clearly shown in Daatland's work (1983). The social productivity of activities of daily life are often undervalued and overlooked. The resulting devaluation of persons in unpaid labor has influenced the position of retirees in modern nations.

More than 20 years ago, when Kleemeier (1961) and associates published their studies of aging and *leisure*, it seemed that the link between time-use research as a method and late life as a topic was about to be established. But it did not happen. Nor did it happen in 1972, when the International Center of Social Gerontology (CIGS) convened a meeting in Yugoslavia to discuss leisure and "le troisième age." There were notable papers, including one by Havighurst, who presented further data analysis both from the 1969 cross-national study of retired men, and the Kansas City studies of adult life, including women. He made one of the first serious attempts to link the division of time among play-study-work to different stages of the life cycle. This was later extended by Rapoport and Rapoport (1975) to a consideration of work and leisure over the family life cycle.

Leisure studies have tended to be of all adult age groups (e.g., Kaplan, 1960; Dumazedier, 1967; Gordon and Gaitz, 1976). Little special attention has been given in most national studies to leisure in old age. Our project supplements existing knowledge by identifying the involvement in creative, diversionary, self-developing, social, and pleasurable activities of older people in several nations.

Older women are of special interest in more developed nations for their involvement in unpaid productivity and for other reasons as well. Women will continue to constitute the majority of old people. Previous research has often omitted women (e.g., studies of retirement) and there is an information gap regarding their activities in later life. Another phenomenon of growing importance is the "woman in the middle"—the middle-aged or older woman who manages her own household and a second one, that of her parents or in-laws. As the generations age together, the number of hours required weekly in the second household increases sharply (Brody et al., 1983). In this volume, gender differences and similarities in daily life are addressed.

Comparative research projects on social aspects of aging and on time use emphasize the *social relationships* individuals maintain. Relations with family, friends, relatives, co-workers, organizational members, service providers, and even strangers integrate the person into a social network (Hill, 1970; Lopata, 1973; Blau, 1973; Shanas, 1968; Unruh, 1984; Altergott, 1980, 1985), but also integrate the community into a social structure. A major comparative study of retirement discovered that men in three nations had three distinctly different patterns of social involvement, emphasizing family and other informal or formal relations to varying degrees (Havighurst et al., 1969). Shanas and her colleagues discovered many cross-national similarities in family and kin involvement. In Britain, Denmark, and the United States, about one-fifth of people 65 and older have no surviving children; those that have children are likely to be in active contact with at least one. This indicates the viability of intergenerational relations in modern society at the same time it alerts us to the variability of the experience of family relations. Time spent with one's spouse has been shown to be higher for older couples in a cross-national analysis (Altergott, 1981). In Hungary, France, and the United States, married couples over 50 spent more time alone with each other than younger couples did.

In this volume, several authors describe the social relations, whether "purely" sociable, care-providing, or formal, for older people in several modern societies. Examining the variations within and across nations provides a comparative contribution to the vast literature on social networks and aging.

The concluding chapter constitutes the comparative analysis. While the nation is the basic research case, age and gender aggregates may show different patterns across nations. Therefore, this chapter considers both national and age and gender aggregate differences in the activities, locales, and companions of daily life. National differences in policy will be summarized, because policy is hypothesized to be a prime differentiator in daily life. Demographic, cultural, and historical characteristics are considered if they seem to account for variations in the way older people live. This exploratory analysis seeks to embellish and develop social theories of aging, and the primary goal is to identify national characteristics that shape the daily lives of older people.

This, then, is the theoretical background and the research designs (the single-nation and cross-national components) that each author relied on in preparing the chapters that follow.

The collaborative and comparative nature of this volume developed out of a long-term commitment by several contributors to understanding aging in society. The common framework was hammered out and the available data sets were used to their fullest. Because cross-national research in gerontology is scarce and limited by methodological challenges and national barriers to cooperation (see Dieck, 1985), this volume describes each national context as well as comparing time-use patterns across nations.

REFERENCES

Aas, D. 1982. "Designs for Large Scale Time-Use Studies of the Twenty-Four Hour Day." Pp. 17-53 in *It's About Time*, edited by Z. Staikov. Sofia: Bulgarian Sociological Association.

Abrams, M. 1978. *Beyond Three Score and Ten: A First Report on a Survey of the Elderly.* London: Age Concern England.

———. 1980. *Beyond Three Score and Ten: A Second Report on a Survey of the Elderly.* London: Age Concern England.

Achenbaum, W. A. 1978. *Old Age in a New Land.* Baltimore: Johns Hopkins University Press.

Altergott, K. 1980. "Variety in Daily Life: Time Allocation and the Structure of Role Relationships." Ph.D. dissertation, University of Minnesota.

———. 1981. "Behavioral Companionship in Marriage." *Journal of Comparative Family Studies* 12:171-85.

———. 1982. "Traditions and Alternatives in Research Design: An Assessment of Time Utilization Studies." Pp. 240-52 in *It's About Time*, edited by Z. Staikov. Sofia: Bulgarian Sociological Association.

———. 1985. "Marriage, Gender, and Social Relations in Late Life." Pp. 51-70 in *Social Bonds in Later Life: Aging and Interdependence*, edited by W. Peterson and J. Quadagno. Beverly Hills, CA: Sage.

Barker, R. and L. Barker. 1968. "The Psychological Ecology of Old People in Midwest, Kansas, and Yoredale, Yorkshire." Pp. 453-60 in *Middle Age and Aging*, edited by B. Neugarten. Chicago: University of Chicago Press.

Barker, R. and H. Wright. 1955. *The Midwest and Its Children.* New York: Harper & Row.

Bengtson, V., J. J. Dowd, D. H. Smith, and A. Inkeles. 1975. "Modernization, Modernity and Perceptions of Aging: A Cross-Cultural Study." *Journal of Gerontology* 30:688-95.

Blau, A. 1973. *Old Age in a Changing Society.* New York: Franklin Watts.

Brody, E. M., P. T. Johnson, M. C. Fulcomer, and A. M. Lang. 1983. "Women's Changing Roles and Help to the Elderly: Attitudes of Three Generations of Women." *Journal of Gerontology* 38:597-607.

Chapin, F. S., Jr. 1974. *Human Activity Patterns in the City: Things People Do in Time and Space.* New York: John Wiley.

Cherry, R. and S. Magnuson-Martinson. 1981. "Modernization and the Status of the Aged in China: Decline or Equalization?" *Sociological Quarterly* 22:253-61.

Cowgill, D. 1974. "Aging and Modernization: A Revision of the Theory." Pp. 123-45 in *Late Life*, edited by J. F. Gubrium. Springfield, IL: Charles C Thomas.

———. 1986. *Aging Around the World.* Belmont, CA: Wadsworth.

———. and L. D. Holmes, eds. 1972. *Aging and Modernization.* New York: Appleton-Century-Crofts.

———. and R. Ogren. 1980. "The International Development of Academic Gerontology." Pp. 501-5 in *International Handbook on Aging*, edited by E. Palmore. Westport, CT: Greenwood.

Cumming, E. and W. Henry. 1961. *Growing Old: The Process of Disengagement.* New York: Basic Books.

Daatland, S. 1983. "Care Systems." *Aging and Society* 3(1):1-21.

Dieck, M. 1985. "Cross-National Research in Gerontology: A Critical Review of Methodology, Theory, and Results." Paper presented at 13th International Congress of Gerontology, New York.

Dumazedier, J. 1967. *Toward a Society of Leisure.* New York: Free Press.

Fischer, D. H. 1977. *Growing Old in America.* New York: Oxford University Press.

Gordon, C. and G. Gaitz. 1976. "Leisure and Lives: Personal Expressivity Across the Life Span." In *Handbook of Aging and the Social Sciences,* edited by R. Binstock and E. Shanas. New York: Van Nostrand Reinhold.

Havighurst, R., J.M.A. Munnichs, B. Neugarten, and H. Thomas. 1969. *Adjustment to Retirement: A Cross-National Study.* Assen, the Netherlands: Van Gorcum.

Hill, R. 1970. *Family Development in Three Generations.* Cambridge, MA: Schenkman.

Hochschild, A. 1975. "Disengagement Theory: A Critique and Proposal." *American Sociological Review* 40:553-69.

Juster, T. and F. Stafford, eds. 1985. *Time, Goods and Well-Being.* Ann Arbor: University of Michigan.

Kantor, D. and W. Lehr. 1975. *Inside the Family: Toward a Theory of Family Process.* New York: Harper & Row.

Kaplan, M. 1960. *Leisure in America: A Social Inquiry.* New York: John Wiley.

Keith, J. 1982. *Old People as People.* Boston: Little, Brown.

Kleemeier, R. 1961. *Aging and Leisure.* New York: Oxford University Press.

Lawton, M. P. 1985. "Activities and Leisure." *Annual Review of Gerontology and Geriatrics* 5:127-164.

Lefevre, H. 1968. *Everyday Life in the Modern World.* New York: Harper & Row.

Lopata, H. 1973. *Widowhood in an American City.* Cambridge, MA: Schenkman.

Little, V. 1984. "An Overview of Research Using the Time-Budget Methodology to Study Age Related Behaviour." *Aging and Society* 4(1):3-20.

Maddox, G. 1969. "Disengagement Theory: A Critical Evaluation." *Gerontologist* 4:80-83.

Michelon, L. C. 1954. "The New Leisure Class." *American Journal of Sociology* 59:371-78.

Moore, W. 1963. *Man, Time, and Society.* New York: John Wiley.

Palmore, E., ed. 1980. *International Handbook on Aging.* Westport, CT: Greenwood.

Rapoport, R. and R. Rapoport. 1975. *Leisure and the Family Life Cycle.* London: Routledge & Kegan Paul.

Riley, M. W. 1976. "Age Strata in Social Systems." Pp. 189-217 in *Aging and the Social Sciences,* edited by R. Binstock and E. Shanas. New York: Van Nostrand Reinhold.

Robinson, J. 1977. *How Americans Use Time.* New York: Praeger.

Shanas, E., P. Townsend, D. Wedderburn, H. Friis, P. Milhoj, and J. Stehouwer. 1968. *Old People in Three Industrial Societies.* New York: Atherton.

———. 1985. "The Validity and Reliability of Diaries Versus Alternative Time Use Measures." Pp. 33-62 in *Time, Goods and Well-being,* edited by T. Juster and F. Stafford. Ann Arbor: University of Michigan.

Sokolovsky, J., ed. 1983. *Growing Old in Different Cultures.* Belmont, CA: Wadsworth.

Szalai, A. 1972. *The Use of Time.* The Hague: Mouton.

Unruh, D. 1984. *Invisible Lives: Social Worlds of the Aged.* Beverly Hills, CA: Sage.

Wariness, K. 1978. "The Invisible Welfare State: Women's Work at Home." *Acta Sociologica* 21:193-208.

2

Use of Time by the
Elderly in Great Britain

MARK ABRAMS

Daily Life

[Mrs. E. Jones, widow, aged 75, in Lindley, Huddersfield[1] (skilled working class); Monday, February 24, 7:30 p.m. to 9:00 p.m.]

What time do you usually get up each day? "Between 8 and 9 a.m. I make my bed have my breakfast around nine o'clock. I didn't do a lot this morning because Hilda [sister-in-law, also a widow] came about quarter past ten, so Hilda had a coffee and I had tea. We sat and nattered[2] until you came—eleven o'clock—before that I washed a pair of tights and prepared my dinner."

Do you get a morning paper? "No I don't."

On a normal week-day morning what other chores would you do— say if you don't have any visitors? "I'd probably straighten up in here, dust and vacuum. Depending on what part of the week it is. One day I might go upstairs and do my bedroom. I don't do the bathroom because the home help[3] does that. One morning I'll probably be washing—one morning I'll probably be ironing, one morning a bit of baking."

What time do you usually have something to eat? "Quarter past twelve to quarter to one. Today I'm reheating a bit of cabbage, potatoes and meat from yesterday."

What do you do in the afternoon? "Oh, nothing—when I've had my mid-day meal I generally sit and watch the news. Then I wash my dinner pots up. Then I have a wash—sometimes I change me,[4] sometimes I don't. Then I'll come back downstairs. I get a paper called *The Weekly News* and I might read some of that, or I might read a book—if I've started one."

How long do you usually read? "An hour and a half to two hours."
Do you fall asleep at all? "Sometimes I do, yes. I nod off . . . I don't always read."
So, how many afternoons do people come and see you? "Oh, I can't tell you, . . ."
Do you go out at all? "No, I haven't been out this month . . . above this month[5]. . . . I've only been out twice under my own steam since Jack[6] died [November 1985]. I've only once been across to the Bay Horse[7] shopping twice. So you can't wonder that I've got fed up, can you?" "Brian[8] has taken me out, in between in the car."

What time do you have your evening meal? "Well, I usually wait until the paper comes, ten past to quarter past four. Depending what's on television, if there's nothing much on, then I read a bit of the paper. Then I make my tea—about quarter to five to quarter past. I sit a bit and then I wash my few pots up—which are hardly worth washing—and then I watch the news. I might watch television then—well, depending what' on. Same as tonight, I should have watched it until eight o'clock. I've never looked what's on after that."

So when you turn television off, what do you do then? "Well, I read. I always finish reading the *Examiner*. I try and make it so that its half past eight—this is a ritual that I do—about half past eight I put my kettle on, full of water. Leave it for half an hour, and then I fill my bottle.[9] Take my bottle up about ten to nine, and I have a kettle upstairs, I make sure I have some water in my kettle. Then I bring my nightdress and dressing gown downstairs to warm. And then if I haven't finished reading the paper I'll finish reading it. If I have, then I might read a couple of chapters of my book." *So you spend a lot of time reading, do you?* "Well, I don't do too bad . . . then I make my supper about quarter past ten."
What sort of thing do you have? "Well, it varies. Sometimes I have a slice of date-loaf, sometimes a buttered scone,[10] sometimes three butter biscuits and a bit of cheese. Always a cup of tea. Then I might read again for about twenty minutes. During this time I've put some water in a little pan and stood a little bottle of oil in this for my knees. And then I start getting undressed—this is turning eleven o'clock—and then I give both my knees a good rub. Then I collect all my stuff up—turn my lamps off—make sure the plugs are out of the television. And I always pull my

curtains back, then—Brian plays pop with me,[11] but I do. He says its silly, because if you were poorly no one would know you were still in bed if you'd pulled your curtain back. But they would, because my upstairs curtains are pulled on, that is until I'm dressed and ready for coming downstairs."

Do you have any favourite television programmes? "Soap operas— *Crossroad, Coronation Street, Emmerdale Farm, Blockbusters, Dynasty, Dallas,* and I love Snooker[12] and I don't mind golf—I used to watch all these with Jack—I hate boxing. I like to watch Harry Seecombe[13] on a Sunday night."

How often do you see your son, Brian? "I contact their house one way or another—Jennifer might phone me [Jennifer is Brian's wife]. I never miss contacting their house two days in succession. I've seen both of them today . . . Jennifer came to do my hair, and Brian will call tonight to collect the hair dryer. I shan't see them tomorrow, but I shall probably see them on Wednesday to go to the supermarket."

How often do you go to the supermarket? "Well that depends on me, I don't want to go every week just for myself. I go about every two weeks."

Do you write any letters? "Yes, I do, not so often though because I don't like writing letters—I have two to do. I keep in very close contact with a friend, she's a widow and lives in Kidderminster . . . I owe her a letter."

How often do you use the telephone? "I did use it four time a day [when Jack died in November], but it's gone off now, if you get me. I might not use it today and I've answered it twice today."

How many friends—who live within half a mile—visit you? "Phyllis every Monday afternoon, Elsie, a lady across occasionally, and a young woman who lives up Willowood, she comes at least once a fortnight."

What about the family? Your nieces or Jack's relatives? "Our Marjorie, if she waits three weeks it's a long time. Norma not so often which is understandable [as she has her father living with her] . . . Thelma; well she's such a lot of places to visit—she comes on for her tea every four or five weeks. Denise doesn't contact me at all."

Disabilities? "Well, I have arthritis, which is why I don't go out much." [Mrs. Jones is very nervous about falling since having an accident two years ago when she was hit by a car speeding down the main road. The hip operation which she had previous to that had been successful, but the accident made her more cautious and nervous about going out again, especially on her own. And since the death of her husband in November, she has lost confidence to do this. One of her nieces has suggested that they go to town together as soon as the weather gets a little better.]

What sort of things do you like doing around the house? "At the moment, I'm not keen on doing anything. I like reading, romances, very light reading."

What sort of things do you enjoy doing outside the house? "I'm just looking forward to getting out—I just want the breeze to blow on my face. I'm not one that enjoys going to town, I never have. I never waste a lot of time looking around. When Jack was alive we used to like to go to the park. Watch the bowling,[14] that sort of thing."

Are Saturdays different from other days? "Well, weekends in general. I'm more on my own at the weekends—nobody comes at weekends." [Note: This is not strictly true, but the isolation and loneliness is felt much more strongly at the weekends when one is more conscious of families being together.]

What about neighbours? "No neighbours come anyway; only the man in the front—he comes in every day—he's been this tea-time. He calls to see if I want anything—he always brings me fish and chips on a Friday tea-time. I haven't seen him since; until half past four today and I was a bit worried because I thought maybe Kathy wasn't so well. Anyways he had a word that he had to fetch her home from hospital on Sunday, so he had to see to her, you see. I probably shan't see as much of him now, because he'll have to look after her." [The neighbour's wife is having treatment for cancer and is in Cookridge Hospital, Leeds.]

So what about Sundays? [Note: I persisted with this question because I already knew that several members of the family had been to see her.] "Brian and family came for tea—all five of them. I go every Wednesday to see them—I think myself, though they've never said anything—I think, they want week-ends to themselves. You see that's the way I look at everybody. That's why you don't get a lot of company—I think, because their husbands are at home. You can't expect people to visit you all the time—week-ends are shocking. You can go for a bus ride on a Saturday, but not Sunday because its a limited service on a Sunday." "Yesterday I felt very low, yes—very low—and then Norma phoned to say that she and Terry would get the bus and call to see me early in the evening—that saved my day, it really did."

So, how satisfied are you with the way you spend your time? "Well, I'm very dissatisfied."

What would make it more satisfying? "Lack of companions, since Jack died in November." [Note: Jack died just before they were to celebrate their golden wedding in early December. The couple led a very quiet and organized life; mainly around their son and his family and also the nieces. Finance was never a problem because they "lived within their income"; holidays were twice a year to Bispham.[15] Mrs. Jones talked about a holiday ... "if only I could persuade Hilda to come with me, but I don't think she will agree." [They owned the small back-to-back[16] terrace house,[17] which includes basement,[18] sitting room, kitchenette at the top of cellar stairs, one bedroom, one bathroom. It is always neat and tidy and in immaculate decorative order.]

Use of Time by the Elderly[19] in Great Britain

The emphasis in this chapter is on the leisure activities of older people in Great Britain. Given the demographic and social conditions that shape the nation, how do people allocate that universally limited resource of time to the social activities commonly referred to as *leisure*? Wherever possible, the conditions and behavior of the elderly are compared with those of the middle-aged—that is, those aged 45 to 64. This is an age band where, compared with the elderly, the average household is larger, more affluent, and more likely—because it contains few young children—to contain a wife who goes out to work. In Britain, the average elderly household also differs from the average middle-aged family in one other respect that might affect comparisons of time use. The elderly will contain a higher proportion of middle-class people because of differential mortality rates related to class. For example, the most recently published official volume on occupational mortality in England and Wales reports that, for the years 1970 to 1972, the death rate among men aged 45 to 64 and described as unskilled manual workers was almost double that among men of the same age and described as professional workers, that is, doctors, lawyers, academics (Office of Population Censuses and Surveys, 1978). The same class gap prevails among women. For their paper "Work, Death and Marriage Go Together Like a Horse and Carriage," Fletcher and colleagues (n.d.) analyzed over a million deaths recorded over an eight-year period and compared the mortality statistics of men with those of married women classified by their husband's occupation; they found that the "correlation between the death rates of men and married women classified by their husband's occupation was of the order of 0.9."

Conditions of Daily Life

Distinctive conditions play an important part in determining the leisure behavior of older people in Great Britain.

Over one-third of them (35%) live alone. Among women the proportion is 45%; among men, 20%. These solitary individuals are dependent on those outside the household for companionship (Her Majesty's Stationery Office [HMSO], 1981).

Of all *men* aged 65 or more, 73% live with a spouse, and 20% live alone. The balance of 7% contains 2% of all elderly men who live with their own children and 5% living with siblings, cousins, and nonrelatives. Of all elderly *women*, 39% live with a spouse and 45% live alone. Another 8% have no spouse but live with their children; the remainder live with siblings, other relatives, or people who are nonrelatives. These gender differences in the households in which elderly people live are related to the differences in the marital status of elderly men and elderly women. Less than 20% of the men are widowers, while 50% of the women are widows. It is unusual for the elderly widowed to live with their children.

Economic Resources

In households where the head is aged 65 or older, the average weekly disposable household income is little more than half (57%) of the average disposable weekly income of households where the head is aged 50 to 64. The latter household's larger income has to meet the needs of more people, but even when household income is turned into disposable income per person, the income of the average person in the average elderly household is 20% less than that of the average person in the average middle-aged household. And because of this fall in income, the elderly person has to cut down expenditure on those leisure activities that cost money—holidays, restaurant meals, visits to theaters and concerts, reading newspapers and books, belonging to clubs, joining adult education classes.

The effect of relative poverty on leisure activities is well documented by the findings of the government's annual *Family Expenditure Survey*. At present, the latest available report deals with the year 1983 and relates to the United Kingdom. The total sample of 6973 households includes 482 households of one retired person mainly dependent on state pensions (i.e., "one in which at least three quarters of the total income of the household is derived from national insurance retirement and similar pensions and state benefits") and 276 households of one man and one woman where the household income is mainly dependent on state retirement pensions. These two types of households are 11% of all U.K. households, and almost half (48%) of all U.K. households where the head is a retired person. Their average weekly expenditure on leisure goods and services is shown in Table 2.1 along with that of all U.K. households.

Health Status

The health of many older people is less than robust. In the government's *General Household Survey 1982*, 58% of elderly men and 62% of elderly women reported that they suffered from some long-standing illness, disability, or infirmity. In the average month, one-third of all elderly people visited or were visited by a doctor. Each year, 10% of the elderly are hospitalized—some merely overnight, others for several weeks. A survey carried out in 1978 on a sample of 1640 elderly people in England found almost the same incidence of long-standing illness, and 68% of those so affected said that this disability kept them from doing some of the things they would like to do. When asked to say what these losses were, 85% answered "getting about outdoors," and 68% said "restricted their leisure activities" (Abrams, 1980).

A government study of home accidents in England and Wales reported that, for the year 1982, "the overall number of home accidents requiring some form of medical treatment is of the order of 3 million," and two-thirds of these accidents received hospital treatment. Over two-fifths (44%) of these hospitalized home accidents were falls of one kind or another (drop falls, falls ascending or descending stairs, and so on). Of all hospitalized home falls experienced by people aged 15 or more, 40% were the falls of people aged 65 or more.

A recent nationwide study of elderly people responsible for household shopping reported that when respondents were asked "Would you say you can walk at a normal pace for half an hour without difficulty?," little more than half (56%) said they could do this without any difficulty; the others said they would have to walk slowly, that they would get breathless and tired, that they would soon get afraid of falling, and so on (Abrams, 1985). It is hardly surprising that on the average weekday

TABLE 2.1   Household Expenditure on Selected Leisure Items, United Kingdom 1983, Weekly Average

	All U.K. Households	Households mainly Dependent on State Retirement Pensions	
		1 Adult	2 Adults
Alcohol consumed away from home	5.04	0.40	1.77
Meals consumed out	2.92	0.48	0.68
Books, newspapers, magazines	2.29	1.01	1.68
TV, radio, and musical instruments	3.91	1.36	2.24
Holidays	4.07	0.81	1.56
Hobbies	0.10	0.02	0
Cinema admissions	0.09	0	0
Dance admissions	0.12	—	—
Theater, concert admissions	0.22	0.01	0.02
Charges to participant sports	0.42	0.01	0.04
Football match admissions	0.08	0	0.01
Admission to other sports	0.02	—	0
Sports goods	0.31	—	—
Other entertainment	0.26	0.03	0.02
Total	19.86	4.14	8.02
Leisure expenditure per person	7.48	4.14	4.01

SOURCE: Her Majesty's Stationery Office (1983); used by permission.
NOTE: — = less than 0.005.

slightly over half of all elderly people do not go outside their dwellings; and when a sample of all elderly in England and Wales were asked: "This last weekend, Saturday and Sunday, did you go out at all?," over one-third (36%) said they had not.

Daily Life: Leisure Time

A summarizing table in the government's publication *Social Trends 1985* reported that the average retired person in Great Britain had on the average 24-hour day (including Saturday and Sunday) 10.3 hours of "free time" (i.e., after 8.6 hours of sleep and 5.1 hours taken up with personal care and domestic work such as cooking, shopping, eating, washing); this was roughly 4 hours more "free time" each day than that experienced by the average nonretired adult.

The present author's survey in 1979 gives a broad picture of how the average elderly person in England and Wales spends this "free time." A list of possible time uses was read out to the respondent and for each item he or she was asked: "Could you tell me how much time you spent on it yesterday?" This was followed by a question in which the respondent was reminded of the amount of time they spent yesterday on each pastime and then was asked if they would like to spend more time on it, and where they said "yes," they were then asked to say what prevented them doing so.

The replies summarized in Table 2.2 indicate that, of the 9.5 hours of free time available to the elderly person, over half is devoted either to watching television or to listening to the radio, and that only a handful of eccentrics would like to spend even more time on these two time uses. Almost another two hours are taken up with just resting, and here the proportion of frustrated consumers is negligible. Less than half an hour is used for taking a walk. Almost one-third of those who had gone for a walk on the day before the interview, however, said they would like to do more walking, but three-quarters of these frustrated walkers said they were unable to do as much as they wanted to because of their physical disabilities. Among those who had spent time reading, there was again a significant minority who would have liked to spend more time on this, but two-thirds of them gave as the main reason for not doing so the fact that they gave up because of poor eyesight and their eyes began to hurt. One of the constant features of the "National Readership Survey" is that the level of newspaper reading is nearly 30% lower among the elderly than among those aged 45 to 64 (HMSO, 1985).

The same issue of *Social Trends* also reports the replies to a question in which respondents were asked if, at any time during the four weeks preceding the interview, they had engaged in any of some 21 sport activities. The replies are shown in Table 2.3 separately for men and women and for two age groups in each sex—those aged 35 to 59, and those aged 60 or more. In the latter age band, all the women would have reached and passed retirement pension age and only 8% still held jobs; among women in the younger group, the "economic activity" rate was 65%. Among men, "the economic activity" rates were much higher: among those aged 60 or more, the rate was almost 20%, and among those aged 35 to 59, it was 90%.

For both sexes, active participation in sports is much lower among people aged 60 or more than it is among those aged 35 to 59. Indeed, among older women, such activity is almost nonexistent except for the 12% who over a four-week period undertake from time to time a walk of two miles or more. Among older men, the relative withdrawal (or

TABLE 2.2   Average Amount of "Free Time" Spent Daily by Elderly,
           in Hours

	Hours	Would Like More Time %
Watching television	3:42	4.7
Listening to radio	1:24	3.8
Reading	1:21	13.5
Resting, relaxing	1:50	1.6
Going for a walk	0:29	30.5
Sewing, knitting	0:22	9.6
Other pastimes	0:28	9.7
Total	9:30	

SOURCE: Abrams (1980); used by permission.

exclusion) from sports activities is even more pronounced. Apart from the 18% who undertake walks of two miles or more, the highest proportions of "activists" are found among participants in the hardly exhausting activities of pool and billiards (4%), golf (3%), and darts (2%).

In the same year, National Opinion Polls (N.O.P.) carried out a similar broad time-use survey and also asked respondents if they were spending more/same/or less time on a wide range of activities now "compared with 12 months ago." Table 2.4 compares the "less" replies of the elderly with those of the "pre-elderly"—that is, those aged 55 to 64; the figures of "less" for the elderly are consistently higher—with two exceptions: watching television and knitting.

Probably the most detailed recent survey of time use carried out in Britain is that by the BBC Broadcasting Research Unit. The fieldwork was carried out in the summer of 1983 (June and July) and the winter of 1984 (February) and published in four volumes under the title *Daily Life in the 1980s* by the BBC. Using an aided recall technique, respondents were questioned about everything they had done on the preceding day; the "day" covered 21 hours; and the questions dealt with respondents' activities in each quarter of an hour from 6:00 a.m. to the quarter of an hour starting at 9:45 a.m.; from 10:00 a.m. until 2:30 a.m., the unit of recording was for each half hour, and the recording "day" ended at 2:59 a.m. The "daily life sheet" sought information on 40 possible activities (counting "sleep" as an activity). Tables 2.5 and 2.6 try to convey a summarized picture of an enormous quantity of information by averaging the findings for six time units spread throughout the 21 hours: the quarter of an hour starting at 7:30 a.m. and the half hours starting at

TABLE 2.3 Participation in Selected Sporting Activities, 1983: Annual Averages of Percentages in Each Age Group Engaging in Each Activity In the Four Weeks Before Interview

	Men		Women	
	35-59	60 or more	35-59	60 or more
Swimming, public outdoor pools	1	—	1	—
Swimming, other outdoor	4	1	3	1
Swimming, indoor	7	1	7	2
Fishing	4	4	1	—
Sailing	1	—	—	—
Football	2	—	—	0
Rugby	—	—	0	0
Golf	5	3	1	—
Cricket	1	—	—	0
Tennis	1	—	1	—
Athletics, outdoor	2	—	1	0
Keep fit, yoga	1	—	5	1
Gymnastics	—	—	—	0
Badminton	2	—	2	—
Squash	3	—	1	0
Table Tennis	2	—	1	—
Darts	9	2	3	1
Billiards, snooker	12	4	1	—
Ten-pin bowling	1	2	1	1
Horse riding	—	—	1	—
Rambling, hiking	1	—	1	—
Walking (2 miles or more)	21	18	20	12
Cycling	2	1	2	1

SOURCE: Her Majesty's Stationery Office (1985); used by permission.
NOTE: — = less than 0.5.

10:30 a.m., 1:00 p.m., 5 p.m., 8:30 p.m., and 11:00 p.m. The figures related to Fridays—a day when (at least in the evening) the weekend's leisure starts—and then to Saturdays and Sundays, the two weekend days when most workers are free to pursue their leisure activities. In Table 2.5, the results relate to the use of time in the summer, and Table 2.6 deals with the winter findings. In both tables, the behavior of the middle-aged (45 to 64 years) is set alongside the findings from elderly respondents.

Friday: (a) Summer

The outstanding difference between the two age groups is, of course, the proportions at work (as employees, employers, or self-employed).

TABLE 2.4   Proportion Reporting Less Participation Than a Year Ago

	Age	
	55-64	65+
	%	%
Listen to radio	5	7
Go to cinema	27	46
Go to theater	12	39
Go to pubs, club	20	27
Watch TV	16	10
Knitting, sewing	19	23
Other handicrafts at home	11	16
Keep fit exercises	—	15
Playing any sport or swimming	15	27
Walking or rambling	12	25
Playing cards, indoor games	15	16
Visits to and from friends	15	16
Going to exhibitions, museums	15	24
Gardening	8	19
Reading books	6	12
Reading magazines	2	12
Going to bingo sessions	9	15

SOURCE: National Opinion Polls (1985a). Used by permission.
NOTE: — = less than 0.5.

By 9:00 a.m., about half all those aged 45 to 64 are either already at work (42%) or traveling to work (6%). At the same hour, only 2% of the elderly are thus engaged. This probably accounts for the fact that the middle-aged wake earlier, do more early morning listening to radio, have less opportunity for relaxing (e.g., sitting in a chair with one's eyes closed), and much less time to spend on watching broadcast television— particularly early evening television; in the half hour starting at 6:30, 57% of the elderly but only 39% of the middle-aged are watching. Apart from these differences, however, the leisure lives of the two age groups, at least in quantitative terms, are very similar. In both groups, over two-fifths of them are, at the selected times, engaged in the four domestic tasks of eating and drinking, preparing meals and washing up, shopping, and housework. For the elderly, the figures are respectively 18%, 10%, 6%, and 7%; for the middle-aged, the corresponding proportions are 18%, 10%, 5%, and 7%—that is, almost identical. In both groups, the average person has very little time for education classes or political meetings, for playing with cats or dogs, for hobbies or the use of craftsmanlike skills.

TABLE 2.5   Use of Time in Summer by Age: Percentages for Average Time Periods

	Fridays 45-64	Fridays 65+	Saturdays 45-64	Saturdays 65+	Sundays 45-64	Sundays 65+
Awake	89	82	88	84	81	80
Watch TV	20	26	23	24	19	21
Eat, drink	18	18	19	17	18	20
Talking	17	18	20	15	19	16
Listen to radio	14	11	15	11	14	9
Prepare food, wash up	10	10	11	12	11	14
Housework	7	7	8	6	5	6
Relaxing	4	7	4	6	6	8
Reading, writing	6	7	5	6	6	8
Shopping, errands	5	6	7	5	1	1
Gardening	3	4	4	4	6	5
Home entertaining	2	3	4	5	5	5
Hobbies, crafts	2	2	3	2	2	3
Pubs, clubs, restaurants	2	1	4	1	3	2
At work	19	1	5	1	2	—
Pets, playing with	1	1	1	1	1	1
A walk, ramble	1	—	—	1	1	—
Adult classes, meetings	—	—	—	—	1	—

SOURCE: Derived from *Daily Life in the 1980s* (BBC, 1985).
NOTE: — = less than 0.5%. Activities omitted from the full schedule (because their incidence is very low) include personal (washing self, dressing, and so on), D.I.Y. (repairs and work to dwelling, and so on), care of children, going to watch live sporting events, fairs, bingo, betting, doing sports, listening to records or cassettes, going to concerts, theaters. The same is true in Table 2.6. Average percentage of participants in a given activity at six selected time periods: the 15-minute period beginning at 7:30 a.m., and the half-hour periods beginning at 10:30 a.m., 1:00 p.m., 5:00 p.m., 8:30, and 11:00 p.m.

Perhaps the most striking figure is the high score of "talking" (this includes telephone talks). The high figure for this activity is all the more surprising because the six averaged time units include two (7:30 a.m. and 11:00 p.m.) when large proportions in both age groups were asleep; both age groups made up for this by talking liberally in the early evening—the average for the half hours extending from 6:00 p.m. to 10:29 found 20% of the elderly and 25% of the middle-aged engaged in talking (the former, it will be remembered, contain a much higher proportion of people living alone).

Friday: (b) Winter

The shift from summer to winter makes very little difference in the time-use behavior of the elderly; the only significant differences—and

TABLE 2.6   Use of Time in Winter by Age: Percentages for Average Time
Periods

	Fridays		Saturdays		Sundays	
	45-64	65+	45-64	65+	45-64	65+
Awake	88	83	86	83	80	80
Watch TV	25	31	28	31	27	31
Eat, drink	18	18	20	20	19	19
Talking	15	16	20	16	20	15
Listen to radio	15	14	13	12	12	11
Prepare food, wash up	13	11	12	12	11	12
Housework	8	8	8	8	6	6
Relaxing	4	8	4	6	6	7
Reading, writing	5	8	5	7	8	10
Shopping, errands	4	5	7	6	1	—
Gardening	—	1	—	1	1	2
Home entertaining	3	3	4	7	7	6
Hobbies, crafts	2	2	3	4	3	2
Pubs, clubs, and so on	3	1	4	2	2	1
At work	17	2	5	—	2	—
Pets, playing with	1	1	1	—	1	1
Walk, ramble	2	2	—	1	1	1
Classes, meetings	—	—	—	1	—	—

SOURCE: Derived from *Daily Life in the 1980s* (BBC, 1985).
NOTE: — = less than 0.5%.

they are comparatively small—are that more of them are watching
television and listening to radio (at the six time units on which Tables 2.5
and 2.6 are based), and fewer are engaged in gardening; and again, fewer
than 0.5% of them spend any time attending educational classes or
meetings. This finding is surprising given that winter is the season
almost invariably set aside for bringing education to the elderly.

The pattern of time use of the middle-aged is similarly much the same
in winter as in summer, but they too show a larger proportion watching
television and practically no one engaged in gardening. And once more,
the only outstanding difference between the two age groups is that,
whereas very few of the elderly are at paid work at the selected time
units, among the middle-aged, the proportion at work at the six time
periods (17%) is almost as high as the proportion engaged in eating and
drinking (18%) but still far behind the proportion (25%) watching
television. Our Victorian forbears might well have described Britain of
the 1980s as a postindustrious society rather than as a postindustrial
society. John Robinson (1977) has applied this term to the United States

after an analysis of declines in active leisure and increases in passive leisure.

Saturday: (a) Summer

It is not surprising that, for the elderly, behavior on Saturdays in the summer is very much the same as Fridays—just another day when practically none of them are at paid work and when the most time-consuming activities are watching television, eating, and talking. The minuscule proportions spending time with pets, taking a walk, and attending classes or meetings show no expansion.

Abrams (1980) shows that the nonmarried spend much more time listening to the radio than married men and women. This was the only significant difference in time use based on marital status.

The middle-aged, however, seem, consciously or unconsciously, to be using some of their extra nonwork time (at the six time periods only 5% were at paid work), to rehearse their retirement life-styles. On Saturdays, compared with Fridays, more of them are watching television, and slightly fewer are taking a walk or reading. But again, the overall impression given by the figures in Table 2.5 is that on Saturdays, as on Fridays, the broad pattern of time use by the middle-aged and the elderly are almost identical in summer.

Saturday: (b) Winter

For the elderly, the pattern of time use in winter is almost identical with that for Fridays in the winter; on both days, at the six selected time periods, nearly one-third (31%) are watching television, and approximately the same proportion are either eating and drinking or preparing food and washing up after meals. There is, comparing the two days, slightly less relaxing on Saturdays, but at the six selected times, some very minor activities show an increase—home entertaining up from 3% to 7%, hobbies and crafts up from 2% to 4%, and attending classes and meetings up from less than 0.5% to 1%.

On Saturdays, the figures for the two age groups are on many activities either identical: eating and drinking (20%), preparing food and washing up (12%), and housework (8%); or almost identical: watching television, listening to the radio, relaxing, reading, shopping, gardening, hobbies, and taking walks. In other words, the patterns for the pre-retired and the retired are very similar, in quantitative terms, on winter Saturdays.

Sunday: (a) Summer

On the traditional day of rest, there are some appropriate, if slight, modifications in time use by the elderly—they wake later in the morning: only 46% are awake by 7:30 a.m. (compared with 56% on Saturdays and 70% on Fridays) and by 2:30 p.m.; 24% are "just relaxing"(compared with 14% on Saturdays and 11% on Fridays). This increase in time spent on sleeping and relaxing enables them to reduce substantially the time they spend on shopping (in any case, practically all shops in Britain are closed on Sundays) and to reduce slightly the time devoted to watching television and listening to radio.

This reduction in television viewing may, however, be due to the fact that Sundays are the day when broadcasting is most prone to devote time to programs that are assumed by producers to be most attractive to elderly people—for example, typical BBC television offerings on one Sunday were *Rediscovering Religious Belief; A Simple Service of Reflection and Prayer; See Hear!* (trips made by the Queen and other members of the Royal Family to places that were once part of the British Empire); *Songs of Praise* (hymns); *Last of the Summer Wine* (adventures of three elderly men one lascivious, one authoritarian, and one moronic). To these could be added on the same Sunday the offerings of commercial television. In addition to various religious broadcasts, there were four silent film comedies "all dating from 1917" and another installment in the series *Getting On* in which a man "who's nearly 70" is helped to "unravel" his life story.

The middle-aged pattern of time use on summer Sundays is as on Saturday very similar to that of the elderly; they sleep and relax more, they rarely do any shopping, they cut down a little on television viewing and radio listening, and the proportion at work is very small.

The outstanding difference in time use between the two age groups on Sundays relates to time spent on religious observances. Among the elderly, the rate of attendance throughout the morning half hours from 10:00 a.m. to 12:29 p.m. rises to an average of slightly over 6% with a second peak (averaging 4%) from 5:30 p.m. to 7:29 p.m. Among the middle-aged, the rates of attendance are well behind—3% in the morning hours and 1% in the evening half hours.

Sunday: (b) Winter

Again, in the winter, the elderly spend a little more time sleeping and relaxing on Sundays as compared with what happens on all other days of the week; however, there is no shopping to be done on Sundays and this enables them to maintain their usual high levels of watching television and listening to radio and also to sustain their church attendance both in the morning and in the early evening at their summertime levels.

One probable explanation for the fact that in the winter the elderly retain their high rates of watching television is that, in the early evening (from 6:30 p.m. to 9:30 p.m.) in the average half hour, 72% are watching the box and that from then on they return to their beds so that the records show that for the half hour starting 10:30 p.m., one-third of the elderly are asleep.

The middle-aged also spend slightly more time sleeping and relaxing on Sundays (as compared with all other days of the week) and this apparently is made possible by equally small reductions in the rates of watching television and listening to the radio and a decline from Saturday low rates of those engaged in paid work or out shopping. Part of the time gained from these two latter reductions is taken up by a little more reading and more home entertaining.

The findings summarized in Tables 2.5 and 2.6 indicate that, as far as people aged 45 or more are concerned, British society is very much in its leisure time a home-centered society. This applies a little more to the elderly than to the middle-aged. This additional time at home is almost certainly related to the constraints upon the elderly referred to at the start of the chapter. The lack of an automobile is an additional constraint that affects 49% of elderly men and 70% of elderly women. Also, substantial majorities of the elderly are afraid to go out in the evening. In January 1985, N.O.P. carried out a survey among 1186 adults living in Greater London and asked two questions bearing on this constraint on the leisure activities of the elderly (N.O.P., 1985b). The first question dealing with this asked: "How safe do you feel walking alone in this area after dark?" Among those aged 65 or more, almost two-thirds replied either "a bit unsafe" (22%) or "very unsafe" (43%). Among those aged 18 to 64, the corresponding figures were 26% and 20%. The second question asked: "How often, if at all, do you go out alone in this area after dark?" Among those aged 65 or more, 50% said "never"; among those aged 18 to 64, the proportion was no more than 22%.

Conclusion

Several patterns in the lives of older people are worth noting. First, the patterns of activity are quite similar for the younger age group, 45 to 64, and the older age group, 65 and older. Given that older individuals face decrements in income, greater physical limitations, a greater prevalence of living alone, and expanded time to engage in leisure, the similarity is surprising. Second, the minor increases reflect in part the opportunity and constraint structure of British society. Fears for personal safety, lack of transportation, limited resources to participate in leisure outside the home do lead to an increase in passive, home-centered leisure for older people. Obviously, nonpassive outdoor leisure activities, before they are adopted by the elderly on a large scale, must be cheap in money terms, require limited physical effort, be undertaken during the daylight hours, and provide companionship for those who live alone. Third, the general pattern of leisure life, at least for middle-aged and older people, is quite passive and homebound. The role of television in drawing attention to home-centered leisure and the consequences of a relatively low level of social and active leisure remain to be fully examined. The concerns of many older people seeking viable relationships and activities may reflect an underlying social issue for other age groups in British society.

NOTES

1. *Lindley* is a working-class extension of the city of *Huddersfield*, which is a woolen textiles town in Yorkshire; it was prosperous up until the Depression of early 1930s, and never really recovered.

2. *Nattered*—trivial chat, for example, about the weather or one's rheumatism.

3. *Home help*—cleaning woman employed by municipal authority; the recipient, if income large enough, would pay the authority part of the wages.

4. *I change me*—local phrase for changing one's clothes.

5. *Above this month*—for more than this month.

6. *Jack*—her dead husband.

7. *Bay Horse*—shopping center named after the pub (saloon) that is part of it.

8. *Brian*—respondent's son.

9. *Fill my bottle*—a hot-water bottle.

10. *Scone*—a heavy plain bun with bicarbonate of soda.

11. *Plays pop with me*—gives me hell about it.

12. *Snooker*—pool; matches are often broadcast on TV.

13. *Harry Seecombe*—a very popular stand-up comic, but now doing a tour of England describing the places he likes.

14. *Watch the bowling*—an outdoor game, somewhat similar to the French game of "boules."

15. *Bispham*—(for holidays) a small village on the coast of northwest England.

16. *Back-to-back*—houses literally built so that they had a common shared back and, therefore, no through ventilation.

17. *Terrace house*—one of an unbroken row of houses.

18. *Basement*—all living quarters below ground level.

19. In this chapter, *the elderly* usually refers to people aged 65 or more; occasionally, however, the available statistics relate to "persons of pensionable age," which in Great Britain means women aged 60 or more and men aged 65 or more. And *Great Britain* excludes Northern Ireland; where the figures include the elderly of the latter area, the description used is *United Kingdom*; some statistics quoted here relate to the elderly of England and Wales and do not include those living in Scotland. Again, sometimes the data relate to those who are described in official statistics as "retired"; this category excludes a small number of people who have passed pensionable age but are still at work, and it includes some who have retired before reaching pensionable age. Wherever any such departures from the usual constituency of the "elderly in Great Britain" occurs in either the text or the tables, they are noted and should be borne in mind because the nonusual category may differ, for example, in its proportions of men and women.

REFERENCES

Abrams, M. 1980. *Beyond Three Score and Ten.* London: Age Concern England.

———. 1985. *A Survey of the Elderly Shopper.* London: Age Concern England.

British Broadcasting Company. 1985. *Daily Life in the 1980s.* Vols 1-4. London: Author.

Fletcher, B., D. Gowler, and R. Payne. n.d. "Work, Death and Marriage Go Together Like a Horse and Carriage." Unpublished paper.

Her Majesty's Stationery Office (HMSO). 1981. *Census Report 1981.* London: Author.

———. 1982. *General Household Survey 1982.* London: Author.

———. 1983. *Family Expenditure Survey 1983.* London: Author.

———. 1985. *Social Trends 1985.* London: Author.

National Opinion Polls (N.O.P.). 1985a. *Political Social and Economic Review.* London: Author.

———. 1985b. *Time Use Study.* London: Author.

Office of Population Censuses and Surveys. 1978. *Occupational Mortality 1970-72.* London: HMSO.

Robinson, J. 1977. *How Americans Use Time.* New York: Praeger.

3

Time Use and Activities of the
Aged in the Netherlands

C.P.M. KNIPSCHEER, L. CLAESSENS,
and M.F.H.G. WIMMERS

A Day in the Life of Mr. D.

Mr. D. is 68 years of age and has been a bookshopkeeper in his small town for 40 years, married for 41 years, and has one son. He retired from his bookshop about three years ago and left it to his son. He has always been involved in a lot of community activities. He served for years as a representative in the community council and served on the boards of several societies.

After his retirement, he immediately joined the local section of the Dutch Society of Protestant Retired People, got on its board, and is now representing the older people on the regional board of Social Welfare and Community Work. In addition, he is the local coordinator of the lectures in the weekly church service.

On a weekday in May, he gets up at 8:00 in the morning and goes through the local newspaper, paying special attention to local social welfare events concerning youth problems and home services as well as activities for the aged. At 10:00, he has an appointment with the board of the local Retirement Society to talk about their yearly summer trip. Before he goes, he has to call a transportation enterprise to find out about rates. When he comes home, his wife tells him about a phone call from the county administrator of the Retirement Society. The administrator is organizing a study trip to Berlin to learn about social work and social services for the aged in Germany. After lunch, both he and his wife take time to rest and at 2:30 they go to work outside. In spring, they organize the vegetable garden for growing vegetables. Their son likes to come and take some fresh food from the garden. After dinner, Mr. D. had to remind the next Sunday's lecturers about the church service. He also goes to talk to a recently retired woman in the community to invite her to become a member of the local board. He likes to be back at 10:00 p.m. to watch the soccer playoffs of the season.

A Day in the Life of Mrs. B.

Mrs. B., 69 years old, has been married for 48 years to a elementary school teacher who is 72 years old. They have three children, the last of which left home nine years ago. Mrs. B. did not have a job. Since her last son left home, she got involved in different kinds of volunteer work such as visiting ill people and transporting them to special events, handicrafts for blind children, and serving as area referee of the women's society. More recently, she got involved in a community center for the aged and started to visit lonely older people. For more than 20 years, she has stayed very active in square dancing. Half a year ago, her husband had a heart attack while she was visiting older people. He has recovered, but not too well and needs a lot of attention.

When Mrs. B. gets up in the morning at 7:30, she goes to prepare breakfast and wakes up her husband at 8:30. They have breakfast together in the bedroom. Then, she assists her husband to get up and stays around when he is washing and dressing. They have coffee at 10:00. Sometimes Mrs. B. invites one of the older neighbors for coffee, depending on the fatigue of her husband. After lunch, her husband goes to sleep for about one hour and a half or two. Mrs. B. goes to do her shopping and sometimes stops in at her daughter's, who lives a few blocks away and has a part-time job. After she comes back home, they have tea together and play cards or do a puzzle. In the meantime, Mrs. B. is preparing dinner and arranges other household affairs. After dinner, she should go to her square dancing evening. She's scared to go sometimes. When her husband does not feel well, she skips it and they watch TV together. Her husband's heart attack has changed her life a lot.

While these individual stories provide a glimpse of what old age might be like, two national studies (1976 and 1982) on the life situation of people 55 years and over will be presented to provide a description of the pattern of later life in the Netherlands.

National Context of the Elderly

The history and economic and social developments of the Dutch society during this century are relevant in understanding the situation of the elderly. Current demographic structures, the socioeconomic situation, housing, and labor participation of the elderly further specify the situation individuals face in old age. The Netherlands is a Western European country with a high standard of living, a very dense population, a well-developed welfare state, and one of the highest life expectancies.

The Netherlands is one of the countries with the highest population density. Since 1900, the birthrate has been very high, and because the health care was of a high standard, child mortality decreased constantly. One of the explanations for the high birthrate was the religious composition of the Netherlands. A classic in Dutch sociology is a study on the emancipation of the Dutch Roman Catholics, based on the development of their birthrate over a period of 50 years (Heek, 1954). The Catholic authorities promoted large families to become, in the long run, a larger portion in the Dutch population. They succeeded up to the 1960s. In comparison to the other Western European countries, this is an exceptional situation. But it explains why the growth in the percentage of older people started later than in most other countries, as we will show later.

Although demographic aging was delayed, policy for the aged developed. In the first year after World War II, a provisional public pension system began. In 1957, a general pension system was introduced for everyone 65 years old and over. In the 1950s and 1960s, the government also developed a housing policy for the aged. Many older people moved to homes for the aged and the first nursing homes were founded (Munnichs, 1978). Popular acceptance and state support affected the growth of these kinds of institutions. The Netherlands has at the moment the highest proportion of institutionalized older people in the world.

The Demographic Situation

Table 3.1 shows the growing number of older people since 1940 and the prospects for increase up to 2030. 1980 was an important turning point and 2010 is expected to be one also. The proportion of those 65 and older grew to 1.5% in 1980 and will be 21.1% in 2030, given projected birth and death rates.

When men and women of different ages and marital statuses are examined separately, several trends become evident. The growth in the number of women 80 years and older is the most spectacular. Over a period of 80 years, the growth is 600%. The proportion of both married men and women above 65 is gradually decreasing between 1980 and 2030 in favor of increasing proportions of the never married and divorced (see Table 3.2). The increase in the absolute number of the elderly in the next decades, in combination with a higher proportion of those never married and divorced, is expected to bring about an exponentially growing need for formal care, especially between 2010 and 2030. The large cohort resulting from the very high birthrate between 1945 and 1965 will have arrived at old age.

The social and economic consequences of this situation in the "near" future need to be reflected on in the next decades. The Dutch welfare state pays a great deal for institutionalized elderly. Its public pension system assures everybody 65 and over an income at the level of the minimum standard of living. Handling the future shift in the age composition of the population will be a real test case. It is just the explosion of births in a two-decade period and the deep decline after this period that creates the problem.[1] A comparison of several Western European countries demonstrates this situation. Table 3.3 shows the low percentage of aged for the Netherlands in 1975. Even in 2005, the percentage will be lower for the Netherlands than for these other countries.

Income

Very low percentages of people over 65 work. Table 3.4 also shows that only 50% of the men between 55 to 65 years have regular jobs. Table 3.4 shows the main sources of income for people 55 years and over in 1983. The income (gross) people get from the general pension system is 1644 guilders for married people and 1146 guilders per month for unmarried people (as of January 3, 1984). Since 1972, benefits from the

TABLE 3.1   The Growth of the Percentage of People Over 54 Years by Age Group and Sex, from 1950 Until 2030

	1950	1980	1990	2000	2030
Men					
55-64 years	4.0	4.4	4.5	5.0	6.8
65-79 years	3.2	3.9	4.1	4.4	7.2
65+	3.7	4.7	5.1	5.4	8.9
80+	0.4	0.8	0.9	1.0	1.7
Women					
55-64 years	4.2	4.8	4.8	5.0	7.0
65-79 years	3.5	5.3	5.6	5.8	9.0
65+	4.0	6.7	7.6	7.9	12.3
80+	0.5	1.4	1.9	2.1	3.2
Total 65+	7.8	11.5	12.6	13.3	21.1

SOURCE: S. Koesobjono (1983). *Leeftÿd*: Dutch Federation on Policy for the Aged, The Hague, Netherlands. Used by permission.

TABLE 3.2   The Growth of the Percentage of People Over 64 Years by Marital Status and Sex

	1950	1980	1990	2000	2030
Men					
never married	8.9	6.5	6.0	6.5	19.7
married	63.1	74.2	73.5	70.9	57.6
widowed	27.2	17.1	17.1	17.5	15.2
divorced	0.8	2.1	3.4	5.0	7.5
total	100	100	100	100	100
Women					
never married	13.3	11.2	9.5	7.6	12.2
married	42.8	39.6	38.8	38.5	33.7
widowed	42.7	46.3	47.6	47.8	41.7
divorced	1.2	2.9	4.2	6.1	12.4
total	100	100	100	100	100

SOURCE: S. Koesobjono (1983). *Leeftÿd*: Dutch Federation on Policy for the Aged, The Hague, Netherlands. Used by permission.

general pension system equal the minimum standard of living as defined each year by the central government. A lot of older people have some income in addition (a private pension, private interest, irregular jobs, and so on) and this makes the mean net income of people above 64 about 1500 guilders per month in one-person households and about 1950 guilders in two- or more person households. Of people 55 years or older who are living independently, 28% find their income amply sufficient;

TABLE 3.3   The Growth in the Percentage of People Over 64 Years in Some Western European Countries

	1975	1990	2005
West Germany	14.3	14.5	17.1
France	13.3	12.7	13.8
Italy	12.0	13.5	15.2
Netherlands	10.7	12.3	13.3*
Belgium	13.9	13.0	13.7
United Kingdom	14.0	14.8	13.9
Denmark	13.2	14.7	13.7
Luxembourg	13.0	12.9	15.3

SOURCE: Commission of the European Communities (1978).
NOTE: Table 3.1 presents a more recent projection. For reasons of comparison, the one of 1978 is maintained here.

49%, sufficient; 15%, insufficient; and 6% find it very insufficient. A total of 39% own their homes; 7% are not provided with a hot-water bath or shower; 7% have no telephone; and 16% receive help from a housekeeper or charwoman. For 21%, financial problems are the reason for not going out more often, although they would like to do so. This percentage rises to 41% for those who want to go on holiday more often but are not able to afford it (C.B.S., 1984).

Because of differences from other Western European countries, the living situation of older people in the Netherlands needs special attention. About 14.5% of the people 65 and over lived in communal accommodations in 1980 (Collot et al., 1982), while in Belgium, the corresponding percentage was 5.0% of people 65 years and older (excluding hospitals); in Denmark, 7.9%; in West Germany, 4.5%; in the United Kingdom, 5.0%; and in France, 5.0% (Collot et al., 1982). In the 1950s and 1960s, the number of homes for the aged in the Netherlands increased very quickly and the first nursing homes were opened. Older people needing nursing care 24 hours a day live in a nursing home. These nursing homes are financed by a social security health system. Older people who are in some lesser degree handicapped in daily activities or in personal care move to a *home* for the aged. Homes for the aged are subsidized in increasing amounts by the government. Since 1972, anyone over 65 can get a subsidized stay in a home for the aged if he or she cannot afford it. At the moment, the government covers the expenses for about 95% of the elderly living in homes for the aged. Since 1976, however, the government's policy has been to reduce the number of people in these homes. A screening system for admission has

TABLE 3.4 Main Source of Income per Household (one-person and more-than-one person households) by Age Group and Sex

	Work	AOW/AWW (1)	Pension (2)	WAO (3)	Other (4)	Total
Men						
55-64 years	50	1	10	20	9	100
65-74 years	4	71	21	1	3	100
75+	2	77	15	0	6	100
Women						
55-64 years	35	30	13	11	11	100
65-79 years	5	71	19	2	3	100
75+	1	90	7	0	2	100

SOURCE: Netherlands Central Bureau of Statistics, Leffsituatie-onderzoek onder de Nederlandse bevolking ran 18 jaar en ouder, kerncijfers (Well-being of the population in the Netherlands of 18 years and older, key figures) (Staatsuitgeverij, 's Gravenhage, 1984); used by permission.
NOTE: (1) general public pension system; (2) private pension; (3) social security for disabled workers; and (4) specific social security fundings, interest of own capital, and so on.

developed. Because of the economic depression, this policy has been strictly enforced since 1980 and the percentage of older people living in homes is gradually decreasing.

Daily Life in Later Years: 1982

In 1982, a national random sample of people 55 years old and over were interviewed about their life situation (income, living arrangements, relationships, health, and so on). This is the Life Situation Study 1982-55+ (L.S.S. '82-55+). Special attention was given to social activities and the time spent in specific activities of life. The older age groups are overrepresented in the sample. The data in the following tables, however, control for this overrepresentation.

The total sample comprised 4283 people 55 years and over, 56% female and 44% male. Of the sample, 70% were married; 4%, divorced; 21%, widowed; and 6%, never married.

Dividing daily life into categories of activity has been attempted by others. By factor analyzing quite a variety of leisure activities, Kelly (1982) got a "core model," a specific group of "activities such as watching television, family interaction, entertaining and visiting, reading and other relatively unscheduled and informal ones." Moss and Lawton (1982) used another distinction between leisure activities in their research. Obligatory activities include personal care, eating, shopping, housework, cooking, and helping others. Social agency and family interaction, social (nonfamily) interaction, religious reading, radio, TV, recreation, and rest are discretionary activities. Gordon and Gaitz (1976) specified five major objectives of leisure activities and placed them on an assumed continuum of expressive involvement intensity. The resulting arrangement of leisure objectives is relaxation, diversion, development, creativity, and sensual transcendence.

The items analyzed in this chapter are arranged in four categories: (1) *nonproductive activities*, including total number of hours spent in leisure activities (gardening, reading, sport, playing cards, and so on) and on mass media (radio, TV); (2) *productive activities*, including total number of hours spend in household activities per week (shopping, cooking, cleaning) and helping other people (children, neighbors), in doing unpaid work (for churches, clubs, unions), and in going out; (3) *companionship*, including how many times one visits other people (own children are not included) or is visited by others per week, how many times one visits a community center for the aged, and the number of organizational memberships; (4) *needs*, including the wish for more work, for education, to have more social contacts, and to go out more often. Our productive activities are closest to the obligatory activities category of Moss and Lawton. The discretionary activities were split into explicit social activities (companionship) and nonproductive and less social activities.

Nonproductive Activities

Table 3.5 indicates minor differences between men and women for the nonproductive activities. More men than women read a newspaper daily. For those aged 75 and older, there is remarkably lower involvement in leisure activities, and Table 3.5 indicates a bigger decline for women than for men. In Table 3.6, showing sex/marital status related to activities, the most consistent pattern is found for the never married. Never-married men and women invest less time in leisure activities, on mass media in general, and they watch TV news less often than other people. This pattern does not show up for daily reading of the newspaper.

In contrast to the never married, the divorced men and women invest more time in leisure activities, but not on mass media. Significantly more divorced women never read a newspaper. There is a general

TABLE 3.5 Nonproductive Activities by Sex and Age (percentages)

		Men			r		Women			r	
	Total N	55-64 Years	65-74 Years	≥75 Years		Significance	55-64 Years	65-74 Years	≥75 Years		Significance
1.1 Number of hours spent in leisure activities per day:											
<2 hours	19	15	12	28	-.11	*	13	16	34	-.24	*
2-4 hours	35	37	32	37			34	32	38		
>4 hours	47	48	56	35			53	52	28		
N	4283	735	674	462			861	845	706		
1.2 Number of hours spent on mass media per day:											
<2 hours	14	18	11	16	.06	*	16	10	14	-.03	—
2-4 hours	43	45	40	42			38	45	47		
>4 hours	43	37	49	42			46	45	39		
N	4257	730	671	457			858	840	701		
1.3 Daily TV news watching:											
yes	87	85	91	86	.00	—	86	88	86	.01	—
sometimes	9	12	5	7			10	9	9		
never	4	3	4	7			4	3	5		
N	4276	734	671	461			860	844	706		
1.4 Daily newspaper reading:											
yes	86	90	89	89	.02	—	85	82	80	.07	*
sometimes	7	5	5	5			9	8	8		
never	8	5	6	6			6	10	12		
N	4278	735	671	462			860	844	706		

NOTE: Pearson's r is used here because most social scientists have become accustomed to this correlation coefficient and because it has the advantage of being easily interpreted.
* p ≤ .01.

TABLE 3.6 Nonproductive Activities by Sex and Marital Status (percentages)

			Men						Women			
	Total N	I	II	III	IV[a]	r Significance	I	II	III	IV[a]	r Significance
1.1 Number of hours spend in leisure activities per day:											
<2 hours	19	17	26	18	22	−.06	17	12	24	24	−.10
2-4 hours	35	34	22	39	43	*	34	31	35	38	*
>4 hours	47	49	52	43	35		49	57	41	38	
N	4283	1523	50	207	91		1293	65	859	195	
1.2 Number of hours spent on mass media per day:											
<2 hours	14	15	10	13	24	.00	12	13	13	22	−.06
2-4 hours	43	43	48	37	37	—	42	50	43	46	*
>4 hours	43	42	42	50	39		46	37	44	32	
N	4257	1512	50	250	91		1289	64	853	193	
1.3 Daily TV news watching:											
yes	87	90	74	84	73	.12	88	91	87	80	.06
sometimes	9	7	20	10	15	*	9	6	9	12	*
never	4	3	6	6	12		3	3	4	8	
N	4276	1519	50	207	90		1292	65	858	195	
1.4 Daily newspaper reading:											
yes	86	91	86	82	90	.07	86	66	80	80	.08
sometimes	7	4	12	6	4	*	7	15	9	10	*
never	8	5	2	12	6		7	19	11	10	
N	4278	1512	50	207	90		1291	65	859	195	

a. marital status: (I) married; (II) divorced; (III) widowed; and (IV) never married.

51

tendency for nonmarried men and women to be less involved in nonproductive activities. The nonmarried watch less TV news and read the newspaper less. It seems to be they are less oriented toward society. Surprisingly little attention is given to the differentiation of activity patterns by marital status (see Gordon and Gaitz, 1976; Kelley, 1982; Moss and Lawton, 1982).

People with a lower education spend less time in most leisure activities but more in TV watching. Fewer of them read the newspaper daily (not shown in the tables).

Productive Activities

For productive activities, the main difference between men and women is in hours spent on housework. Two-thirds of older men are involved in household activities for less than 5 hours per week, while 70% of the older women are involved for more than 15 hours. The traditional sex roles seem to be maintained in old age. The people over 75 years of age decrease their time investment in household activities. This may be because of caring activities by others. The same trend is seen in helping activities, in unpaid work, and in times gone out. The consistency of this trend is apparent from the age of 55 (see Figure 3.1). Table 3.7 confirms this trend between age groups for men and women separately, with the exception of one case. Men invest more time in household activities as they reach older age (Figures 3.2 and 3.3).

Table 3.8 shows that this is especially true for divorced and widowed men. The never-married older people tend to invest less time in productive activities, parallel to what was shown for most of the nonproductive activities. A comparison of two other subgroups demonstrates again the traditional sex role differentiation. Women *not* living alone invest more time in household activities than women living alone, while men not living alone invest much less time in it than men living alone. As for the correlation of productive activities and education level, only minor trends can be seen. People of the higher education level invest somewhat more time in helping other people, in unpaid work, and in going out. A cohort effect may be involved here.

Companionship

Very few people 65 years and older visit a service center for the aged weekly or more often. There is a minor increase for both men and women after the age of 75 (Table 3.9). There are few but consistent

TABLE 3.7 Productive Activities by Sex and Age (percentages)

	Men 55-64 Years	Men 65-74 Years	Men ≥75 Years	r	Significance	Women 55-64 Years	Women 65-74 Years	Women ≥75 Years	r	Significance
2.1 Number of hours spent on household activities per week:										
< 1 hour	12	33	20	.17		1	1	4	-.28	
1-5 hours	18	36	33		*	3	6	11		*
5-15 hours	23	22	31			13	19	29		
15-25 hours	23	6	11			32	33	32		
25-35 hours	13	2	2			26	22	15		
> 35 hours	11	1	3			26	19	9		
N	4196	727	662			848	829	681		
2.2 Number of hours helping other people per week:										
0 hours	90	90	89	-.04		83	90	98	-.18	
0, 5-3 hours	6	6	6	—		10	6	1		*
> 3 hours	4	4	5			7	4	1		
N	4267	728	669			860	842	706		
2.3 Number of hours doing unpaid work for organizations, clubs, and so on per week:										
0 hours	86	76	84	-.15		82	90	94	-.14	
0, 5-3 hours	8	14	8		*	11	6	4		*
> 3 hours	6	10	8			7	4	2		
N	4272	730	672			859	845	706		
2.4 Times going out per month:										
0	15	7	15	-.26		7	10	29	-.28	
1-2 times	31	28	28		*	28	32	36		*
3-7 times	36	41	35			44	38	27		
> 7 times	18	24	22			21	20	8		
N	4264	734	672			857	844	703		

PERCENT

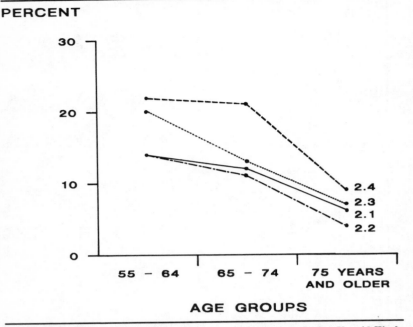

Figure 3.1   **Time Invested in Household Activities, Helping Activities, Unpaid Work, and Times Gone Out: Total Sample**

differences between men and women in socializing activities. Women visit other people more often and are visited more often too. In terms of age groups, both men and women 75 and over pay fewer visits to others (Table 3.10). The number of memberships is also lower for older age groups. Divorced, widowed, and never-married men and women visit other people more often than married people 55 years and over. But only divorced, widowed, and never-married *women* are visited more by others than the married women, while married men get more visits than the divorced, widowed, and never-married men (Table 3.10). Earlier analysis of the social network showed that widows, divorced, and never-married women socialize more (both being visited by others and paying visits to others) than men (Knipscheer, 1980). Comparing, in current data, people living alone and people not living alone, the same trend shows up. In addition, men and women who live alone visit a service center for the aged more often.

The main association between companionship and educational level

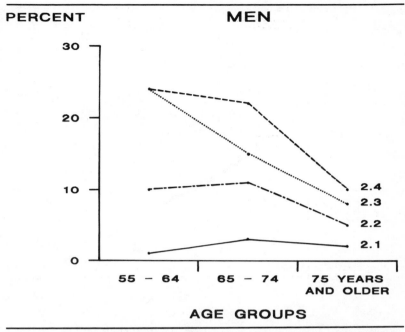

PERCENT   MEN

Figure 3.2   Time Invested in Household Activities, Helping Activities, Unpaid Work, and Times Gone Out: Men

is in the number of memberships. The higher the educational level, the more numerous the memberships. Also, those with higher educational levels visit services centers for the aged less often and get visits less often.

The questionnaire included some questions about what older people would like to do more frequently. Table 3.11 shows that more older women than older men would like to participate in education, have more social contacts, and go out more often. This has to be stressed, because in the last paragraph, it was shown that older women are already more active in socializing activities than men. There is no differentiation between age groups in the expressed need for more social contacts. Younger age groups would like more work, more education, and more going out than older ones. Table 3.11 indicates the same age group differentiation for both men and women. As demonstrated in Table 3.12, more divorced older people would like more work, education, more social contacts, and more going out than those older men and women who are married or widowed. The never-married older

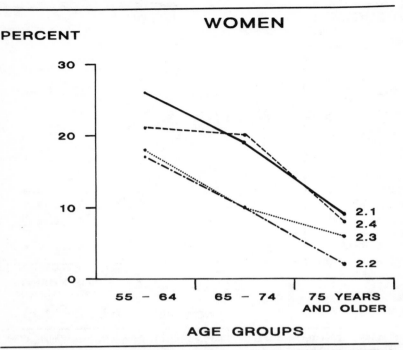

Figure 3.3   Time Invested in Household Activities, Helping Activities, Unpaid Work, and Times Gone Out: Women

people are similar to the divorced in the need for more social contacts and more going out. Here again, the higher scores of the divorced and never married in socializing activities do not mean their needs are being met. Among the older men and women living alone, a significantly higher percentage wish to have more social contacts than among those living with someone. The higher the education, the more older people wish to participate in work, education, and going out.

Summary

In summarizing the main trends in these data, age differences in time use and activities are obvious. In the productive activities, in companionship, and in needs, we see a steady decline by age, with two significant exceptions. People 75 and over do not have less need for social contacts and they do not indicate a decrease in being visited by

TABLE 3.8 Productive Activities by Sex and Marital Status (percentages)

		Men					Women				
	Total N	I	II	III	IV	r / Significance	I	II	III	IV	r / Significance
2.1 Number of hours spent on household activities per week:											
< 1 hour	12	27	10	11	33	.18	1	1	2	4	−.26
1-5 hours	18	36	14	19	22	*	4	2	8	16	*
5-15 hours	23	25	45	36	28		14	24	27	30	
15-25 hours	23	8	22	23	11		32	45	33	27	
25-35 hours	13	2	6	6	5		25	10	18	13	
> 35 hours	11	1	2	5	1		24	18	12	9	
N	4196	1496	49	204	89		1275	62	830	191	
2.2 Number of hours helping other people per week:											
0 hours	90	90	100	92	99	−.06	89	78	91	94	−.03
0, 5-3 hours	6	6	0	6	0	*	7	13	5	0	—
> 3 hours	4	4	0	2	1		4	9	4	5	
N	4267	1513	50	205	91		1291	64	859	194	
2.3 Number of hours doing unpaid work for organizations, clubs, and so on per week:											
0 hours	86	81	84	93	87	−.09	89	86	90	80	.03
0, 5-3 hours	8	11	10	5	5	*	7	9	6	13	—
> 3 hours	6	8	6	2	8		4	5	4	7	
N	4272	1515	50	207	90		1291	65	859	195	
2.4 Times going out per month:											
0	15	15	6	24	21	−.03	11	5	19	17	−.09
1-2 times	31	30	18	22	27	—	31	37	35	24	*
3-7 times	36	35	48	33	34		40	42	31	38	
> 7 times	18	20	28	20	17		18	16	15	21	
N	4264	1516	50	207	91		1291	64	854	195	

TABLE 3.9 Companionship by Sex and Age (percentages)

	Total N	Men					Women			
		55-64 Years	65-74 Years	≥75 Years	r	Significance	55-64 Years	65-74 Years	≥75 Years	r	Significance
3.1 Times one visits other people per week:											
1 time	51	51	55	65	-.09		44	45	56	-.09	
1-3 times	29	30	30	20		*	33	31	27		*
> 3 times	19	19	15	15			23	24	17		
N	4215	719	662	459			847	835	693		
3.2 Times visited by others per week:											
1 time	30	33	31	35	.00		28	26	28	.03	
1-3 times	41	42	40	40		—	45	40	39		—
> 3 times	29	25	29	25			27	34	32		
N	4229	726	661	457			852	836	697		
3.3 Times visiting a service center for the aged per week:											
never	92	97	91	90	.13		96	89	88	.12	
1 time	1	1	3	5		*	1	3	4		*
1-3 times	4	2	4	4			3	7	7		
> 3 times	3	0	2	1			0	1	1		
N	4275	733	673	460			861	844	704		
3.4 Number of memberships:											
0	40	28	38	40	-.13		46	38	49	-.03	
1	30	32	29	34		*	28	32	29		—
> 1	30	40	33	26			27	30	22		
N	4283	735	674	462			861	845	706		

TABLE 3.10 Companionship by Sex and Marital Status (percentages)

	Total N	Men				r Significance	Women				r Significance
		I	II	III	IV		I	II	III	IV	
3.1 Times one visits other people per week:											
1 time	51	57	59	50	26	.07	53	47	43	37	.14
1-3 times	29	28	22	26	22	*	30	20	32	31	*
>3 times	19	15	19	24	26		17	33	25	32	
N	4215	1498	49	204	89		1273	61	849	192	
3.2 Times visited by others per week:											
1 time	30	30	63	42	52	-.12	27	35	26	31	.03
1-3 times	41	42	27	37	26	*	44	39	39	37	—
>3 times	29	28	10	21	22		29	26	35	31	
N	4229	1507	48	202	87		1285	62	843	195	
3.3 Times visiting a service center for the aged per week:											
never	92	94	94	88	89	.10	94	86	87	94	.07
1 time	1	2	4	6	7	*	2	9	4	1	*
1-3 times	4	3	0	3	2		4	3	8	4	
>3 times	3	1	2	2	2		0	2	1	1	
N	4275	1518	50	207	91		1292	65	858	194	
3.4 Number of memberships:											
0	40	33	44	44	45	-.10	44	52	42	46	.02
1	30	31	30	32	30	*	30	26	31	24	—
>1	30	36	26	25	25		26	22	27	30	
N	4283	1523	50	207	91		1293	65	859	195	

TABLE 3.11 Needs by Sex and Age (percentages)

	Total N	Men 55-64 Years	65-74 Years	≥75 Years	r Significance	Women 55-64 Years	65-74 Years	≥75 Years	r Significance
4.1 Wish to perform more work:									
yes/it may be	12	22	12	4	.21 *	18	8	1	.24 *
no	89	78	88	96		82	92	99	
N	4253	727	668	459		854	841	704	
4.2 Wish for education:									
yes	11	17	6	2	.21 *	22	11	2	.24 *
no	89	83	94	98		78	89	98	
N	4240	728	665	459		851	838	699	
4.3 Wish to have more social contacts:									
yes	15	11	11	12	.00 —	17	17	17	.01 —
no	85	89	89	88		83	83	83	
N	4167	720	658	451		838	811	689	
4.4 Wish to get out more often:									
yes/it may be	27	28	21	15	.12 *	38	31	25	.12 *
no	73	72	79	85		62	69	75	
N	4266	733	669	460		860	839	705	

TABLE 3.12 Needs by Sex and Marital Status (percentages)

	Men							Women					
	Total N	I	II	III	IV	r	Significance	I	II	III	IV	r	Significance
4.1 Wish to perform more work: %													
yes/it may be	12	15	23	6	15	.05		11	20	6	9	.07	
no	89	85	77	94	85		—	89	80	94	91		*
N	4253	1510	49	206	89			1287	64	854	194		
4.2 Wish for education:													
yes	11	10	14	4	6	.06		13	27	9	16	.03	
no	89	90	86	96	94		*	87	73	91	84		—
N	4240	1507	49	207	89			1285	62	849	192		
4.3 Wish to have more social contacts:													
yes	15	10	35	16	7	-.04		15	33	19	21	-.06	
no	85	90	65	84	93		—	85	67	81	79		*
N	4167	1493	48	201	87			1258	63	832	185		
4.4 Wish to go out more often:													
yes/it may be	27	23	31	16	13	.07		32	40	30	35	.00	
no	73	77	69	84	87		*	68	60	70	65		—
N	4266	1516	48	207	91			1290	65	855	194		

others. The number of hours spent in leisure activities, however, decreases after 75. The differentiation by age, however, is not the most surprising in our data (see Gordon and Gait, 1976; Kelly, 1982). The differences between men and women are mainly in the amount of companionship and the need for more activities or social contacts. Despite the fact that women invest more time in companionship activities, they indicate a need for still more. These findings are not particularly surprising given similar findings in other research (Rosow, 1976; Blau, 1973; Knipscheer, 1980).

The differences between divorced and never-married women in comparison to the married and the widowed women are of interest. Divorced and never-married women spend less time on mass media per day, do more unpaid work for organizations and clubs, visit more people, and are visited by others less. More of these women wish to engage in more educational activities, more social contacts, and would like to go out more often. In comparison to men, women seem to be more involved in social activities and at the same time express a need for even more. This seems to be the case with an exponential factor for never-married and divorced women in comparison to the married and widowed women. This finding may be more related to marital status than to aging.

In earlier research, Knipscheer (1974) pointed out that women living alone between 30 and 60, especially those never married and divorced, felt neglected by other people and indicated they had to invest more time and energy in maintaining their relationships. The situation for older divorced women is different. Divorce is many times a disruptive event, not only for someone's social network but also for the family network (Hagestad, 1984; Bengtson and Robertson, 1985). This situation may explain the remarkable involvement of divorced women in many activities and their need for more.

More highly educated older people are more involved in leisure activities, do more unpaid work, go out more, and have more memberships. In addition, they would like more work and educational activity.

Daily Life in Later Life:
A Panel Study (1976-1982)

The preceding analysis shows that the young-old people have a more active time-use pattern than the old-old people. A longitudinal design, however, is needed to conclude that with growing older, activity diminishes. Fortunately, a panel study attached to the national Life Situation Survey 1982-55+ is available. This panel study consists of 1020 respondents who took part in the Life Situation Survey for the Elderly in 1976. At that time, they were 55 to 65 years old.

In 1982, the respondents from the panel study were 60 to 73 years old and the average age was 66.3. The L.S.S. 1982-55+ is extended to the entire population of 55 years and older. As a consequence, the average age of this sample is somewhat higher, namely, 68.5 years. Because of this difference in age structure, the two samples differ slightly from each other in several aspects. In this section, we will first investigate the development of the time-use pattern of the so-called young old within a period of six years (1976 to 1982) for the whole sample, and also for men and women separately.

The changes that appear, however, cannot simply be ascribed to growing older. Other factors probably play a part in it as well. In the course of six years, one has not only grown older, but important life events may have occurred. In this period, 305 out of the 1020 respondents stopped working, 66 persons lost their husband or wife, 44 people became impaired between 1976 and 1982, and for 224 people, the (last) child(ren) left the parental home. Other important life events could be added to this list, but not all the changes were measured in this survey or they apply to only a few respondents. We will restrict our attention to the four mentioned events and their impact on the development of time use.

Aside from this, we will check the probability that people who went through more than one of these events have changed more than the others. The number of years one has been retired or widowed is known, so the time since the occurrence of the event shall be considered also.

Changes in Time Use

Tables 3.13 to 3.15 show percentages for several groups of people remaining stable, spending more time or spending less time on 12 time-use items. Table 3.16 shows stability and change in four needs concerning time use. The percentages are obtained from turnover tables (e.g., a cross-table with the variables hours spent in household duties in 1976 and hours spent in household duties in 1982). The significance of differences observed between the two groups is tested by chi-square. The asterisks point to significant differences.

In the first column of Table 3.13, we see that more than 40% of the

TABLE 3.13 Changes in Nonproductive Activities Between 1976 and 1982 for Several Groups (percentages)

The Situation in 1982 Compared with the Situation in 1976	Whole Sample	Men	Women	People Who Became Impaired	People Who Remained Able	People Who Retired	People Who Kept Working	Women Whose (Last) child(ren) Left Home	Women Still Having (a) child(ren) at Home	Women Who Became Widows	Women Still Married
	(1020)	(473)	(544)	(44)	(809)	(305)	(108)	(112)	(59)	(50)	(322)
Number of hours spent in leisure activities:											
the same	42	42	41	38	33	38	50	43	44	26	46
more	40	41	40	41	56	48	36	40	40	45	35
less	18	16	19	21	11	14	16	17	16	29	19
χ^2		$\chi^2 = 2.135$	$p > .3438$	$\chi^2 = .429$	$p > .5$	$\chi^2 = 3.097$	$p = .2126$	$\chi^2 = .113$	$p > .5$	$\chi^2 = 6.663$	$p = .0357**$
χ^2 after correction		$\chi^2 = 1.362$	$p > .5$	$\chi^2 = 6.006$	$p > .0496***$	$\chi^2 = 5.704$	$p = .0577*$	$\chi^2 = .053$	$p > .5$	$\chi^2 = 6.846$	$p = .0326**$
Number of hours spent on mass media:											
the same	48	47	46	43	51	49	56	44	32	46	50
more	39	43	40	45	35	41	36	41	38	35	29
less	13	10	13	12	14	10	8	16	30	19	21
χ^2		$\chi^2 = 9.418$	$p = .009***$	$\chi^2 = .665$	$p > .5$	$\chi^2 = 1.534$	$p = .4645$	$\chi^2 = 3.137$	$p = .2084$	$\chi^2 = .085$	$p > .5$
χ^2 after correction		$\chi^2 = 3.068$	$p = .2157$	$\chi^2 = 1.749$	$p = .4170$	$\chi^2 = 1.540$	$p = .4631$	$\chi^2 = 5.239$	$p = .0728*$	$\chi^2 = .776$	$p > .5$
Daily watching TV news:											
the same	87	88	86	93	91	88	82	84	87	80	83
started watching	10	10	9	0	4	10	10	6	5	12	13
stopped watching	4	3	5	7	5	2	7	9	8	8	4
χ^2		$\chi^2 = 5.037$	$p = .0806*$	$\chi^2 = 5.261$	$p = .0721*$	$\chi^2 = 10.737$	$p = .0047***$	$\chi^2 = 1.791$	$p = .4083$	$\chi^2 = 3.647$	$p = .1615$
χ^2 after correction		$\chi^2 = 4.801$	$p = .0907*$	$\chi^2 = 2.427$	$p = .2971$	$\chi^2 = 8.679$	$p = .0130**$	$\chi^2 = .126$	$p > .5$	$\chi^2 = 1.759$	$p = .4150$
Daily newspaper reading											
the same	90	91	89	74	91	90	91	91	90	84	91
started reading	4	4	3	7	4	5	5	3	4	2	4
stopped reading	6	4	8	19	4	6	4	6	5	14	5
χ^2		$\chi^2 = 6.088$	$p = .0476**$	$\chi^2 = 18.049$	$p = .0001***$	$\chi^2 = .553$	$p > .5$	$\chi^2 = .756$	$p > .5$	$\chi^2 = 5.541$	$p = .0626*$
χ^2 after correction		$\chi^2 = 8.175$	$p = .0168**$	$\chi^2 = 17.514$	$p = .0002***$	$\chi^2 = 1.031$	$p > .5$	$\chi^2 = .153$	$p > .5$	$\chi^2 = 5.632$	$p = .0598*$

total sample remains stable between 1976 and 1982 in the total number of hours spent in leisure activities and in radio/television. The number of hours spent in leisure activities more often increases than decreases. This is also the case for listening to the radio and for watching television. Some examples of increased leisure activities are as follows: 22% of the people weren't involved in round games in 1976, but were in 1982; a fairly high percentage of people started doing needlework, little jobs, gardening, walking, and cycling. Most people watch the TV news and read the newspaper every day in 1976 and in 1982, so many changes didn't occur on these points.

In Table 3.14, we see that 37% of all respondents spent the same amount of time on household activities in 1976 and in 1982, 30% spent more time and 33% spent less time. Doing small repairs and cleaning the house are the activities one abandons most often.

Most people didn't help others and didn't do unpaid work for associations, churches, and so on in 1976. This hasn't changed in 1982, so the percentage of people remaining the same is very high (77% and 79%). The total number of times one goes out decreased more often than it increased. This is particularly true for making an excursion and for shopping. These two activities, however, mostly show an increase as well. So, these activities represent one of the areas where the patterns of time use have changed, increasing for some and decreasing for others. The visits one pays and is paid have decreased and increased in the same amount (27%-29%). The number of times attending a service center for the aged has increased somewhat more often than decreased. For more than half of the people, the number of memberships stays the same. For one-quarter, the number grows, and for almost one-quarter, it declines. Most striking are the increases in people who have become members of an association for the aged (16%) and the decreases for those who are members of a labor union or employers' organization in 1982 (14%).

The wishes one expresses concerning more work, more social contacts, education, and going out remain stable for most people.

One cannot conclude from these figures that the people have become less active in their general use of time. Only the number of times going out declined for a fairly large minority of the sample (35%). The number of hours spent in leisure activities even increased for 40% of them. According to Kelly (1982), leisure demonstrates more continuity than discontinuity in later life. Palmore (1968) suggests that normal aging persons tend to compensate for reductions in some activities by increases in others, so the net effect is no or little change. He finds a

(text continues on p. 72)

TABLE 3.14 Changes in Productive Activities Between 1976 and 1982 for Several Groups (percentages)

The Situation in 1982 Compared with the Situation in 1976	Whole Sample	Men	Women	People Who Became Impaired	People Who Remained Able	People Who Retired	People Who Kept Working	Women Whose (Last) child(ren) Left Home	Women Still Having (a) child(ren) at Home	Women Who Became Widows	Women Still Married
	(1020)	(473)	(544)	(44)	(809)	(305)	(108)	(112)	(59)	(50)	(322)
Number of hours spent in household activities:											
the same	37	51	32	19	37	45	53	27	25	10	28
more	30	34	62	28	28	40	24	19	29	19	22
less	33	15	6	53	35	15	23	54	46	71	50
χ^2		$\chi^2 = 103.845$	$p = .00$***	$\chi^2 = 8.5141$	$p = .0140$**	$\chi^2 = 7.259$	$p = .0265$**	$\chi^2 = 2.738$	$p = .2243$	$\chi^2 = 12.572$	$p = .0019$***
χ^2 after correction		$\chi^2 = 74.229$	$p = .00$***	$\chi^2 = 5.877$	$p = .0529$*	$\chi^2 = 8.642$	$p = .0133$**	$\chi^2 = 1.958$	$p = .3757$	$\chi^2 = 8.448$	$p = .0146$**
Number of hours helping other people:											
the same	77	80	77	86	80	77	76	73	82	69	82
more	11	11	13	9	13	12	9	15	11	25	11

	C1	C2	C3	C4	C5	C6	C7	C8	C9	C10	C11
less	11	10	10	5	7	12	14	12	7	6	7
χ^2		$\chi^2 = 3.767$	$p = .1520$	$\chi^2 = 2.604$	$p = .2720$	$\chi^2 = 1.860$	$p = .3946$	$\chi^2 = 4.143$	$p = .1260$	$\chi^2 = 8.450$	$p > .0146$**
χ^2 after correction		$\chi^2 = 1.290$	$p = .5$	$\chi^2 = 1.011$	$p = .5$	$\chi^2 = 1.168$	$p = .5$	$\chi^2 = 2.135$	$p = .3439$	$\chi^2 = 7.489$	$p > .0237$**
Number of hours doing unpaid work for organizations, clubs, and so on:											
the same	79	76	78	93	83	76	75	80	85	84	84
more	10	12	9	2	11	14	13	10	7	12	8
less	11	12	13	5	5	10	12	10	8	4	8
χ^2		$\chi^2 = 3.021$	$p = .2208$	$\chi^2 = 6.046$	$p = .0487$**	$\chi^2 = 3.906$	$p = .1418$	$\chi^2 = .906$	$p > .5$	$\chi^2 = 2.752$	$p = .2526$
χ^2 after correction		$\chi^2 = 1.822$	$p = .4022$	$\chi^2 = 3.564$	$p = .1683$**	$\chi^2 = .252$	$p > .5$	$\chi^2 = .513$	$p > .5$	$\chi^2 = 1.764$	$p = .4140$
Times gone out:											
the same	38	41	37	34	40	38	42	38	37	44	35
more	26	24	29	21	32	26	22	24	31	28	33
less	35	35	33	46	28	36	36	38	32	28	31
χ^2		$\chi^2 = 2.349$	$p = .3090$	$\chi^2 = 2.795$	$p = .2472$	$\chi^2 = .736$	$p > .5$	$\chi^2 = 4.668$	$p = .0969$*	$\chi^2 = 1.256$	$p > .5$
χ^2 after correction		$\chi^2 = 3.758$	$p = .1528$	$\chi^2 = 6.283$	$p = .0432$**	$\chi^2 = .708$	$p > .5$	$\chi^2 = 1.282$	$p > .5$	$\chi^2 = 1.404$	$p = .4956$

TABLE 3.15 Changes in Companionship Between 1976 and 1982 for Several Groups (percentages)

The Situation in 1982 Compared with the Situation in 1976	Whole Sample	Men	Women	People Who Became Impaired	People Who Are Not Disabled	People Who Retired	People Who Kept Working	Women Whose (Last) child(ren) Left Home	Women Still Having (a) child(ren) at Home	Women Who Became Widows	Women Still Married
	(1020)	(473)	(544)	(44)	(809)	(305)	(108)	(112)	(59)	(50)	(322)
Times one visits other people:											
the same	45	48	43	48	47	46	56	51	46	38	41
more	27	24	33	16	30	28	18	25	20	40	22
less	29	28	23	36	23	26	26	24	34	23	37
χ^2		$\chi^2 = 43.546$	p = .0***	$\chi^2 = 3.187$	p = .2033	$\chi^2 = 4.068$	p = .1308	$\chi^2 = .647$	p > .5	$\chi^2 = 3.394$	p = .1833
χ^2 after correction		$\chi^2 = 10.073$	p=.0065***	$\chi^2 = 6.205$	p = .0449**	$\chi^2 = 4.165$	p = .1246	$\chi^2 = 1.712$	p = .4248	$\chi^2 = 7.463$	p = .0240**
Times visited by others:											
the same	43	43	43	45	42	43	47	43	40	36	47
more	29	28	34	36	38	30	26	29	22	40	25
less	27	29	23	19	20	27	26	29	37	23	28

	a	b	a	b	a	b	a	b	a	b
χ^2	$\chi^2 = 2.134$	p = .3440	$\chi^2 = 1.672$	p = .4334	$\chi^2 = 1.465$	p = .4806	$\chi^2 = 2.866$	p = .2362	$\chi^2 = 2.173$	p = .3373
χ^2 after correction	$\chi^2 = 7.553$	p = .0229**	$\chi^2 = .158$	p > .5	$\chi^2 = .852$	p > .5	$\chi^2 = 1.315$	p > .5	$\chi^2 = 4.806$	p = .0905*
Times visiting a service center for the aged:										
the same	91	90	91	91*	92	98	94	97	84	92
more	7	8	7	7	6	2	7	3	16	6
less	2	2	2	2	3	0	0	0	0	2
χ^2	$\chi^2 = 3.329$	p = .1893	$\chi^2 = .020$	p > .5	$\chi^2 = 3.606$	p = .1648	$\chi^2 = 2.507$	p = .2855	$\chi^2 = 6.222$	p = .0445**
χ^2 after correction	$\chi^2 = 2.683$	p = .2615			$\chi^2 = 5.241$	p = .0728*			$\chi^2 = 6.477$	p = .0392**
Number of memberships:										
the same	52	51	48	51	53	54	50	59	52	53
more	25	22	30	31	23	27	29	16	28	26
less	22	27	23	18	24	19	21	25	20	21
χ^2	$\chi^2 = 3.170$	p = .2049	$\chi^2 = .454$	p > .5	$\chi^2 = .881$	p > .5	$\chi^2 = 1.671$	p = .4337	$\chi^2 = 1.66$	p > .5
χ^2 after correction	$\chi^2 = 1.090$	p > .5	$\chi^2 = .580$	p > .5	$\chi^2 = 1.382$	p > .5	$\chi^2 = 3.000$	p = .2231	$\chi^2 = .069$	p > .5

TABLE 3.16 Changes in Needs Concerning Time Use Between 1976 and 1982 for Several Groups (percentages)

The Situation in 1982 Compared with the Situation in 1976	Whole Sample	Men	Women	People Who Became Impaired	People Who Are Not Disabled	People Who Retired	People Who Kept Working	Women Whose (Last) child(ren) Left Home	Women Still Having (a) child(ren) at Home	Women Who Became Widows	Women Still Married
	(1020)	(473)	(544)	(44)	(809)	(305)	(108)	(112)	(59)	(50)	(322)
Wish to Perform More Work:											
the same	78	77	79	74	78	80	75	71	72	84	85
wish appeared in 1982	8	10	7	10	8	9	16	6	4	8	6
wish disappeared in 1982	13	13	14	17	14	11	9	23	24	8	9
χ^2		$\chi^2 = 4.552$	$p = .1027$	$\chi^2 = .615$	$p > .5$	$\chi^2 = 4.100$	$p = .1287$	$\chi^2 = 5.489$	$p = .0643^*$	$\chi^2 = 1.550$	$p = .4606$
χ^2 after correction		$\chi^2 = 4.552$	$p = .1027$	$\chi^2 = .440$	$p > .5$	$\chi^2 = 3.766$	$p = .1521$	$\chi^2 = .123$	$p > .5$	$\chi^2 = .247$	$p > .5$
Wish for Education:											
the same	82	86	83	89	88	81	74	77	98	74	83
wish appeared in 1982	7	6	9	9	9	8	14	5	1	16	7
wish disappeared											

in 1982	11	8	8	2	3	11	12	18	0	10	9
χ^2		$\chi^2 = 9.066$	$p = .0107^{**}$	$\chi^2 = 3.576$	$p > .1673$	$\chi^2 = 3.426$	$p = .1803$	$\chi^2 = 12.772$	$p = .0017^{***}$	$\chi^2 = 4.507$	$p > .1050$
χ^2 after correction		$\chi^2 = 3.227$	$p = .1992^{**}$	$\chi^2 = .104$	$p = .5$	$\chi^2 = 3.191$	$p = .2028$	$\chi^2 = 12.772$	$p = .0017^{***}$	$\chi^2 = 4.264$	$p > .1186$
Wish to have more social contact:											
the same	87	90	87	73	83	91	89	85	74	88	86
wish appeared in 1982	8	6	10	14	7	6	7	6	9	10	10
wish disappeared in 1982	5	4	3	14	10	3	4	9	17	2	5
χ^2		$\chi^2 = 8.837$	$p = .0121^{**}$	$\chi^2 = 10.807$	$p = .0045^{**}$	$\chi^2 = .330$	$p > .5$	$\chi^2 = 1.569$	$p = .4563$	$\chi^2 = .638$	$p > .5$
χ^2 after correction		$\chi^2 = 6.541$	$p = .0380^{**}$	$\chi^2 = 4.006$	$p = .1349$	$\chi^2 = .306$	$p > .5$	$\chi^2 = 3.395$	$p = .1831$	$\chi^2 = .765$	$p > .5$
Wish to go out more often:											
the same	69	69	69	64	71	72	71	70	69	58	68
wish appeared in 1982	14	13	17	23	14	13	13	13	14	18	14
wish disappeared in 1982	17	18	14	14	14	15	16	17	17	24	18
χ^2		$\chi^2 = 1.477$	$p = .4778$	$\chi^2 = 2.979$	$p = .2255$	$\chi^2 = .887$	$p > .5$	$\chi^2 = 1.767$	$p = .4133$	$\chi^2 = 3.172$	$p = .2048$
χ^2 after correction		$\chi^2 = 4.332$	$p = .1146$	$\chi^2 = 2.574$	$p = .2762$	$\chi^2 = .065$	$p > .5$	$\chi^2 = .064$	$p > .5$	$\chi^2 = 1.871$	$p = .3924$

positive correlation between total activities and attitudes toward the activities. According to him, this correlation supports the activity theory of aging. In a later article (Palmore, 1979), he proposes that secondary-group and physical activity may help prolong healthy and happy aging. In general, our data support a high amount of continuity in the time use and activities of the "young old" within a period of six years.

Gender and Changes in Time Use

Distinctions on gender (see the second column in Tables 3.13 to 3.16), however, produce a more differentiated picture for several items. We will only pay attention to the percentages that are obtained after correction.[2] The difference between the chi-square before and after correction for time spent on mass media indicates that women already spent more time on mass media in 1976, so their opportunity to increase the time is smaller. Women stopped following the daily news somewhat more often than men.

After correction, it appears that women have increased the number of hours spent on household duties more often than men: for 62% of the women and 34% of the men, the time increased.

The number of visits paid to men declined significantly more often and the number of visits to women increased more often. Already in 1976, women were visited more often. The same pattern is seen for the number of visits one pays to others. After correction, 33% of the women show an increase in these visits as opposed to 24% of the men; 23% of the women decreased the number of visits to others, while 28% of the men did so. Women more often expressed the need to have more social contacts and to go out. Men more often wished to do more work. It is probably useful to keep in mind that 237 out of 473 men stopped working and 112 out of the 544 women went into the so-called empty nest stage during the period 1976-1982. The differences in gender are most striking for changes in household activities and social contacts.

Life Events and Changes in Time Use and Activities

Ferraro (1984) and others state that "aging per se generally is not seen as a causal factor for understanding changes throughout the life course but, rather, as an indicator of other phenomena that actually initiate change." That is why we will now shift our attention to the effects of four important life events (impairment, retirement, the empty nest, and widowhood) on time use. According to Kelly (1982), there are a series of critical transitions in the life course that may change the orientations as well as the contexts of leisure. Changes in leisure are related to changing resources (especially health and income), opportunities, and so on throughout the life course. Leisure, by providing a context for social interaction, may help people adapt to change.

Do certain types of role loss influence time use? And if so, how do they? Does role loss lead to inactivity and social isolation (the decremental model), or can activity be a compensation for role loss (the compensation model)?

Lemon et al. (cited in Ferraro, 1984) state that "the greater the role loss, the less activity one is likely to engage in." Ferraro et al. (1984), however, suggest that "the more stressful the life event, the more likely individuals are to seek activities which provide for affectivity and emotional support." Palmore (1968) and Atchley (1971) also prefer the compensation to the decremental model.

It is not likely that the four life events represent comparable amounts of role loss. Holmes and Rahe (1967) have constructed a social readjustment rating scale, which contains 43 events. They have asked respondents to estimate the intensity and length of time necessary to accommodate to a life event, regardless of the desirability of this event. There was a high degree of consensus within the sample on the magnitude of these events. Death of a spouse stands at the head of the list with a mean value of 100. It is followed by personal injury or illness (53), retirement (45), and son or daughter leaving home (29).

Thijssen (1985) asked, using the same panel data: What are the effects of widowhood, impairment, retirement, and the empty nest on life satisfaction? He concludes that becoming widowed or disabled can be called stressful. Retirement and empty nest transitions are less likely to cause a decrease in life satisfaction. Some people may experience these two events as a liberation.

We examined the correlation of these four role losses with changes in 16 time-use indicators. The results are shown in columns 3 to 6 of Tables 3.13 to 3.16.

(1) Disability. Between 1976 and 1982, 44 out of the 1020 respondents were not disabled in 1976 and had become disabled by 1982, as indicated by having difficulties with more than one activity of daily life or needing help to perform one or more of these activities; however, 809 were neither impaired in 1976 nor in 1982.[3] The persons who became disabled are more often female, older than 64 years, less educated, and members

of the lower income classes. In 1976, their health probably was worse already, because they judged it more often in a negative way. The two groups differ significantly on time-use items in 1976: wish to take a course (less often) and to have more social contacts (more often), time spent in leisure activities (fewer hours), and the number of visits one gets (fewer). It may be that the two observations (1976 and 1982) captured a process that began before 1976 and continued until 1982 or later.

(2) Retirement. By 1982, 305 persons had stopped working and 108 persons still worked. Compared with the latter, the retired people are more often older than 64, widowed, and with less education. They are less likely to belong to the highest income classes. The working and retiring groups are similar concerning the 16 time-use items in 1976. Both groups consist primarily of men.

(3) Launching. During the period of 1976-1982, the last child of 112 women[4] left the parental home. In 1982, 59 women still had one or more children living at home. The other women in the sample had already had all their children living independently by 1976, or they did not have any children. The women whose child(ren) left the parental home between 1976 and 1982 are older, more likely to be widowed, and have a lower income than the women still having (a) child(ren) at home. They differ on several time-use aspects in 1976.

(4) Widowhood. Finally, 50 women were widowed between 1976 and 1982, while 322 women were still married in 1982.[5] The widowed women are slightly more often 65 years or older and their income is much more often on the lowest level than the income of the still-married women (43% compared with 2%!).

The amount of impact on time use and activities from these role losses is quite different. The fact that one has become a widow influences the time-use pattern to the greatest extent. On 7 out of the 16 items, the widowed and still-married groups deviate significantly from each other. This event is directly followed, concerning the impact on time use, by the fact that one has become disabled. These people differ significantly from the people who remained able on 6 time-use items.

The influence of retirement and of the empty nest phase seem to be less dramatic. The people who experienced these events differed on four time-use items.

These findings run parallel to those of Thijssen (1985) concerning the amount of stress caused by the four life events. The more stressful the event, the greater the difference with the control group concerning changes in time use or vice versa. The statement of Heyman and

Gianturco (1973) that "life style changes in the elderly may more often result from the cumulative effect of chronic illnesses and limitations in physical functioning than from bereavement" cannot be confirmed by our findings. They found that the adaptation to widowhood was characterized by relatively few life changes.

We found that becoming a widow had a strong influence on time use and activities. The women widowed between 1976 and 1982 changed their investment in leisure activities a lot. Some showed a decrease and some an increase in leisure activities. They more often stopped reading the newspaper (almost) every day. In spite of the fact that in most cases they had to shoulder more domestic tasks than before they lost their husbands, the total time spent in household duties diminished more often for them than for the still-married women (71% against 50%). The widows, however, increased the amount of time in helping others.

In 1976, the widows maintained more frequent social contacts than the women who were still married. In 1982, the difference between them has only grown wider. The widows also more often increased the number of visits paid to a service center for the aged and they somewhat more often (nearly significant) took up the wish to attend a course or something like that. Despite the fact they have become lonely much more often (49% of the widows, as opposed to 7% of the still-married women), the wish to maintain more social contacts isn't expressed much more often.

Kelly (1982) argues that, in case of widowhood, the presence of intimate others may help to facilitate the readjustment. The widows studied here have indeed augmented the amount of social interaction (visits, assistance to others, frequenting a service center) more often than the married women. This is in favor of the compensation model of role loss. Ferraro et al. (1984) conclude that most individuals experiencing life events such as widowhood compensate for the loss in certain realms of social integration by augmenting their relationships in other dimensions (e.g., with other widows).

It is possible that the number of years one is widowed plays a part in the development of time use. Therefore, the women widowed less than two years have been separated from the women widowed two to six years. The first group consists of 17 and the second group of 37 women. Because of the small numbers of people, the results from this subanalysis cannot be generalized.

The two groups of widows do not differ significantly for any of seven time use items (time spent in leisure, mass media, household duties, times going out, visits active and passive, and number of memberships). The differences between paying visits and spending time on radio and TV are evident but not significant. The women widowed the shortest time increased the number of visits to others more often than the women widowed a longer time. The latter have relatively more often augmented the time spent on radio and TV.

The increase of visits during the first period of widowhood fits in with the findings of Ferraro (1984), who points out that most of the research shows a considerable familial stability immediately after widowhood. He further states that several studies find that friendship participation is higher for those widowed for a short time than for either married persons or those widowed for a long time. Interaction with neighbors is stable and more likely to increase than decrease during the first few years after the death of spouse.

As was to be expected, the people who became disabled participated less in the energetic time-use activities, such as leisure activities, working on household activities, going out, and visiting people. They did not change as often as the people who remained fit in terms of unpaid work for organizations. In other words, they stayed out of it just as often. They also were more likely to stop reading the newspaper. Their wish to have more contacts changed more often, both in positive and negative directions.

Retirement usually causes a great amount of spare time. In spite of this, the impact of widowhood and impairment on time use seems to be greater than the impact of having stopped working. The people who retired between 1976 and 1982 more often started to spend more time in leisure activities than the people who had a paid job both in 1976 and 1982. This is particularly the case for time spent on puzzles (e.g., crosswords), fishing, and walking for pleasure. The people who retired remained stable more often as far as watching the daily television news is concerned. In 1982, 40% of the retired people spent more time in household duties than they did in 1976. For the still-working people, this percentage is only 24%. The retired people more often augmented the amount of visits paid to others (nearly significant), and the amount of visits paid to a service center for the aged. Perhaps not according to expectations, the still-working people were somewhat more likely (although not significantly) to express the wish to have more work to do.

Retired people do not differ much from those who are working in terms of time use. Atchley (1976) states that most retirees show continuity in their activities. Bosse and Ekerdt (1981) found a relative continuity in perception of leisure activity levels over the transition from work to retirement. According to Atchley (1971), most people expand their leisure involvement when they retire. Leisure can positively function as a bridge between pre- and postretirement life. Peppers (1976) also found a significant rise in the absolute number of activities after retirement, but no major change in their nature. The retired persons from our panel study more often augmented the amount of time spent in leisure activities than the still-working people (48% as opposed to 36%).

Bosse and Ekerdt (1981) suspect that increased nonwork time may be swallowed up in maintenance activities like personal care and household duties. This assumption is verified by our finding that 40% of the retirees as opposed to 24% of the still-working people raised the number of hours spent in household activities. Leisure time, however, also increased.

A distinction could be made between the ones who retired longer than and less than two years ago. In our analysis, this distinction didn't result in any significant differences in the seven examined items. The people retired less than two years increased the number of hours spent on radio, television, and household duties more often, and those retired more than two years decreased the amount of time spent at these activities more frequently, although even this difference was not significant.

The women who entered the empty nest phase between 1976 and 1982 hardly show any difference in actual time use from the women who still had a child(ren) at home in 1982. The latter were only more likely to decrease the number of hours spent in watching television.

The chi-squares before and after correction differ from each other rather often. This means that the two groups deviated from each other in 1976 (before the "empty nest" occurred). The difference in time-use items in 1976 is indeed significant for 6 out of the 16 items. The women who still had children at home in 1982 watched the news on TV less often in 1976 and they went out less often. It is worth noting that the women whose (last) child(ren) left the parental home between 1976 and 1982 wanted to have more work and social contacts in 1976, to take a course, and to go out more frequently. Possibly they expected their child(ren) to leave the parental home in the near future and because of this anticipation they felt the need to occupy themselves with other things.

We see that launching one's children can be considered less stressful than other life events. Deutcher (1968) said that the postparental phase in the family cycle is not generally defined unfavorably by those involved in it. Many people consider it as a time of freedom. Neither its impact on life satisfaction nor its impact on time use seems to be great.

It seems plausible that going through more than one life event in the same period is more disruptive of daily life than the occurrence of one event. Between 1976 and 1982, 493 people (48%) weren't involved in any of the four discussed life events; while 427 persons (42%) went through one of these life events and 100 persons (10%) went through two or three events (88 people through two and 12 people through three).

In a comparative analysis of these three subgroups, it appears that the more life events one has gone through, the more likely one is to increase the amount of time spent on leisure activities, on radio, and on TV. The people to whom two or three life events happened received visits much more often than the others. Other than these differences, however, the three groups are relatively equal.

Conclusions

This panel study suggests that people in their sixties do not change their time use and activities dramatically within a period of six years. Only beyond the age of 75 does a decline in level of activity seem apparent, according to our cross-sectional study. We investigated the possible effect of four life events on the use of time for people aged 55 to 73 years. Becoming a widow or becoming impaired have a rather large impact on time use. The influence of retiring has a much smaller effect and the launching of the last child seems hardly to have an effect on the use of time. Widowhood does not generally lead to inactivity and isolation, as stated by the decremental model of role loss. The findings are generally in favor of the compensation model.

Summary

The data on time use and activities analyzed in this chapter are descriptive (they are not related to a dependent variable such as life satisfaction, well-being, or mental health). From them, we can examine the style of life for older people in the Netherlands.

Older people in the Netherlands are involved in many activities. The distribution over the different possible activities, however, is very unequal. A great deal of time is used for leisure activities such as gardening, reading, walking, collecting stamps, handicraft, playing cards, sports, and care for animals. Nearly 50% spend more than four hours per day in these kind of activities. About the same amount of time is spent on mass media. Both leisure activities and mass media take more time than household activities. The time spent in helping other people and in unpaid work is, in comparison, very low. This could be related to our highly developed welfare state as we showed in the beginning of this chapter.

Social life seems to be well developed for the elderly in the Netherlands. Most of them visit other people weekly and are visited weekly too. Nevertheless, about 15% express a need for more social contacts. Most of them are women, and the divorced women are especially affected.

Many activities studied in this chapter involve social relationships. The women in our study with the most unfavorable situation in terms of social relationships are often the most involved in specific activities and even look forward to more involvement. In an earlier section, we pointed out this apparent contradiction for the divorced and never-married women. For the widowed women, the situation is in some way comparable, but seems to work out in variable ways. In the cross-sectional data presented in an earlier section, the time-use and activity patterns of the widows were more in line with the married women than with those of the divorced and never-married women. The longitudinal analysis of the women widowed between 1976 and 1982 shows many shifts in their time-use and activity patterns, both decreases and increases. It is striking, for example, that there is little change in the expressed need for more contact and that, for 40%, an increase in people visiting them occurs. Their social world seems to be less disrupted than for the divorced older women. There remain more possibilities for compensation for the widowed.

Since 1961, the year of the publication of *Growing Old: The Process of Disengagement* by Cumming and Henry, social gerontology has been involved in a discussion of disengagement and activity theory. Some people have stated, however, that the question is not "either/or" but that successful aging requires continuity. "Activity patterns are highly individualized and show a high degree of stability across the life course. Nevertheless, options are sometimes limited in later life by physical, financial and transportation factors" (Atchley, 1983). Our data support, to a certain degree, the stability or continuity hypothesis. Our data, however, urge us to add marital status as one of the important factors. We have referred to the notion of compensation; Atchley uses the notion of consolidation. Both concepts imply the effective use of present resources.

Compensation is one way to maintain continuity in life. Our data support this continuity in time use and activities, in general, at least between the ages of 55 and 75. Handicaps or disruptive changes in someone's social network, and not the individual aging process, seem to explain most of the decrease in time use and activities. Social structural variables are critical in understanding daily life in later life, as they are in understanding lonely people (Jong-Gierveld, 1984). The demographic changes in the next 50 years in the Netherlands will lead to a large increase in divorced and never-married older people. This compositional change may alter the way people age in the Netherlands. Preparing for this situation will be the challenge for the next decades.

NOTES

1. Between 1900 and 1978, the birthrate per 1000 population decreased from 31.6 to 12.6 in the Netherlands, and for about the same period, from 30.1 to 15.5 in the United States. From 1940 to 1943, it increased slightly, and from 1943 to 1946, it increased a lot. From 1947, it decreased very slowly; after 1965, it decreased quickly.

2. To avoid regression to the mean (in case the two groups differ from each other in 1976), the following correction was made: Starting points are two turnover tables for an item (1976-1982), one table for male and one for female respondents. The marginals for 1976 from the turnover table for men are divided by the marginals for the women. The obtained quotients are multiplied by the marginals for the women. The obtained quotients are multiplied by the absolute numbers in the corresponding cells (cells in the same row) of the table for women. In this way, one gets a new turnover table for the women.

3. This doesn't add up to 1020 because the people who were already disabled in 1976, and 63 people who had trouble with only one of the activities of daily life, were eliminated from the analysis.

4. In this analysis, the "empty nest" event is restricted to women only, because it probably is a much more radical change for the Dutch women, who are mostly housewives, than for the men.

5. The 172 women, left out of the analysis, were not married in 1976. Three-quarters of the widowed people are female, so the 16 widowers were dropped from the analysis.

REFERENCES

Atchley, R. C. 1971. "Retirement and Leisure Participation: Continuity or Crisis?" *Gerontologist* 11(1):13-17.
———. 1976. *The Sociology of Retirement*. New York: Halsted.

————. 1983. *Aging: Continuity and Change.* Belmont, CA: Wadsworth.

Bengtson, V. L. and J. F. Robertson. 1985. *Grandparenthood.* Beverly Hills, CA: Sage.

Blau, Z. S. 1973. *Old Age in a Changing Society.* New York: Franklin Watts.

Bosse, R. and D. Ekerdt 1981. "Change in Self-Perception of Leisure Activities with Retirement." *Gerontologist* 21(6):650-54.

C.B.S. 1983. *Leefsituatie-onderzoek onder de Nederlandse Bevolking van 18 jaar en ouder* (Life Situation Survey of people 18 and over). 's Gravenhage, Staatsuitgeverij.

————. 1984. *Leefsituatie van de Nederlandse Bevolking van 55 jaar en ouder. Deel Ia Kerncijfers* (Life situation survey of people 55 and over, part Ia). 's Gravenhage, Staatsuitgeverij.

Collot, C., H. Jani-le Bris, and A. Ridoux. 1982. *Towards an Improvement in Self-Reliance in the Elderly: Innovation and New Guidelines for the Future.* Paris: CLEIRPPA.

Commission of the European Communities. 1978. *The Economic Implications of Demographic Change in the European Community.* Brussels: Author.

Cumming, E. and W. E. Henry. 1961. *Growing Old: The Process of Disengagement.* New York: Basic Books.

Deutcher, J. 1968. "Postparental Life." Pp. 263-68 in *Middle Age and Aging,* edited by B. Neugarten. Chicago: University of Chicago Press.

Ferraro, K. 1984. "Widowhood and Social Participation in Later Life." *Research on Aging* 6(4):451-68.

————, E. Mutran, and C. Barresi. 1984. "Widowhood, Health and Friendship Support in Later Life." *Journal of Health and Social Behavior* 25(2):245-59.

Gordon, C. and C. Gaitz. 1976. "Leisure and Life: Personal Expressivity Across the Life Span." Pp. 310-41 in *Handbook of Aging and the Social Sciences,* edited by R. Binstock and E. Shanas. New York: Van Hostrand Reinhold.

Hagestad, G. O. 1984. "Multi-Generational Families: Socialization, Support and Strain." Pp. 105-14 in *Intergenerational Relationships,* edited by V. Garms-Homolova, E. M. Hoerning, and D. Schaeffer. Lewiston, NY: C. J. Hogrefe.

Heek, F. van. 1954. *Het geboorte-niveau der Nederlandse Rooms-Katholieken. Een demografisch-sociologische studie van een geemancipeerde minderheidsgroep* (The birthrate of the Dutch Roman Catholics, a demographic-sociological study of emancipation of a minority group). Leiden: H. E. Stenfert Kroese.

Heyman, K. and D. Gianturco. 1973. "Longterm Adaptation by the Elderly to Bereavement." *Journal of Gerontology* 28(3):359-62.

Holmes, T. and R. Rahe. 1967. "The Social Readjustment Rating Scale." *Journal of Psychosomatic Research* 11(2):213-18.

Jong-Gierveld, J. de. 1984. *Eenzaamheid: een meersporig onderzoek.* (Loneliness: A research approach with multiple strategies). Deventer, the Netherlands: Van Loghem Slaterus.

Kelley, J. 1982. "Leisure in Later Life: Roles and Identities." Pp. 30-46 in *Life After Work: Retirement, Leisure, Recreation and the Elderly,* edited by N. Osgood. New York: Praeger.

Knipscheer, C. 1974. *Eenzaamheid onder alleenstaanden* (Loneliness of nonmarried) (Internal paper). Nijmegen, the Netherlands: Sociological Institute.

————. 1980. *Oude mensen en hun sociale omgeving. Een studie van het primair sociaal netwerk* (Elderly people and their social environment: A study of the primary social network). Den Haag: Vuga.

————. In press. "Family Care of the Impaired Elderly: Possibilities for Innovations." In *Innovations in Health Care for the Elderly*, edited by W.J.A. van den Heuvel and G. Schrijvers. Lochem, the Netherlands: Tijdstroom.

Moss, M. and M. Powell Lawton. 1982. "Time Budgets of Older People: A Window on Four Lifestyles." *Journal of Gerontology* 37(1):115-23.

Munnichs, J.M.A. 1978. *Voorzieningen voor ouderen: visie op ouderdom* (Provisions for the elderly: A vision on age). Cahiers Ouderdom en Levensloop, Deventer, the Netherlands: Van Loghum Slaterus.

Palmore, E. 1968. "The Effects of Aging on Activities and Attitudes." *Gerontologist* 8(3):259-64.

————. 1979. "Predictors of Successful Aging." *Gerontologist* 19(5):427-31.

Peppers, L. 1976. "Patterns of Leisure and Adjustment to Retirement." *Gerontologist* 16(5):441-46.

Rosow, I. 1976. *Social Integration of the Aged*. New York: Free Press.

Thijssen, L. 1985. "Belangrijke levensgebeurtenissen en welbevinden bij ouderen" (Important life events and well-being among the elderly). *Sociaal-Cultureel Kwartaalbericht* 3:34-41.

4

Daily Life of Elderly Persons in Hungary

RUDOLF ANDORKA

A Typical Life

An old man after being pensioned usually continues to work at his earlier place of employment for several hours per day or some months in a year. In addition, he works rather intensively to supplement the family income in the second economy. This consists, most of all, in small-scale agricultural production. The time spent in household chores also increases as compared to his employed years. In consequence, the leisure activities increase relatively little. The most important increase in leisure activity is television viewing. As he grows older, the time spent in working activities diminishes. This, however, causes serious problems for the family income.

National Context

In this chapter, the *aged population* is defined as the population aged over the legal age of pensioning, that is, 60 for men and 55 for women. For some special occupational groups, the age of pensioning is lower. In the Hungarian population (10,679,000 in January 1984), there were 777,000 men aged 60 and over and 1,482,000 women aged 55 and over (or 21% of the total population, combined). The percentage of the population aged 65 and older is 12.3%.

As can be seen from these figures, women are strongly overrepresented in the old age groups. The sex ratio of the population aged 60 and over is 1.90. In the oldest age groups, over 80, the sex ratio is higher than 2. In consequence, while the majority (78% in 1980) of old men are married, the majority of women above the age of pensioning are unmarried (43% widows, 6% single, and 5% divorced). From these data, it might be concluded that the old widows actually constitute the largest group of older people.

The main cause of the high percentage of elderly persons is, as in other countries, that the birth rate has been relatively low since the second half of the 1950s, the level of the total fertility rate being only in some exceptional years higher than the level necessary for simple reproduction. Therefore, the percentage of all age groups below 30 is rather low. The changes in mortality played only a minor role in the increase of the share of old population. The expectancy of life at birth of men has not improved since 1965, while that of women increased slightly, and the mortality conditions of adult men deteriorated to an important degree. Recently, some deterioration also appeared among adult women. According to the life table of 1983, men who reach 60 live 15 more years and women who reach 60 live 19 more years, on the average. The increase in the gap of life expectancy of men and women, however, has strongly contributed to the growth of the number of elderly widows (Klinger, 1983).

The percentage of elderly persons was highest in the capital city— Budapest, with 20% aged 60 and more in 1980 (because of a long-lasting low birth rate)—but was higher than the average in the villages (18%), because of the overrepresentation of younger adults among the out-migrants to the cities, and lowest in the smaller urban places (14%).

The problems of old persons are somewhat different in Budapest. There, they often do not have living children who could care for them, but the possibilities for social care are relatively abundant. In the villages, the problems from aging are often caused by the out-migration of the living children to urban places and the distance from places where social care could be available.

The problems of care are also somewhat differentiated by age, older persons being more often ill than the younger pensioners.

Income and Living Conditions

The most important source of income of elderly persons is the pension. People who worked for at least ten years before attaining the

TABLE 4.1   Gender- and Age-Specific Life Expectancies

Life Expectancy Age the Age of	Men	Women
	Years	
0	65.59	73.49
30	38.34	45.45
60	15.02	18.95

SOURCE: *Demographic Yearbook* (Central Statistical Office, 1983).

TABLE 4.2   Sex, Age, and Indicators of Physical Health (percentages)

Sex and Age	Chronically Ill	Confined to Bed for Longer than One Month	In Hospital for More than Two Weeks
Men			
60-69	47	10	9
70-74	53	13	12
75+	56	13	10
Women			
55-59	49	8	8
60-69	58	10	10
70-74	66	12	9
75+	68	16	10

SOURCE: Central Statistical Office (1984).

age of pensioning are entitled to the pension, which is determined on the basis of the wage of the last five years. The pension might be as high as 75% of the level of the previous wage. Widows of deceased persons who had a right to a pension receive the so-called widow's pension after a certain age. The widow's pension amounts to 50% of the pension of the wage earner. Therefore, persons receiving a pension are in a relatively advantageous position in their first years. They can also supplement their income by working each year for 840 working hours (usually at their previous job), and 30% of pensioners (not including the women receiving a widow's pension) supplement their income in this way. The wage they received for this work amounted to more than 50% of the average pension.

These advantageous possibilities explained why most of the people having attained the age of pensioning did not utilize the possibility of remaining full-time workers for additional one to five years, although in that case they obtained a supplement to their pension in later years. In

1980, about 8% of the persons over 55 were still active, most of them males in the age group of 60 to 64.

With the passage of the years, however, the economic situation of pensioners slowly deteriorates. On the one hand, as their physical fitness declines, they are less and less able to be engaged in the above-mentioned supplementary wage work, and also the working places are less and less willing to employ them. Manual workers, most of all those doing heavy and unskilled work, are in a more disadvantaged situation, from this point of view, than nonmanuals, most of all professionals, who are able to perform more similarly to their younger ages.

Meanwhile, the real value of all their pension diminishes. Pensions are automatically increased each year by 2% and from time to time the lowest pensions are increased with further additions. They are, however, not indexed to the price level. Because for many years the price level has increased by more than 2% yearly, somebody who became a pensioner two decades earlier with a relatively advantageous pension might belong today to the stratum having the lowest per capita income.

This explains the fact that in 1981 the average pension for all was 51% of the average wage, although the average of the pensions of persons beginning to receive a pension in this year was 72% of the average wage. The inequality of pensions was higher that the inequality of wages.

This also explains why, according to the household income survey of 1982, 25% of the persons belonging to the households in the lowest per capita income category (below 1800 Ft. monthly, amounting to 6.4% of the total population) lived in households of pensioners. An important part of the poorest stratum consisted of pensioners and their dependents. The oldest pensioners, the women receiving the widow's pension, and the former members of agricultural cooperatives were most likely to fall into this most disadvantaged category. Old couples where only one person, usually the husband, received a pension with the supplement for the spouse rather low were often in the stratum of lowest per capita income. Finally, there are some old families having neither wage nor pension income.

There are several possibilities for old people to cope with this situation. First of all, about 40% of the pensioners lived in households of active earners, mostly their children. These active earners shared their wage income with the old parents. At the other extreme, old people having nobody to help them financially might ask for the so-called social allowance, the amount of which, however, is not permitted to exceed the minimal widow's pension. It is very low. Only about 15% of the old persons having neither wage nor pension income receive this kind of social allowance. The most frequent way of supplementing the low income from pensions is to engage in some kind of supplementary work in order to earn extra income.

The most common possibility to do so is provided by the system of so-called household and auxiliary plots in agriculture. Each member of an agricultural cooperative, including each pensioned member, is entitled to a so-called household plot of 0.6 hectare, on which he or she can produce some food, either for household consumption or for the market. In the villages, the gardens around the houses as well as the stables, pigsties, and so on are also used for production of fruit and vegetables and animal husbandry. These and other small parcels are called the "auxiliary plots." Almost all rural households and many households living on the outskirts of urban areas are engaged in this small-scale production. According to the survey of 1982, 25% of these small households and family plots belonged to pensioner families, and 19% of the total production of these plots was provided by the plots of the pensioners (Oros and Schindele, 1984).

Although the average income per hour gained by the work of pensioners on these plots was much lower than the average wage per hour obtained in the large agricultural units (state farms and cooperatives), the work on these plots supplemented to an important degree the income of these families. In 1982, these earnings contributed 10% of the total personal income of all households in Hungary, but 16% of the income of all pensioner households and 27% of the income of the pensioner households residing in the villages. As a consequence, they were able to diminish their disadvantage in terms of income as compared to the average household income. Nevertheless, the old rural family households are, on the average, the poorest part of the Hungarian society.

The relative disadvantages of pensioners, especially the pensioned cooperative peasants, can be clearly seen from any indicator of living conditions. Four indicators were selected here that strongly characterize and differentiate the living conditions of social strata in present-day Hungary. Pensioners, especially pensioned cooperative peasants, are more likely than others to live in dwellings built of sun-dried bricks without solid foundations, usually moist and unhealthy, and to have no piped water inside. Few of them have an automatic washing machine and a personal car in their household.

Therefore, the daily life of old persons in Hungary is strongly

TABLE 4.3   Indicators of the Living Conditions of Pensioners, 1981
(percentages)

	Active Earners	Pensioners		
		Total	Workers	Cooperative Peasants
No solid foundations; house of sun-dried brick	7.1	8.5	12.9	22.9
No running water in the dwelling	25.8	35.1	31.6	65.2
Automatic washing machine in household	11.8	5.6	4.4	1.3
Personal car in household	37.2	12.7	13.6	13.6

SOURCE: Central Statistical Office (1984).

influenced, on the one hand, by their relatively disadvantaged position, and on the other, by their great efforts to overcome these disadvantages.

Daily Time Budget of
Old Persons

In 1976-1977, a time-budget survey was performed by the Central Statistical Office on a sample of the population aged 15-69 (Andorka and Falussy, 1982; Andorka, Falussy, and Harcsa, 1982). Four times during the year, each person in the sample was interviewed concerning the time budget of the previous day. Altogether, 27,607 time budgets were collected, processed, and analyzed by the methods elaborated in the international comparative time-budget survey (Szalai, 1972). Unfortunately, the population aged 70 and older was not included in the sample because it was thought that it would be more difficult to interview them on their exact time use. Only those below 70 can be examined here.

It is not surprising that the daily use of time of the persons above the age of pensioning differ in many respects from the time budgets of the economically active persons.

Aging itself causes gradual changes in the use of time, and the sudden cessation of regular employment might change life-styles completely.

TABLE 4.4   Time Spent in Different Activities by All Economically Active Persons and by Men Aged 60-69 and Women Aged 55-69 (mean minutes per day)

Activity	All Economically Active		Aged	
	Men	Women	Men 60-69	Women 55-69
Work and productive activities:				
work in main occupation	341	259	87	44
income supplementing work	3	2	6	0
work in household plot	58	50	118	82
building	15	3	11	3
maintenance of consumer durables	10	0	3	0
transport	77	72	52	54
Household chores:				
cooking, washing up	11	106	19	145
tidying of dwelling	12	48	33	63
heating	8	3	19	6
bringing water	1	1	2	1
washing, ironing, mending clothes	1	44	2	46
other household chores	16	6	31	16
Shopping and services:				
shopping	7	18	15	21
utilization of services	3	5	5	5
visits to offices	1	1	1	1
Personal and physiological needs:				
sleeping	482	488	553	555
personal hygiene, dressing	56	52	49	44
eating	77	73	89	81
passive resting, resting because of illness	28	22	75	64
Care and education of children:				
care	6	16	3	7
education, playing	7	6	4	5
learning	8	5	3	0
Social activities, human relations:				
conversation	23	19	36	32
visiting friends, entertaining guests	14	15	13	19
social entertainment	6	2	6	1
social work	2	1	1	0
other social activities	2	2	2	5
Cultural and entertainment activities at home:				
reading newspapers and periodicals	18	7	33	12
reading books	13	11	26	12

(continued)

TABLE 4.4 Continued

Activity	All Economically Active		Aged	
	Men	Women	Men 60-69	Women 55-69
radio	5	2	15	8
television	86	75	98	82
tape recorder and phonograph	2	1	1	0
traditional needlework	0	13	0	19
hobbies	7	3	7	2
Cultural and entertainment activities at institutions	7	3	2	1
Outdoor activities, sports	15	11	21	9
Other activities:				
religious activities	0	1	2	3
drinking in inns	6	c	7	0
other	3	2	2	2
Total	1440	1440	1440	1440

SOURCE: Andorka et al. (1982).

Nevertheless, in the case of Hungary, I would like to stress some of the similarities of the time use of active workers and those over the age of retirement.

Activities

First of all, working at some working place in the form of a main occupation still plays an important role in the lives of men aged 60-69 and women aged 55-69. In all, 19% of the men and 11% of the women mentioned this kind of activity in the time budget of the previous day. Taking into consideration that weekend days and working days were included into the surveys, this might be considered a high percentage. The main reason for it is not the continuation of working regularly instead of going to pension after attaining the age of pensioning, but rather the frequency of pensioners engaging in part-time work. It ought to be added that, at the time of the survey, the age of retirement of members of agricultural cooperatives was still somewhat higher than their present age of retirement.

More remarkable, however, men and women in pensionable age used an important part of the time set free by the cessation of regular wage work to increase the working time input into the household and auxiliary plots. Obviously, this work serves also to alleviate the psychological problems caused by the loss of involvement in a regular gainful job. The increase of the time of household chores probably also has similar functions. The main motivation of the increased input into small-scale agriculture is, however, the supplementary income derived from it, which helps to avoid the decline of the living standard after retirement. As the possibility to work in the household plot and the productivity of this work slowly decline with age, this is only a temporary solution for the difficulties caused by the deterioration of the economic situation of the family.

Not all aged persons have the possibility to work in household and auxiliary plots. A total of 53% of the men and 49% of the women in the investigated age groups mentioned this kind of work in the time budget of the previous day. This constitutes about 65%-70% of those living in households that have such a plot. The men who actually worked in the household plot on the previous day did so for 4 hours and 38 minutes, and the women for 3 hours and 13 minutes, that is, for rather long hours. They are predominantly former cooperative peasants and workers residing in villages, members of the lower strata of the Hungarian society. Pensioned workers in urban areas have much less opportunity to supplement their income in this way. Nevertheless, the per capita income of pensioner households in Budapest is somewhat higher than that of the pensioner households in other towns and is almost equal to that of the pensioners in villages. Thus it is clear that those pensioners having the lowest pensions compensate for part of this disadvantage by doing a great deal of extra work in small-scale agricultural production in plots belonging to their households.

Two other types of working activities that contribute to the material well-being of the households appeared frequently in the time budgets: building of dwellings by private efforts, and the repair and maintenance of consumer durables, including the maintenance of personal cars.

In the mid-1970s, about half of the new dwellings were built by private resources, especially in the villages. The private housing system utilized the work of the family, other kin, friends, colleagues, neighbors, without paying monetary wages, but in the framework of a system of mutual help. Each person who gives his manpower to a friend or colleague can surely count on reciprocal help when he or any member of his family is building his dwelling. Only a few activities necessitating a special skill are performed by paid wage workers. The maintenance of dwellings is mostly done in a similar framework of mutual help. Therefore, it is not surprising that 5.4% of the interviewed men mentioned some building work in the time budget of the previous day. It is, however, remarkable that the men aged 60 and above also actively participate in this kind of building work, with 4.2% of them having done it on the previous day. Obviously, most of them helped in the building of the dwelling of some other person, a child, grandchild, and so on.

Maintenance of consumer durables is widely practiced in Hungary on a "do-it-yourself" basis because of the high cost and shortage of wage labor in the field of services. Old men also participate in these activities, although much less often than the adults of working age. This may be true because the latter possess more consumer durables (e.g., cars) and are most acquainted with the necessary skills to care for durables.

In spite of the growth of the time spent in small agricultural production and of the frequency of other income-supplementing activities among the old persons, the time set free by the cessation of regular work in some main occupation and the related shortening of transportation time provides the possibility to spend more time in other activities. First of all, the time spent in the satisfaction of personal physical needs increases by about two hours after retirement: old people sleep and rest for longer hours and spend somewhat more time in eating meals. They also spend more time in household chores. Men participate to a larger degree in household chores, such as in tidying the dwelling and shopping.

They also use more time for the different cultural activities that can be done at home and usually do not cause important extra expenses, like reading newspapers, journals, and books, seeing the programs on the television, listening to the radio, doing some hobby, and doing the traditional needlework (among women). On the one hand, this might be interpreted as a very positive phenomenon, because these old people— after having lived a very stressed life, full of hard work—at the end of their lives are able to participate again in the cultural life of the society. On the other hand, however, they reduce the time spent in cultural activities outside of the home (i.e., going to the movies, theaters, sporting events), which require transportation from the home to these institutions and entail some costs, although tickets for cultural institutions are still very inexpensive in Hungary. Thus their participation in culture is rather one-sided. Walking and hiking, as well as other active sports and movement in the open air, which are very rare among the adults of working age, increase only slightly among older men and diminish among older women, although they could spare more time for it than the active earners.

We would expect also that pensioned persons, having more time, would spend more time in social activities such as visiting each other and so on. This would compensate for the loss of the human contact that was usually found at the workplace. Only time spent in conversation, the most superficial type of social activity and involving usually no movement out of the home, is, however, clearly greater among the old persons. The visits of relatives and friends increase somewhat among old women, but decrease among old men. This probably reflects changes in visits with family members, children, and grandchildren.

The diminishing time spent on care and education of children is due to the fact that these old couples usually do not have young children. They might care for grandchildren. There would be a great need for that, because both parents usually work a full day. Grandparents care for their grandchildren only when living in the same household or in the neighborhood. Because of the mass migrations of the previous decades, however, this residential proximity is often not the case. In these conditions, the grandparents became more and more isolated, while their children often have great problems in assuring the care of their small children.

The decline in leaving the home, that is, the dwelling, the courtyard, the garden and the small plot around it, is also displayed by the distribution of time spent in different locations.

Human Contacts of Old People

The deterioration of the social aspects of the lives of elderly persons is seen in the time spent with different kinds of persons. The possibilities to meet colleagues and friends at workplaces diminishes with the cessation of regular work. We might expect, however, that this loss of human contact is compensated for by an increasing role of family members in the same household and outside the household, by more frequent contact with friends outside of the workplace, and so on. Except for neighbors and other "acquaintances"—the more superficial types of contacts—however, the time spent with all categories of persons diminishes among the old people. There are several reasons for this social isolation.

First of all, 7% of the men and 20% of the women over the year of pensioning live alone, in one-member households. Some of them—2.3% of the men over 60 and 3.7% of the women above 55—not only live alone, but also have personal contact with relatives and friends less often than once a month.

TABLE 4.5   Time Spent in Different Locations by All Economically
Active Persons and by Men Aged 60-69 and Women Aged
55-69 (mean minutes per day)

Location	All Economically Active		Aged	
	Men	Women	Men 60-69	Women 55-69
Home:				
sleeping time	481	484	556	555
kitchen	100	232	155	289
other room in dwelling	53	107	54	70
courtyard, garden, household				
plot, weekend house	139	71	179	104
total home time				
Workplace	232	149	91	42
Other:				
someone else's home	62	48	35	45
shops, service institutions	18	34	25	30
cultural institutions	14	7	6	2
open-air recreation	15	9	6	4
restaurant and so on	19	5	9	1
street, vehicle	89	68	72	51
other	4	3	5	6
Total	1440	1440	1440	1440

SOURCE: Andorka et al. (1982).

About 20% of these old persons have no living child (Cseh-Szombathy and Hutas, 1984). This high percentage is caused by the higher percentage of never-married persons, by the higher percentage of childless couples in the older age groups, and by the great loss of human life among the children of these old persons during the war.

The intensive migration of the postwar years caused parents and adult children to reside in different communities, often at great distances from each other. Because adults of working age are usually strongly overburdened by working activities and by supplementary work in second jobs, they are not able to travel long distances in order to visit their parents frequently. This is especially true if they do not have a personal car.

The contacts with friends and colleagues living in the same community, however, become less and less frequent among the old persons.

TABLE 4.6   Time Spent with Different Types of Persons for All Economically
Active Persons and for Men Aged 60-69 and Women Aged
55-69 (mean minutes per day)

Persons Who Were Participating or Present	All Economically Active		Aged	
	Men	Women	Men 60-69	Women 55-69
Members of family in the same household	399	450	385	375
Relatives not living in the same household	43	37	24	35
Friends, colleagues not at workplace	58	26	18	11
Neighbors and acquaintances	38	31	49	48
Friends, colleagues at workplace	181	117	47	29
Official persons	35	38	33	29
Other, unknown person, and crowds	142	124	101	80
Alone, not sleeping	232	284	337	371

SOURCE: Andorka et al. (1982).

Conclusions and the Aims of Social Policy

Thus it might be concluded that the daily lives of old people in Hungary raise several problems. On the one hand, the standard of living of many old persons is still significantly below the average, even below the level considered to be the socially desirable minimum standard. It ought to be added that in this respect the situation has improved very much in the last two decades. During this time, the per capita income of old persons approached the national average.

This improvement is partly due to the efforts of social policy, such as the increase of pensions and to their extension to almost the total population, but partly also to the consequence of the efforts of the old persons themselves to supplement their income by different working activities. Therefore, the old members of the Hungarian society live— similarly to the young and middle-aged adults—a very stressed way of life, overburdened by working activities, or—in terms of the concepts of time-budget analysis—by contracted and committed types of activities (Andorka, Harcsa, and Niemi, 1983). This leaves little time and energy for cultural activities—especially outside of the home—for social contacts and for recreation. Physical and mental health problems, a relatively disadvantageous mortality of adults, and social isolation might be considered, hypothetically, consequences of this way of life, reflected in the time-budget data. This requires further sociological and demographic analyses.

It ought to be stressed that the remarkable performance of the Hungarian economy in the last two decades and the improvement of the level of personal income and of living conditions is to an important degree the product of the willingness of the population—including the old members of the society—to engage in such long working hours and in different income-supplementing working activities. Therefore, the aim of social policy should not be the diminishing of these efforts, but the alleviation as far as possible of its eventual negative consequence and side effects.

The main goals of social policy remain the avoidance of the deterioration of the living standard of old persons and the improvement of the conditions of the part of old population that has the lowest income level. It is an explicit goal of the government to maintain the real value of the lower pensions, even in rather difficult macroeconomic circumstances. In the short term, the amount of money available for the local administration to provide social help on individual basis was increased. In the longer perspective, the indexation of pensions is envisaged.

The improvement of the quality of life of old persons is getting more and more consideration in social policy (Cseh-Szombathy, 1983). The ideal is to assure the adequate care of old persons in their own families and dwellings. Therefore, homes for the aged people are considered to be only a second best solution, used if care in the family and the dwelling cannot be realized. Therefore, use of social care in people's own homes by adequately trained nurses and others, use of the day-care centers, and clubs for old people will be further developed. All these measures will be integrated into a system of social care by social workers. This system ought to deal with all kinds of social and family problems, from poverty to the maladjustment of children (Cseh-Szombathy and Hutás, 1984). The complex studies on the situation of old persons (Szalai et al., 1982) contributed to an important degree to the development of the ideas of such a social policy.

REFERENCES

Andorka, R. and B. Falussy. 1982. "The Way of Life of the Hungarian Society on the Basis of the Time Budget Survey of 1976-1977." *Social Indicators Research* 11:31-73.

————. and I. Harcsa. 1982. *Idömerlèg. Rèszletes adatok* (Time budget: Detailed data). Vols. 1-2. Budapest: Central Statistical Office.

Andorka, R., I. Harcsa, and I. Niemi. 1983. *Use of Time in Hungary and in Finland.* Helsinki: Central Statistical Office of Finland.

Central Statistical Office. 1983. *Demographic Yearbook.* Budapest: Author.

————. 1984. *Stratification, Living Conditions, Way of Life.* Budapest: Author.

Cseh-Szombathy, L. 1983. "The Sociological and Socio-Political Aspects of Aging." Pp. 69-80 in *The Demographic Situation and Problems of the Older Population in Hungary,* edited by A. Klinger. Luxenburg: International Institute for Applied Systems Analysis.

————. and I. Hutás. 1984. "A nepesseg eloregedesenek tarsadalmi kovetkezmenyei" (Social consequence of the aging of the population). *Nagyar Tduomany* 29 (7-8):497-509.

Klinger, A. 1983. "Demographic Aspects of Aging." Pp. 12-56 in *The Demographic Situation and Problems of the Older Population in Hungary,* edited by A. Klinger. Luxenburg: International Institute for Applied Systems Analysis.

————., ed. 1983. *The Demographic Situation and Problems of the Old Population in Hungary.* Luxenburg: International Institute for Applied Systems Analysis.

Oros, I. and M. Schindele. 1984. *Idofelhasznalas a mezogazdasagi kistermelesben I* (Time use in small-scale agricultural production). Vol. 1. Budapest: Central Statistical Office.

Szalai, A., ed. 1972. *The use of time: Daily activities of urban and suburban population in twelve countries.* The Hague: Mouton.

————. et al., eds. 1982. *Magyar nemzeti beszamolo az oregsengrol es az idos nepesseg helyzeterol* (Hungarian national report on aging and the situation of the aged population). Budapest: Hungarian National Academy of Sciences.

5

Elderly People in Nordic Time-Use Studies

LARS ANDERSSON

A Day in the Life of a Swedish Elder

Perhaps no day is typical, and the typical day might not seem very exciting. A Swedish elder might awaken at around 8:00 on weekdays and at 9:00 on weekends. Free time activities are scattered throughout the day, with more leisure between 6:00 p.m. and midnight for the young-old and between noon and 6:00 p.m. for the old-old. Reading is one activity the elderly participate in a great deal more than younger age groups, so some part of the free time in a typical day is allocated to reading. Most of the household work that needs to be done is finished by 6:00 p.m. In the evenings, most free time is spent watching TV. At 10:00 p.m., one-third of the young-old, one-half of the middle-old, and two-thirds of the old-old are asleep.

This chapter focuses on Swedish conditions and studies. Because there are great similarities among the Nordic countries, some attention is also paid to time-use studies from Denmark, Finland, and Norway.[1] After a general introduction to the national contexts, the chapter concentrates on an analysis of some Nordic time-use studies, with specific reference to the elderly. The chapter also brings to the fore some issues concerning the amount and meaningfulness of certain activities.

AUTHOR'S NOTE: For assistance in collecting and reviewing the background material, I wish to thank Ms. Katarina Florin.

For most elderly people in the Nordic countries, retirement offers a possibility to engage in desirable activities—both obligatory and leisure—and to attain an optimal distribution of time. In the highest age groups, disabilities become more common. Help and services increase as well, which has the side effect of creating more free time for the individual. The indispensable help in itself most likely enhances well-being. More free time does not necessarily benefit older people, however, if disabilities prevent a meaningful or optimal use of time. In this case, adding time even to desirable and often practiced activities may not increase well-being. Nevertheless, time has to be filled somehow and the resulting time budget can present a portrait of more or less time spent on activities than is actually preferred. Some data concerning the issue of actual versus ideal time use will be presented.

Demographic and Structural Background with Particular Reference to Sweden

In all the Nordic countries, the population has grown slowly but steadily during the last century. From 1900 to 1980, for instance, the increase for Denmark was from 2.5 to 5.2 million; for Finland, 2.7 to 4.8 million; Norway, 2.2 to 4.1 million; and Sweden, 5.1 to 8.3 million. According to forecasts, the Swedish population will be stable at just over 8 million for the next 50 years.

The proportion of the Swedish population aged 65 or over has increased from 10.2% in 1950 to 16.4% in 1980. The increase will continue to a first peak of 17.5% around 1990. After that, the proportion of elderly will fall back to the 1980 level and remain there until the large birth cohorts from the late 1940s reach retirement age around the year 2010, when the proportion of elderly will reach an all-time high of 20%.

Life expectancy at birth for Swedish males and females has increased from 54.5 and 57.0 in 1900 to 73.1 and 79.1 in 1982. In the other Nordic countries, the figures today are much the same except for Finnish males, whose life expectancy at birth is now 69.5 (National Commission on Aging, 1982; Swedish National Central Bureau of Statistics, 1984).

As shown in Table 5.1, approximately 88% of the elderly in the Nordic countries live in ordinary dwellings, the standard of which is comparatively very good. In Sweden, only about 3% lack water or a bathroom.

The overall employment level is fairly high but there is a marked drop at retirement age. Table 5.2 shows the percentages gainfully employed in

TABLE 5.1   Housing Conditions for the Elderly (65+) in the Nordic Countries 1982 (approximate numbers)

	Denmark		Finland		Norway		Sweden	
Housing Context	n	%	n	%	n	%	n	%
Institution	46,000	6.1	37,000	6.2	42,000	6.7	105,000	7.5
Congregate housing	8,000	1.1	3,200	0.5	24,000	3.8	28,000	2.0
Congregate housing without service	31,500	4.2	39,000	6.5			43,000	3.1
Independent living	669,500	88.7	516,300	86.7	562,500	89.5	1,219,000	87.4
Total	755,000	100.1	595,500	99.9	628,500	100.0	1,395,000	100.0

SOURCE: Adapted from Daatland and Sundström (1985).

upper age groups in the Nordic countries in 1982-1983. In the adjoining years, the pattern in Norway and Sweden is rather stable.

The higher level of employment at ages 65-74 in Norway compared to Sweden reflects a higher official retirement age (67 versus 65 years) in Norway. Due to labor market conditions, the figures for Denmark at 55-59 and 60-64 years are part of declines in overall level of employment, while the opposite applies to Finland.

In all Nordic countries, value is placed on the elderly being able to live in as normal a setting as possible. To this end, various social services are provided by formal agencies. The most common service is clearly home help, that is, assistance with cleaning, cooking, laundry, and shopping. Both the level and the intensity of home help are highest in Denmark.

The level of home help is defined by Daatland and Sundström (1985) as the annual number of man-hours in elderly households in relation to the population aged 65 and over (in Denmark and Norway, 67 and over). Measured in this way, the level of home help in 1982 was 57 hours in Denmark compared to 36 hours in Sweden, 27 hours in Norway, and 14 hours in Finland.

The intensity of home help, measured as the annual number of man-hours in elderly households per helped household, was 304 hours in Denmark compared to 205 hours in Sweden, 161 hours in Norway, and only 82 hours in Finland. I would like to note that the intensity is strikingly stable over the years.

To get a better understanding of the life-styles of older people as affected by factors such as employment level, and level of social services, the time budget offers an intriguing approach. As noted by Moss and Lawton (1982), time budgets have the advantage of relative objectivity while preserving much of the content that defines the experiences of everyday living.

TABLE 5.2   Gainfully Employed by Age, 1982-1983 (percentage of age group)

Age Group	Denmark	Finland	Norway	Sweden
55-59	63	61	74	78
60-64	38	34	60	54
65-74	12	9	22	8

SOURCE: *Yearbook of Nordic Statistics 1983* (Nordic Statistical Secretariat and the Nordic Council, 1984).

Nordic Time-Budget Studies

Large-scale studies of time use in the Nordic countries are scarce. Findings from some major investigations in each of the countries are compiled in Table 5.3.

The Danish study (Kühl & Munk, 1976) is based on a national random sample of adult Danes living independently. A sequential record of the individual's behavior during the day before the interview was obtained. Only the primary activity was recorded. Results were presented for eight groups with different positions in relation to professional life. The two groups of primary interest here are the male (n = 254) and the female (n = 312) retirees.

The population of the Finnish study (Niemi et al., 1979) consists of individuals aged 10 to 64, living independently. The national random sample numbered 6057 persons (the nonresponse rate was 17.6%). Respondents kept time-diary records for two successive days; most of them filled in the records for both days. Primary and secondary activities were recorded.

The Norwegian study, conducted by the Norwegian Central Bureau of Statistics (Statistisk sentralbyrå, 1975a), was based on a national random sample of individuals aged 15 to 74. The sample numbered 3040 persons (the nonresponse rate was 42%). Respondents kept time-diary records for two or three days. Primary and secondary activities were recorded.

The population of the Swedish study (Gahlin, 1983; Wigren, 1984) consists of individuals aged 9 to 79. The national random sample numbered 3301 persons (the nonresponse rate was 11.7%). Respondents were interviewed by telephone about their activities the day before the interview (in most cases). Primary activity was recorded. As an extra control, respondents were asked whether they also listened to the radio, and whether they engaged in any further activity.

TABLE 5.3   A Compilation of Some Nordic Time Use Studies, with Specific Reference to Late Life.[a] Use of Time—Average for All Days

	Denmark: Kühl & Munk (1975, January)	Finland: Niemi et al. (1979, September-November)	Norway: Statistisk sentralbyrå (1971-1972, September-August)			Sweden: Wigren (1981-1982, November and May)		
	"Retirees" 67 and above	55-64	45-64	65-74	"Retirees" 74 and Below	65-69	70-74	75-79
	%	%	%	%	%	%	%	%
Sleeping, meals, personal care	50.5	44	44.5	49.5	50.0	41.0	43.0	43.0
Gainful employment, education	2.5	12	16.5	7.5	2.5	1.0	0.5	0
Domestic work	9.0	16	17.5	17.0	19.0	18.5	16.5	14.5
Free time	34.0	28	20.5	24.0	26.5	39.5	40.0	42.5
Unknown	4.0	—	1.0	2.0	2.0	—	—	—
Total	100[b]	100	100	100	100	100	100	100
n	566	750[c]	1065	298	211	480[d]		

a. The figures are not necessarily presented in this way in the original sources. The original figures have been recalculated by the author in order to facilitate comparison.
b. The respondents filled in records covering 21 hours, leaving out 3 hours in the middle of the night. In this table, these hours have been added to the first category (Sleeping . . .).
c. Approximate figure: The number of responses (days) equals 1511, but most respondents filled in records for two days.
d. No exact figure is given. The three age-groups together make up about 480 respondents.

The present review is based on the published reports. Thus I have not had access to the original data files.

Table 5.3 utilizes the following broad categories specified by Aas (1978):

(1) necessary time related to basic physiological needs, including sleep, meals, and personal health and hygiene;
(2) contracted time related to gainful employment and school attendance;
(3) committed time related to domestic work; and
(4) free time.

This is a convenient categorization that can be applied to almost all time-use studies.

When necessary, the figures in the table have been recalculated to facilitate comparisons, that is, some of the original sources present the figures divided into weekdays and weekends, or by gender. In most cases, the presentation is more detailed in the original sources. Clearly one should not make direct comparisons between the countries because the surveys were designed and carried out separately. Several differences have to be taken into account. For example, the diminishing number of elderly people in the work force limits comparisons because the studies refer to different years. Also, the age ranges differ, as do the definitions of *retirees*. In the Danish study, *retiree* is defined as retired individuals aged 67 and over. In the Norwegian study, however, individuals are classified as retirees if they engage less than 15 hours per week in income-producing work and receive a pension as their principal source of income or if they were born before 1901 (that is, aged approximately 70-74). Nevertheless, the results of each of the four studies will be discussed, using the other studies as reference points.

Use of Time

Almost half of the day is taken up by sleeping, meals, and personal care. The retirees in Denmark and Norway spend around 50% of their time on this class of activities, the elderly in Sweden only 43%. In the Swedish study, approximately one hour less is recorded for sleep—8.5 versus 9.5 hours—which explains this difference. (The Norwegian data sum sleep and personal hygiene into a single category; assuming that the latter amounts, as in the other countries, to approximately 30 minutes, this holds true.)

How should this difference be interpreted? One possibility is a cohort difference. The Swedish study was done about a decade after the Norwegian study and the later retirees might be less worn out than the earlier. Still, there is no difference between the preretirement groups from Norway and Finland, though almost a decade separates these studies too. Another explanation could be that the studies were conducted in different seasons: the Danish study in the "dark" season (January); the Norwegian study during a whole year; and the Swedish study both in May—when the Nordic night is very short—and in November—when nights are long. If November is considered more "average," as suggested by Statistisk sentralbyrå (1975a, pp. 48-49), and the weeks around midsummer "exceptional," sleep patterns could perhaps be expected to vary accordingly. A third explanation concerns the definition of "sleeping, meals, and personal care." In the Norwegian study, this item also includes "bed rest in connection with illness," which might add to the total figure. A corresponding category is probably not included in the other studies, however, so that would not explain the Danish figure.

Gainful employment occupies very few hours in the retirement years, as already shown in the introduction.

For domestic work, the Danish figure differs from the rest, being especially low. Perhaps the comparatively high level of Danish home help for the elderly (Daatland and Sundström, 1985) contributes to this. The Swedish data show a falling trend of involvement in housework with age. Here too one explanation could be that an increasing part of domestic work is done by home-helpers.

Finally, with regard to free time, it is interesting to note that the figure for Norway, which is ten years older, is about two-thirds of the Swedish figure. Before taking a closer look at the leisure activities, we will examine two other aspects of time use, termed quite simply "where" and "with whom" (Little, 1984).

Where

A general observation from the Nordic time-budget studies is that a large part of the day is spent at home—for the elderly about 80% to 85%, that is, 20 out of the 24 hours (Stockholms läns Landsting, 1974; Walldén, 1975a, 1975b; Statistisk sentralbyrå, 1975a). A similar percentage was found in Moss and Lawton's (1982) four nonrepresentative groups of elderly in Philadelphia (75% to 85% of the day). The distribution of time spent at home can be illustrated with data from Walldén (1975a, 1975b), who investigated activities among groups of Swedish townspeople. Two groups are relevant here: (1) singles born 1894 to 1901, that is, aged 67-75 at the time of the study; and (2) spouses with husbands born from 1894 to 1901. The material was collected in October 1969. Results showed that elderly women spend more time at home than do elderly men. One woman in three had not been outdoors at all on the days studied, with no difference by marital status. Married men, on the other hand, stayed at home *less* than singles, before and after lunch time, that is, between 10:00 a.m. and noon and between 2:00 and 4:00 p.m. The married male retirees had on average been at home 80 minutes less per day than their wives.

The time spent at home also varies with age. Figure 5.1, adapted from Wigren's (1984) study, shows three subgroups of elderly persons: 65-69, 70-74, and 75-79 years of age. It will be seen that the proportion of elderly who are at home at different hours on *weekdays* increases with age. The difference is greatest in the middle of the day (between 10:00 a.m. and 5:00 p.m.). The mornings and evenings are spent at home to a large extent in all these age groups. Before lunch (approximately 10:00 a.m. to noon) the "young-old" (aged 65-69) differ from the other two groups, with a great tendency to be away from home. After lunch (approximately 1:00 to 5:00 p.m.) all three groups differ, one reason being that the oldest group has no lunch time "peak" (representing the tendency to be at home then to a greater extent than before or after lunch). After about 10:00 a.m.—when the proportion not at home is largest—the proportion at home continuously increases during the rest of the day.

On *weekends*, the elderly spend more time at home than on weekdays. There are no pronounced differences between subgroups, except that after 6:00 p.m. the "young-old" are away to a somewhat greater extent than the older age groups. This is similar for the interval between 10:00 a.m. and 1:00 p.m., except that the proportion away from home is then also somewhat greater for the oldest group (aged 75-79) compared to the "middle-old" group (aged 70-74). Perhaps church attendance is more common in the oldest group, though this cannot be inferred from the data.

It is perhaps not remarkable that such a large part of the day is spent at home. Middle-aged and younger people also spend much of their time at home. The category spending least time at home according to another Swedish study (Stockholms läns Landsting, 1974) are males in house-

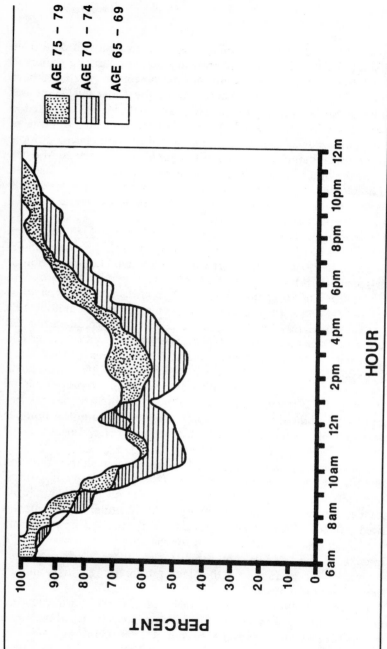

Figure 5.1 Percentage of Elderly Swedes (Aged 65-79) Who Are at Home at Different Hours During Weekdays

holds with children, where the spouse works part-time. These men still are at home 53% of weekdays. The average Swede aged 9-79 spends 66% of the week at home (Gahlin, 1983). Time at home is dominated by basic needs (sleep, personal hygiene, and meals), and as we have seen, these occupy half or almost half of the average day. The proportion is much the same for all age groups above 14 (Gahlin, 1983).

How time for sleep is reflected in the daily rhythm, and how the elderly differ from the population at large in this respect, can be illustrated by the Danish and Swedish data.

On weekdays, one in two of the population at large is awake at about 6:30 a.m., while about 90% of the elderly are still asleep. One elderly person in two is awake at about 7:45 a.m. In the evening, when 60% of the elderly have gone to bed, one in two of the population at large has done so. This happens at about 11:00 p.m. according to the Danish data and about 10:30 according to the Swedish. On weekend evenings, the situation is about the same. On weekend mornings, though, the situation is reversed, with only about 30% of the elderly in Denmark (20% in Sweden) asleep at a time when one in two of the population at large is still asleep.

As we have seen, the home is, quite naturally, the dominant *location* of activities. On an average day, the most common locations, in descending order after the home, are (1) in nature, parks, streets; (2) in someone's apartment; (3) traveling; and (4) in shops (Wigren, 1984). The young-old spend more time than the old-old in all locations except the home. For example, the young-old spend 1.75 hours in "nature, parks, streets," while the old-old spend just about one hour there.

With Whom

The question of with whom older people spend time can be conceived of as the social context. If someone else is present during certain activities, or if an activity has socializing as its main purpose, the social context becomes an important aspect of the activity. The obvious difficulties involved in delimiting this aspect of time use are reflected in the varying definitions. According to the reviewed reports, socializing has been understood as in these different categories:

Denmark
(Retirees—2.2 hours per day):
    socializing with spouse and children

visits by relatives
visits by others
visits to relatives
visits to others

Finland
(55-64 age group—1.1 hours per day):
   socializing with children
   socializing with other family members
   visiting acquaintances
   socializing with acquaintances at home
   socializing with acquaintances outdoors
   telephone conversations
   visits to restaurants and dances
   visiting cafes and the like
   other socializing
   traveling related to socializing

Norway
(Retirees—2.1 hours per day;
65-74 age group—1.7 hours per day)
   play with children
   conversation with children, reading to children
   other socializing with children
   visits with family or friends
   parties
   other gatherings
   games, dancing
   conversations
   other socializing

Sweden
(65-69 age group—2.1 hours per day;
70-74 age group—2.1 hours per day;
75-79 age group—2.3 hours per day)
   socializing

As shown above, the retirees spend about 2.1 hours per day on socializing. The figure is the same irrespective of the degree of specification in the questionnaires. At first glance, this might look like a shortcoming but it could just as well be interpreted as a successful test of the reliability and a validation of the instruments. The detailed questionnaires show, not surprisingly, that in the course of one or two days—the usual duration of time diaries—a particular individual uses only a few of the alternative social activities. This may help to explain why respondents can make a fairly good overall estimate of what should be included in more general categories. In the end, the degree of specification of activities should be determined by the study's particular purpose.

In sum, rather than answering the question "with whom," directly, the Nordic studies give estimates of time spent on activities whose main purpose is to socialize.

Thus socializing as shown here is presented in the reports as one of the categories constituting leisure—together with mass media, the most time absorbing one. But how much time is spent on leisure in general?

Leisure Time

It is easy to conclude with, for example, Wigren (1984) that time spent on leisure is largest among retirees. But the difference from younger age groups is not as great as might be supposed. Time for child care and for education decreases substantially after age 40. The number of gainfully employed falls gradually from around age 50. Thus the possibilities of reserving time for leisure grow long before the official retirement age. Gahlin's (1983) data show that, on an average day, leisure time is as follows:

Age Group	Hours
15-24	6.36
25-44	5.53
45-64	6.39
65-79	9.40

Niemi et al. (1979) found a similar trend, though their figures are somewhat lower. Figure 5.2 shows how the retirees in Gahlin's study schedule their leisure. Leisure activities outside the apartment primarily take place between 9:00 a.m. and noon and between 1:00 p.m. and 5:00 p.m. On Saturdays, the total amount of leisure is somewhat greater than on weekdays, and a larger part of it is spent at home.

Because most of the time from 6:00 p.m. until bedtime is spent at home, it is no surprise that mass media take up a good part of the elderly's leisure time—40%. They do not differ dramatically from younger age groups, however, where at least 30% of leisure time is spent on mass media (Gahlin, 1983). For retirees, watching TV occupies about

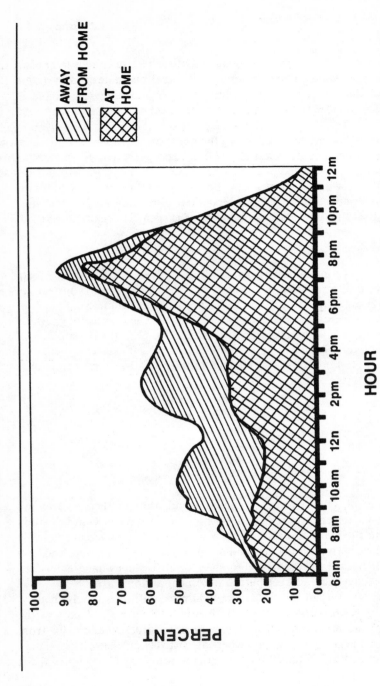

Figure 5.2 Percentage of Elderly Swedes (Aged 65-79) Who Engage in Leisure Activities at Different Hours During Weekdays

45% of total mass media time in all age groups. Listening to the radio decreases with age from 38% of total mass media time for the young-old, to 27% for the old-old. Reading increases from 22% to 28%. The latter difference can be interpreted as a cohort difference. The old-old might not have developed the habit of listening to the radio to the same extent as the young-old, because they were between 17 and 21 years old when broadcasting was introduced. An alternative explanation might be that it is easier to compensate for impaired eyesight than for impaired hearing.

Mass media is an *indoor* activity of considerable range, while walks should be mentioned as a frequent *outdoor* activity. According to Walldén (1975a), male retirees—both married and single—go for a walk more often than female retirees. About one married man in two walks alone; one in four walks the dog, but very few are accompanied by their wives. Single male retirees almost exclusively walk alone. Female retirees—married as well as single—very seldom go for a walk for its own sake, while elderly husbands are the category with the largest amount of walks. One hypothesis as to the sex difference in number of walks is that the wives get their share of walking from the necessary errands. Data showed, however, that the elderly husbands actually take care of more errands requiring a walk. No other leisure activities compensate for the scarcity of walks among retired women. Another explanation might be that husbands use walks as escapes from conflicts at home. Single male retirees, however, go for a walk more often than single female retirees. Either there is a sex difference in need achievement for this activity or a difference in norms. Women may regard walking as "futile or unprofitable" or the males of this generation may consider it unnatural to spend a whole day in the apartment. One might add that women probably have had fewer opportunities to acquire the habit earlier in life. At the turn of the century, a "good girl" was not supposed to take walks alone.

Actual Versus Ideal
Use of Time

The activities just mentioned illustrate a common question concerning studies of time use. Is there a relationship between the time spent on an activity and the interest taken in it? For example, among the relatively few elderly who feel lonely, both reading and walks are reported as activities intended to repress feelings of loneliness (Andersson, 1983). Moss and Lawton (1982) claim that "the frequency of time devoted to an activity is not a good measure of the satisfaction or pleasure obtained."

This aspect has attracted little attention, but a small-scale attempt will be reported here. The study (Andersson et al., 1979) was done in production plants belonging to a large Swedish company. A total sample was drawn from (1) former employees who had been retired for three years, and (2) employees who were about to retire. Most of the participants were blue-collar workers and, due to the character of the company (metal manufacturing), only 6% of the participants were women. The retirees were divided into old-age pensioners and disability pensioners.

The interviewer first asked how much time was spent on leisure activities, summarized into eight categories: (1) mass media; (2) games, competitions, culture; (3) excursions and travel; (4) house, gardening, weekend cottage care, boat; (5) indoor activities such as woodwork, handicraft, playing music, crosswords, repairs; (6) outdoor activities such as fishing, hunting, sports, walks; (7) socializing; and (8) club and social activities and courses. A detailed interview followed for the *three* categories on which the participant had spent most time. Thus limitation was dictated by the length of the interview. In view of the dominant role of the three most time-consuming classes of activities, this procedure gave a fairly clear picture of daily life.

The results showed only minor differences between workers, old-age pensioners, and disability pensioners for activities in the categories (2) games, competitions, culture; (3) excursions and travel; (7) socializing; and (8) club and social activities and courses. Old-age pensioners, however, spend 5 hours more per week than workers on mass media (1) while disability pensioners spend a further 3 hours, totaling 47 hours, on such activities. Similarly, workers spend the least time (3 hours per week) on indoor activities (5) and disability pensioners spend the most (6 hours per week). Outdoor activities (6), as well as being busy with the house and so on (4), are more frequent for old-age pensioners (13 hours per week and 7 hours per week, respectively), compared to disability pensioners (10 hours per week and 5 hours per week, respectively), and workers (7 hours per week and 5 hours per week, respectively). The two groups of retirees spend more time on leisure than the workers, of course, but the difference in time use is even somewhat smaller than it is in Gahlin's (1983) data presented earlier. The two groups of retirees also spend more time than workers on domestic work—12 hours per week compared to 9.5 hours per week. The predominance of males in the study accounts for the generally low figures for domestic work.

To catch a glimpse of what time use actually meant to the participants, the following question was asked: "Would you say that your life would be more pleasant/happy and more meaningful if you could spend more time on this?"

For a fifth of the respondents, indoor activities was one of the categories that was investigated further. As mentioned, workers spent the least and disability pensioners the most time on this. Because only those who devoted the most time to a certain activity were questioned in detail about it, the reported hours exceed those of the total group. The ranking order between the groups is still the same in this material. The proportion of the participants who answered affirmatively to the above question, about indoor activities, was highest for workers (84%), somewhat lower for old-age pensioners (65%), and lowest for disability pensioners (33%). Thus these answers support the hypothesis that the more time that is spent on a pleasurable activity, the less probable it becomes that further time would add to well-being. The categories "outdoor activities" and "being busy with the house and so on," however, give a slightly different picture. Workers, again, are more prone to report that more available time would increase well-being— 94% for both categories; but old-age pensioners hold this view more than disability pensioners (66% and 65% versus 58% and 55%). This suggests a certain "saturation" among disability pensioners, considering that they actually spend less time than old-age pensioners on these activities but are not so inclined to think that having more time would increase their well-being. It is, of course, difficult to say to what extent the disabilities as such influence the answers of disability pensioners in a more "realistic" direction, even though they were asked to imagine ideal situations.

Regarding mass media, only reading was followed up. The percentages here are much lower—35% of the workers stated that their well-being would increase if they had more time for reading. The corresponding figures for old-age and disability pensioners are 14% and 19%, respectively.

In sum, the results of that study give some support to the notion that things are less enjoyable when one is not feeling well (Moss and Lawton, 1982).

The importance of investigating the subjective aspects of time use is further underlined by the fact that free time increases for the elderly particularly in welfare societies, as illustrated by the Swedish data (Wigren, 1984). The necessity of working decreases drastically; help with domestic work is provided by the community-based home-help service, relatives, or welfare agencies; and transportation is provided by the municipal transportation service. Thus activities that would otherwise take up a large part of the day are handled more effectively with the assistance of others. The effect is also that the older (and more frail) the retiree, the more free time is available. More free time can also imply a less structured pattern of living. Gahlin (1977) writes that retirees are the group with the greatest possibility of using mass media flexibly. Still, they show—to a larger extent than other groups—a regular and structured pattern. He concludes that this seems to contradict the hypothesis of mass media consumption and its dependence on other activities.

Gahlin suggests that the regularity of timing and content of mass media impart confidence. Reading the newspaper and watching TV become important goals and events to look forward to, in an uneventful and unstructured life. This seems to support Robinson's (1983) assumption that "having too much free time makes for a highly unsatisfying lifestyle for most people." One indicator of less satisfying free time might be the proportion of passing the time—that is, doing nothing in particular. According to Wigren (1984), this category occupies about one-seventh of free time—somewhat less among the young-old, somewhat more among the old-old. An interesting finding is that among the elderly living alone, the figure is fairly constant, just below 1.5 hours per day in all elderly age groups. In households of two or more persons, the figure rises with age—one hour among those aged 65 to 69 and two hours among those aged 75 to 79.

In total, the amount of passing the time does not seem to be considerable. In any event, the percentage is comparable to what Moss and Lawton (1982) found for "rest and relaxation," defined as a relatively passive discretionary activity, in their four groups. If we expand the concept to include other passive sedentary activities, such as watching television, we can conclude with Abrams (as cited in Little, 1984) that considerable time is spent on this. Wigren (1984) observes, however, that the elderly more than other age groups choose actively among the television programs offered.

In sum, it is important to take a closer look at the interplay between objective time use, the subjective experience of time, and individual well-being. This includes studying the prerequisites for being able to enjoy an increasing share of free time in an optimal way.

NOTE

1. Although a Nordic country, Iceland is not included in this chapter due to a lack of relevant time-budget data.

REFERENCES

Aas, Dagfinn. 1978. "Studies of Time-Use: Problems and Prospects." *Acta Sociologica* 21(2):125-41.

Andersson, Lars. 1983. "Aldrande och ensamhet—ett interventionsforsok." Pp. 111-26 in *Ensamhet och Isolering—Rapport fran ett seminarium*. Rapport nr 51 fran Institutet for Gerontologi. Jonkoping: Institutet for Gerontologi.

————, Bengt Edren, Thord Ericsson, Sture Lind, Gote Lindahl, Goran Olhagen, and Bengt Sparrow. 1979. *Arbetsliv och pensionering. Delrapport 2. Resultat fran intervju-och halsoundersokning. Beskrivande data*. Rapport nr 104 fran Laboratoriet for klinisk stressforskning. Stockholm: Karolinska Institutet.

Daatland, Svein Olav and Gerdt Sundström. 1985. *Gammal i Norden. Boende, omsorg och service 1965-1982. Del-rapport 1 fran projektet: Atgarder inom service- och bostadssektorn for aldre*. Stockholm: Nordiska ministerradet.

Gahlin, Anders. 1977. *Radio, TV och tidningar bland tre generationer*. SR/PUB nr 10. Stockholm: Sveriges Radio.

————. 1983. *Levnadsvanor i Sverige. Dagliga aktiviteter*. SR/PUB nr 10. Stockholm: Sveriges Radio.

Kühl, P. H. and Jens K. Munk. 1976. *Dognsrytme. Befolkningens tidsanvendelse pa ugens dage*. Socialforskningsinstitutet, Meddelelse nr. 15. Kobenhavn: Statens trykningskontor.

Little, Virginia C. 1984. "An Overview of Research Using Time-Budget Methodology to Study Age-Related Behaviour." *Aging and Society* 4(1):3-20.

Moss, Miriam S. and M. Powell Lawton. 1982. "Time Budgets of Older People: A Window on Four Life Styles." *Journal of Gerontology* 37(1):115-23.

National Commission on Aging. 1982. *Just Another Age: A Swedish Report to the World Assembly on Aging 1982*. Stockholm: Departementens reprocentral.

Niemi, Iiris, Salme Kiiski, and Mirja Liikkanen. 1979. *Use of Time in Finland*. Central Statistical Office of Finland, No. 65. Helsinki: Government Printing Centre.

The Nordic Statistical Secretariat and the Nordic Council. 1984. *Yearbook of Nordic Statistics 1983*. Stockholm: Author.

Robinson, John P. 1983. "Environmental Differences in How Americans Use Time: The Case for Subjective *and* Objective Indicators." *Journal of Community Psychology* 11:171-81.

Statistisk sentralbyrå. 1975a. *Tidsnyttingsunderskelsen 1971-72. Hefte 1. Norges offisielle statistik A 692*. Oslo: Norwegian National Central Bureau of Statistics.

————. 1975b. *Tid nyttet til egenarbeid*. Statistiska analyser nr 19. Oslo: Norwegian National Central Bureau of Statistics.

————. 1977. *Dognets 24 timer. En analyse av tidsnytting i 1971-72*. Statistiske analyser nr 30. Oslo: Norwegian National Central Bureau of Statistics.

Stockholms läns Landsting. 1974. *TU71. Resultatrapport nr 2. Hushallens tid, sysslor, forflyttningar*. Vardag, lordag, sondag. Stockholm: Author, Trafiknamnden.

Swedish National Central Bureau of Statistics. 1984. *Statistical Abstract of Sweden 1985*. Official Statistics of Sweden. Stockholm: Statistics Sweden.

Walldén, Marja. 1975a. *Individers aktivitetsmonster—en studie av ett urval stadsborisma och mellanstora stader. Del 2. Frekvensen aktiviteter utanfor bostaden.* Rapport R9: 1975. Stockholm: Byggforskningen.

———. 1975b. *Individers aktivitetsmonster—en studie av ett urval stadsbor i sma och mellanstora stader. Del 3. Tidsanvandning.* Rapport R10: 1975. Stockholm: Byggforskningen.

Wigren, Gunnila. 1984. *Levnadsvanor i Sverige. Pensionarer.* SR/PUB nr 9. Stockholm: Sveriges Radio.

6

Social Action and Interaction in Later Life

Aging in the United States

KAREN ALTERGOTT

A Day in the Life

Mrs. Blue is 72 years old and married. One day in April, Mrs. Blue awakes at 7:30. She spends 20 minutes getting ready for the day. After cooking breakfast for herself and her husband, she joins him for brief devotions. They then have breakfast together. Around 8:30, Mrs. Blue spends a bit of time reading the newspaper and listening to the radio. Then, as she begins an hour and a half of housework, she turns on the TV to keep her company as she does her chores. Around 10:30, she joins her husband in the garden and they work together for about a half hour. Going inside alone, she prepares lunch, reads the mail, and watches a bit of TV. Around 12, her husband comes in and joins her for lunch. They rest together for about an hour and a half after lunch, while reading and talking. After this, Mrs. Blue goes outside alone to work on the flowers. Coming in, she joins her husband for another hour of rest and reading. She spends a half hour preparing supper in the company of the TV and

AUTHOR'S NOTE: The data utilized in this study were made available by the Inter-University Consortium for Political and Social Research. Neither the original collectors of the data nor the Consortium bear any responsibility for the analyses or interpretation presented here.

enjoys supper with her husband, with the TV on in the background. She and her husband wash the dishes together while listening to TV, then devote one hour to watching TV together. Mrs. Blue spends about an hour reading in the early evening. Then she dresses to go to a neighbor's house. She and her husband show travel slides to her neighbor and a group of teenagers until about 10:00. When they return home, the Blues watch more TV, share evening devotionals, get ready for bed, and go to bed at 11:00.

Dr. Green is 70 years old and remarried after being widowed. Before he remarried, he was closest to his dog, enjoyed being with his children, turned to his son in a crisis, and felt important because of his patients. Now, his wife is his closest, most enjoyable companion. It is her he turns to in a crisis and she makes him feel important.

One day in May, Dr. Green awakes at 6:00, showers, and readies himself for the day. He takes the garbage out while his wife cooks breakfast. They eat together, and because they read the paper and talk over breakfast, this breakfast lasts from 7:00 to 8:00. After breakfast, he leaves home to take the car to be repaired at a downtown garage. His wife accompanies him and they talk while driving downtown and walk around while the car is being repaired. Once home, he begins working on a project for his part-time job. As a retired professional, he was able to find rewarding part-time work in a field related to his earlier career in medicine. He has lunch with his wife around noon, and they talk until 1:00. Then, he returns to his work until three. About an hour is spent in traveling to the grocery store and shopping. Back at home, he installed an attic light. A brief nap was followed by a leisurely supper with his wife and an evening full of TV viewing with his wife. Dr. and Mrs. Green went to bed around 10:00.

Nation as Context for
Daily Life

What could national context have to do with the daily life of Dr. Green and Mrs. Blue? First, the structural and contextual features of a nation set the stage for the individual's life. Are there high or low proportions of older people in society? What are their living arrangements? Opportunities to engage in activities, accomplish tasks, and involve oneself with others are shaped by the social environment. Second, national policy, whether implicit or explicit, provides resources and constraints that are often age specific. Are economic resources or opportunities to acquire them sufficient? Are the lives and roles of the aged central or peripheral to the policymakers? It is through direct manipulation of policies that governments further structure the lives of their older citizens.

Demography

In the United States, 12% of the population is 65 years of age or older (AARP, 1984). Of the 25.5 million Americans 65 and older in 1980, 61% were 65 to 74 years old, 30% were 75 to 84 years old, and 9% were 85 years old or older (U.S. Select Committee on Aging, 1982a). The oldest segment, those 85 and older, consisted of 2.2 million people in 1980 and is a rapidly growing aggregate. As in other developed countries, fertility reductions and life expectancy increases have led to the greater proportion of older citizens.

Lower fertility rates increase the proportion of older people in a population. This is perhaps best illustrated by population projections based on different assumptions about childbearing. If American women bear 2.7 children on the average, the American population will double by 2040, but the percentage of older people will remain about the same. If fertility reaches as low as 1.7 children per woman, other things being equal, the American population size will remain the same and the proportion of people over the age of 65 will be about 23% (U.S. Bureau of the Census, 1977).

There has also been an increase in life expectancy since the early 1900s. Much of the increase is due to reductions in infant and maternal mortality, but since 1960, the life expectancy for someone who reached age 65 increased 2.5 years (AARP, 1984). Life expectancy at birth in 1980 was 78 for a white female, 71 for a white male, 74 for a black female, and 65 for a black male. This lifelong mortality advantage for women results in an increasingly disbalanced gender ratio. There are 88 men for each 100 women aged 55-64, 76 men for 100 women aged 65-74, 66 men for each 100 women aged 75-84, and 44 men for 100 women aged 85 or older (U.S. Bureau of the Census, 1980). The predictable period of widowhood for most American women at the end of their lives is part of the demographic reality of aging. Most older men are married, while most older women are not. In 1983, there were five times as many widows as widowers (AARP, 1984). In 1981, 82% of men 55-64 were married, compared to 67% of women that age. For those 65 to 74, 81%

of men and 48% of women were married. For those 75 and older, 70% of men were married while only 22% of women were married. Another demographic reality that sheds light on the family situation of older Americans is the fact that 12% of the married and 17% of the unmarried older people live in the same household as their child (Schorr, 1980). These intergenerational households may be parent-headed or the parent may have joined the child's household.

Stages of life have expanded during the twentieth century and many demographic realities facing Americans are new. Social responses of innovation and changes in the role structure seem inevitable.

Cowgill suggested, however, that the responses to demographic aging have not produced integrative social changes for the aged. His thesis, that modern societies have economic structures and cultural consequences that are disadvantageous to the aged, cannot be directly explored in the current volume because all societies are at a relatively high level of modernity. We can, however, examine how particular modern societies vary in the opportunities they create for action and interaction of older adults in daily life. The same structural and cultural forces Cowgill discussed are relevant to this question (Cowgill, 1986).

Economic Structures

General economic forces include the economic status of older people, the transformation of the labor force, and the institutionalization of retirement. Whether the economic situation in modern societies is favorable or unfavorable to older people has been described in various ways.

The institutionalization of retirement as a stage of life has been an important social change of the twentieth century. About 20% of men and 8% of women over the age of 65 are employed. Access to work is highly limited, depending upon prior work experience and overcoming barriers to employment such as age discrimination and the lack of part-time work. Social security is the most important single source of income for older Americans (Barberis, 1981). According to Bader (1986), 43% of income received by those 65 and older came from social security, 16% came from earnings, 15% came from interest on savings, and 18% came from pensions. Private pensions are available to only about one-fifth of the elderly and their value is low and often decreases with inflation. It is clear that the economic situation of the older population in the United States is determined, to a large extent, by government action.

While improvements have been made in the poverty level among older Americans, millions live in poverty. In 1959, 35% lived below the poverty level; in 1985, 12.6% did (U.S. Bureau of the Census, 1986). Perhaps because of the wide variety of living conditions, the poverty of older people is somewhat invisible. Everyone knows of the retirement communities for the well-off and retired, but the invisible suffering of the older people living alone or with equally impoverished kin are less familiar realities. The aged are overrepresented among the wealthy and this has misled many to assume that economic situations for the aged are nonproblematic. The eroding policies and programs to sustain the well-being of American elders may be threatened in the future, because of the myths of elder's economic resourcefulness (Villers Foundation, 1987).

Other social conditions that Cowgill (1986) suggests are present in modern societies, especially Western societies, are trends toward greater urbanization, high levels of mobility, separate living quarters for elders, and increasing reliance on formal education. Each of these has the potential to shape the daily lives of older people in the United States.

Cultural Context

The American society has been considered youth oriented by many. According to social historians, such as Fischer, this is a cultural perspective that has been with us since the late 170Cs when regard for elders gave way to the admiration of youth (Fischer, 1977). Of course, economic resources and political power were relevant to the status of any man in the early decades of the nation. But from the era of this nation's formation to the present, a youth orientation seems predominant.

Modern societies often foster value systems that either equalize age groups or result in lower status for older people (Cowgill, 1986). The effect this has on the life-styles of older people is channeled through ageism (Levin and Levin, 1980), stereotypes that restrict opportunities to engage in activities and interactions, and through limited planning to facilitate activities of the aged.

A final cultural factor shaping the life-style of older people is the life-style dominant in the nation as a whole. That is, in spite of the different positions and statuses older people hold, they share in a general way of living that dominates their communities. Culture consists of the way of living of a people, and a good part of culture is captured and reflected in the daily lives of individuals. In some way, then, we can only understand the life-style of older people in relation to the life-style of a nation. In Table 6.1, the activities and interactions of Americans aged 18 to 88 are recorded. These figures come from the same study on which the analysis of later life is based.

Time spent in TV viewing and social leisure reflect dominant free time activities. Paid work and housework are equally salient obligatory activities. Americans spend a good deal of time in solitude, and have most of their social interactions with family members.

Policies

The socioeconomic status of older people is defined by policies for many older people. Social security, Supplemental Security Income, rent subsidy programs, and food stamps are some of the policies that define the social position of older people who participate in them. These programs have been insufficient, given the levels of need, to equalize the status of older people. Inequalities among the elderly are maintained and decrements in socioeconomic status for the older population are defined by the policies in place. Resources available effect the activities that are possible.

Medical benefits are provided through Medicare on the basis of age, by Medicaid on the basis of indigence, and through a few preventative (e.g., nutritional and service) programs. Social programs and home services are not highly developed in the United States, relative to other countries (Amann, 1980). When functional limitations inhibit participation in interactions and activities, services are not provided to compensate for these limitations. The lifestyles of the very old are likely to be most affected. The amount of activity engaged in as well as social interactions are influenced by the needs and the ways we meet the needs of older adults. The care system in American society is primarily private and this will influence daily life.

Previous Research on Life-Styles of Older Men and Women

What fills the daily lives of American elders? What are the gender differences that exist in the daily lives of older people? What are the patterns across the age groups within the older population? Since the early days of social gerontology in the United States, examining the

TABLE 6.1   Participation in Activities and Interactions by American Adults Aged 18-88: Daily Average

Leisure Activities (872)	X	Obligatory Activities (872)	X	Social Activities (872)	X
Active leisure	:20	Paid work	2:33	Spouse	3:56
Passive leisure	:56	Housework	2:14	Child	2:34
TV	2:03	Helping	:08	Other household adult	:32
Social leisure	1:14	Child care	:22	Friends and relatives	2:37
Religious practice	:13	Personal care	2:11	Colleagues	1:56
Voluntary organizations	:08	Sleep	8:34	Organization members	:07
Creative leisure	:13			Neighbors	:07
Entertainment	:09			Service providers	:05
Education	:12			Strangers or acquaintances	:29
Travel for leisure	:27			Solitude	4:34

daily lives of older people has been a central task. Palmore's (1981) work with the Duke Longitudinal Study documents the changes in many activities over the individual lifetime. Only through accumulation of evidence from both longitudinal and cross-sectional studies will a clear picture of later life emerge.

Studies of time use by older people often emphasize leisure time (Cowgill and Baulch, 1962; Havighurst, 1957; Lawton, 1978; Gordon and Gaitz, 1976). The focus on leisure may stem from the assumption that retirement has produced a new leisure class (Michelon, 1954). Some studies of social relationships have also taken a daily life perspective (Larson et al., 1985; Altergott, 1985). Only a few studies use the approach of taking all activities and experiences into account in describing the life-style of older people (Moss and Lawton, 1982).

In the previous work on lifestyles of older people, many voices called for more "rigorous" methods, including Peter Townsend (1968) in a chapter on problems in the cross-national study of old people in the family. His concern was to determine the differences between older people integrated into the family, those integrated into extrafamilial social circles, those who were "doubly integrated," and those who were isolates. Without a method that captured all the activities and inter-actions, it would be difficult to classify individuals accurately.

In recent years, the breakthrough in data collection and analysis techniques that the pioneers in gerontology sought seems to be found in time-budget methods. The advantages of this method at getting a clear picture of the lifestyles of older people include the recording of "the totality of roles in which they engage in daily life" (Robinson, 1988) and the collection of data for a period of time that is "maximally understandable to them and accessible to memory" (Robinson, 1988).

The detail and completeness captured by the time-budget data collection process and the ease with which many kinds of behavioral measures can be constructed combine to provide rich insight into the characteristics of daily life.

Within the constraints of national context, subcultures of aging (Rose, 1965), and life-course continuities and discontinuities, themes and variations can be observed. The purpose of this chapter is to analyze the patterns of activity and interaction in daily life, circa 1975, for older men and women. Time-budget concepts and measures will be relied on.

Methods

Sample and Data Collection

In 1975-1976, Dr. Juster and his colleagues at the University of Michigan, Institute for Social Research, conducted a national study of time use by American adults (Juster et al., 1976). Their study provided the data set for this analysis. A multistage random sampling procedure resulted in interviews with 1519 respondents. Each respondent was invited to complete four separate interviews during a one-year period. Each interview included survey questions and a time-use interview. In a time-use interview, the interviewer gathers a sequential record of activities for a particular 24-hour period of time. Information for each event in a person's day included

> primary activity,
> time that activity began and ended,
> social companions during the activity,
> location, and
> whether the person was doing anything else at the same time.

For two reasons, however, the sample of 1519 in the original study was truncated to 872. First, panel attrition from the first interview to the fourth resulted in 947 respondents in the final interview. In addition, it was important to have a Saturday, a Sunday, and two weekdays available for each respondent in order to capture comparable information on life-style for all respondents. Of the 947 respondents, 872 had complete information on each weekend day and two weekdays. Finally, because this analysis concerns the time use of men and women 55 years of age and older, the 260 respondents in this age range were selected.

Measurement

The coding of the primary activities and companions are most relevant to this analysis. Original coding of the data was conducted and supervised by the Institute of Social Research staff. The process was highly systematic, and a coding scheme with hundreds of precise activity labels was used based on the international standard for coding the time budget, as developed by Alexander Szalai (1972) and colleagues. For the current project, the coded activity records were used to create 17 categories of primary activity, and nine types of social companions plus solitude. The decision to collapse the categories was based on a goal to tap central elements of life-style.

Primary Activities

Basic activities that are considered obligatory included sleep (including naps and night sleep) and personal care (including time spent washing, dressing, eating, and caring for oneself). Other activities that are somewhat obligatory include paid work, child care, helping, and housework. Once the roles of worker, parent (or grandparent), helper, or home care provider are taken, some level of activity is required. For work, all paid work on a first or second job is included as well as paid work done at home. For child care, all time spent caring for children who live in the household was included. This may include one's own grandchildren. For housework, all time spent doing indoor and outdoor chores are included. Helping included giving help and care to adults in and out of the household. Any of these activities, except sleep, can be considered productive activities, because services and goods with value are produced.

All the other activities analyzed here are considered leisure activities because they allow a high degree of choice. While the differences are not rigid, leisure activities such as passive leisure (radio or other listening, reading, writing letters), TV watching time, active leisure (sports), religious practices, entertainment (attending sports and music events, going to movies, theaters, and museums), social activities (visiting, conversing, parties, social gatherings in bars, lounges, or other places of leisure) are generally not productive, while creative leisure (hobbies, arts and crafts) and voluntary organizational participation (identity, political, helping religious organizations, and so on) are somewhat more productive forms of leisure.

Social Interaction

Time spent alone as well as in the company of one's spouse, one's children, other adults in the household, with friends and relatives, with co-workers, with organization members, with neighbors, with service providers, and with others (strangers, acquaintances, and crowds) were analyzed. The three clusters of relevance to themes in the convergence literature are solitude; close and personal relations (spouse, children, other household adults, friends, and relatives); and more distant, integrative relations (neighbors, colleagues, organization members, service providers, and others).

Measures of Involvement

There are three ways to describe involvement in actions and interactions: overall averages, percentage of participants, and average amount of time per participant. All three figures are valuable.

The involvement of an age strata in a particular activity can be assessed by the time devoted to that activity by members of the age strata. The overall average is the total amount of time spent on an activity by all people in a particular aggregate divided by the number of people in that aggregate. In this study, each individual was interviewed four times for different days of the week (Saturday, Sunday, and two weekdays) and the overall average was divided by four to produce an *overall daily average*.

The intensity of involvement by older people in certain activities can also be measured by examining just those who participate in activities. The *percentage of participants* is the proportion of people in an aggregate who participated in a certain activity sometime during the four days that were observed for each person. The *daily average per participant* is the mean amount of time spent on an activity by people in a particular aggregate divided by four to provide a daily average. If all members of an aggregate participated in an activity (such as sleep), then the overall average will be the same as the participants' average. If only a few people participate in an activity, such as education, however, the participants' average will be considerably higher than the overall average.

Daily Life in Later Life: American Patterns

The 260 men and women who provided information for this study follow patterns commonly found in national samples of older people. The older Americans in this analysis felt relatively healthy and had an average educational attainment of 11-12 years of formal schooling. The average age for the women was 66, with a range of 55 to 88, and 65 for men, with a range of 55 to 87. Men in this study had higher family incomes than women, due in part to the different family structures in which they lived. Only 41% of the women in this study were married, while 90% of the men were. The latter two points highlight some of the differences between older men and older women. Men are much more likely to be married and have greater economic resources. For these reasons, and for anticipated differences in lifestyles of men and women, the analyses were conducted separately for men and women.

Leisure

(1) Overall gender patterns. Men and women were very similar in the amounts of time they spent in five of the leisure activities. The daily averages for men and women 55 to 88 years of age were over one hour for social leisure. Men and women were also similar and spent very little time overall in religious practices, voluntary organizations, entertainment, and education.

Gender differences in involvement were found for the other leisure activities. Men, overall, spent more time than women did in active leisure, such as golf, walking for pleasure, and exercising. Men also spent more time traveling to and from leisure activities than women did. More time was devoted to TV viewing and to other forms of passive leisure, such as listening to music, reading, relaxing, by men than by women. The only leisure activity women devoted more time to than men, overall, is creative leisure, such as knitting, hobbies, and artistic production. In general, men devoted about 50 minutes more time to the leisure activities considered here than women in this age group did.

TABLE 6.2 Time Spent in Leisure Activities by Men and Women, 55 and Older, in 1975: Daily Average Hours and Minutes

	Daily Averages: Overall		Percentage of Participants During Four Days		Daily Averages for Participants	
	Men (106)	Women (154)	Men (106)	Women (154)	Men	Women
Active leisure	:27	:08***	49%	27%***	:55	:29
Passive leisure	1:36	1:18*	96%	96%	1:40	1:22
TV	2:55	2:18***	97%	96%	3:00	2:24
Social leisure	1:14	1:22	87%	92%	1:25	1:28
Religious practice	:14	:19	47%	55%	:30	:35
Voluntary organizations	:09	:12	25%	32%	:36	:37
Creative leisure	:08	:28***	20%	47%***	:38	:59
Entertainment	:04	:04	13%	8%	:32	:52
Education	:06	:03	18%	14%	:35	:22
Travel for leisure	:26	:20*	82%	84%	:32	:23
Total leisure	7:19	6:31				

*p ≤ .05; **p ≤ .01; ***p ≤ .001

For most leisure activities, the percentages of men and of women who participate are quite similar. Almost all men and women participated in some passive leisure, TV viewing, social leisure, and travel for leisure, during the days observed. The percentages of participants for other activities were lower than this but similar for men and women. About half of men and women engaged in religious practices such as attending services or Bible study. One-quarter of men and one-third of women participated in voluntary organizations during the four days. About one in five to one in six people over 55 participated in educational activities such as attending courses or working on homework for classes. About one in ten participated in entertainment out of the household, such as going to a movie, museum, or fair.

Significant differences between men and women did emerge in the percentage of participants in active leisure and creative leisure. About half of the men participated in some form of active leisure while only one out of four women engaged in any active leisure during the four days observed. One half of women, on the other hand, participated in creative leisure while only one in five men did so.

Can we learn anything new about the lifestyles of older men and women by examining the amount of time each *participant* devotes to leisure activities? Those men who engage in active leisure spend about an hour a day (or four hours in four days), which is twice as much as the average for women who engage in this leisure activity. That is, the overall average is higher for men than for women because more men participate in active leisure and those who do participate spend more time at active leisure than women who participate. For entertainment, fewer women participate, but those who do participate spend more time at the activity than men do (one hour versus one half hour).

(2) Gender and age patterns. Are there life-style differences for the young-old, the old, and the old-old in terms of leisure participation? For men, the total amount of leisure peaks in the 65-74 age range at just over eight hours each day. This is only about two hours more than the daily average for men and women aged 18 to 88 in the national sample. Among women, leisure is higher for older age groups, reaching a daily average of seven and a half hours for women 75 and over. How does the allocation of this leisure time differ for the three age groups considered?

Men 75 and older had lower levels of social leisure and active leisure than young-old men, while passive leisure was higher among the old-old. TV viewing peaked in the 65- to 74-year-old group at just over three hours a day. These four activities constituted stable or increasing

TABLE 6.3   Gender and Age Patterns in Time Spent in Leisure Activities: Daily Average Hours and Minutes

	Men			Women		
	55-64 (51)	65-74 (44)	75 and Older (11)	55-64 (70)	65-74 (59)	75 and Older (25)
Active leisure	:32	:26	:09	:08	:08	:06
Passive leisure	1:13	2:06	1:26	1:02	1:24	1:52
TV	2:34	3:08	3:40	2:10	2:24	2:28
Social leisure	1:13	1:18	:59	1:23	1:20	1:22
Religious practice	:14	:14	:18	:16	:20	:30
Voluntary organizations	:08	:10	:09	:12	:14	:04
Creative leisure	:04	:06	:29	:24	:28	:38
Entertainment	:03	:06	:01	:03	:04	:07
Education	:07	:07	:01	:03	:02	:05
Travel for leisure	:26	:26	:26	:17	:25	:13
Total leisure	6:34	8:05	7:35	5:49	6:49	7:23

portions of older women's daily time. Active leisure was similar across age groups for women, but dropped sharply for men at age 75. Social leisure was similar across age groups, but men 75 and older had the lowest levels of these activities. Passive leisure was higher in the oldest group of women as was TV viewing. Women did not watch as much TV as their male counterparts.

Other daily activities varied across the age groups examined. Men 75 and older spent slightly more time in religious practice, while women in that age group spent twice as much time as their younger counterparts in religious activity. Men of each age group had similar (and low) levels of voluntary association participation; women over 75 had much lower levels of participation in voluntary organization activity than younger women. Both men and women in the oldest age group had higher levels of creative leisure than their younger counterparts. Women remained more active in this type of leisure. The other activities were fairly constant across age groups.

(3) Gender and marital status patterns. Some of the age differences between men and women may be due to marital status differences. Most men are married; more women are widowed. In the comparisons of married men with widowed men and married women with widowed women, some insight into the effects of absence of a spouse on the lifestyles of older men and women can be gained. Divorced and never-married women and men were omitted from this analysis, because very few in the sample fell into these categories.

Marital status differences emerge for different activities for men and women. Widowed men spent much more time in active leisure, passive leisure, TV viewing, and a little more time in creative leisure and travel for leisure activities than older married men did. Widowed women spent more time in social leisure, religious practice, voluntary organizations, and a little more in passive leisure when compared to their married counterparts. For both men and women, the amount of time devoted to the leisure activities considered here were higher for women and especially for men who had lost their spouses. In terms of leisure life-style and particular activities engaged in, the widowed status had quite different effects on men than on women.

Obligatory Activities

(1) Overall gender patterns. The total amount of time devoted to the obligatory activities considered here was somewhat greater for women than for men overall. Women 55 and older spend less time in paid work than men do and these women spend considerably more time in housework than men do. Taken together, the two types of work absorb almost equal amounts of time for men and women. Helping is another activity with a significant difference in involvement for men and women, with women devoting much more time to help and care for adults in and out of the household. Very little difference exists for personal care (about two hours) or for sleep (about nine hours).

One significant difference in the percentage of participants in obligatory activity is for work, because 44% of men and only 30% of women worked for pay in the four days mentioned. Almost all men participate in housework, so no difference in participation emerged. A great difference in the percentage of women helping adults emerged, with twice the proportion of women providing such help as men. Almost one in five men and one in six women participated in some child care during the four days observed.

Daily averages for participants reflect the greater absorption of men into paid employment. Actually, the figure of 3:37 averaged across four days probably reflects about seven hours devoted to work during two days, and little or no time devoted to work on Saturday and Sunday. Likewise, the figure of 2:30 for women reflects about five hours of work during two days. Of all the activities showing a weekly pattern of involvement, work time is most obvious. We can see, however, that devotion of time to work is greater for employed men than for employed women.

TABLE 6.4   Gender and Marital Status Patterns in Time Spent in Leisure
Activities: Daily Average Hours and Minutes

	Men		Women	
	Married (85)	Widowed (10)	Married (56)	Widowed (81)
Active leisure	:20	1:09	:06	:10
Passive leisure	1:30	2:04	1:13	1:25
TV	2:55	3:24	2:22	2:14
Social leisure	1:12	1:04	1:10	1:30
Religious practice	:16	:15	:17	:23
Voluntary organizations	:10	:12	:08	:15
Creative leisure	:05	:12	:28	:29
Entertainment	:05	:02	:06	:03
Education	:06	:06	:02	:04
Travel	:26	:36	:22	:19
Total	7:05	9:04	6:15	6:52

A second new observation based on the participants' daily average
time concerns helping. Not only are women more likely to be helpers of
other adults, they are also likely to devote more time to helping than
those men who are helpers. Women who help others spend almost three
times as much time in this activity as men who help others.

Finally, although a minority of both older men and older women
provide child care, among those who do provide care, women devote
more time to this activity than men do.

(2) Gender and age patterns. For both men and women, the young-
old are the age group most involved in work. The very low averages for
those 65 and older reflect the institutionalization of retirement in
American society. The level of involvement is similar for men and
women beyond 65. Housework involvement is similar for men of all
three age groups, and is only slightly lower for the women over 65 than
for the younger women. Helping others is an activity that is pursued by
women until the age of 75 and older, but even among those over 75,
women devote more time to helping than men of any age group do.
Child care is rare among women over 65 and nonexistent for men over
75 in this study.

The amount of time devoted to personal care is similar for all age
groups and for men and women. Sleep, which includes naps during the
day, is more time absorbing for older men and women than for younger
men and women.

TABLE 6.5 Time Spent in Obligatory Activities by Men and Women 55 and Older in 1975: Daily Average Hours and Minutes

	Daily Averages: Overall		Percentage of Participants During Four Days		Daily Averages for Participants	
	Men (106)	Women (154)	Men (106)	Women (154)	Men	Women
Paid work	1:36	:46***	44%	30%*	:37	2:30
Housework	1:49	3:12***	98%	100%	1:51	3:09
Helping	:02	:12***	18%	37%***	:12	:33
Child care	:03	:05	18%	16%	:18	:32
Personal care	2:16	2:10	100%	100%	2:16	2:10
Sleep	9:04	9:06	100%	100%	9:04	9:06
Total leisure	14:13	14:55				

*p ≤ .05; **p ≤ .01; ***p ≤ .001

TABLE 6.6   Gender and Age Patterns in Time Spent in Obligatory
Activities: Daily Average Hours and Minutes

	Men			Women		
	55-64 (51)	65-74 (44)	75 and Older (11)	55-64 (70)	65-74 (59)	75 and Older (25)
Paid work	2:54	:28	:05	1:17	:25	:04
Housework	1:41	1:58	1:47	3:20	3:03	3:05
Helping	:03	:01	:02	:12	:16	:06
Child care	:03	:04	:00	:10	:02	:02
Personal care	2:18	2:12	2:20	2:05	2:21	2:00
Sleep	8:33	9:21	10:16	8:58	9:06	9:26
Total	15:32	14:05	14:30	16:02	15:13	14:43

Considering all these obligatory activities together, about one hour
more is devoted to obligatory activities for the younger age group than
for the older age groups. Differences in sleep and in paid work are most
important.

(3) Gender and marital status patterns. Marriage is linked to work for
pay for both men and women, with married men especially involved in
this type of work. On the other hand, widowed men spend more time on
household tasks while widowed women reduce the time spent on
housework. Helping shows no difference across marital status, nor does
personal care or sleep. Overall, married men and women spend about
one hour more time in the obligatory activities examined here than their
widowed counterparts do.

Social Interaction

(1) Overall gender patterns. Many differences exist in the social lives
of older men and women. First, women spend more time in solitude.
This is, as will be seen, linked to marital status differences between men
and women. Men spent two and a half hours more than women in
marital interaction, more time with their children who share the same
household, and more time with their work colleagues than women.
Women spent more time with friends and relatives and spent more time
with neighbors than men did.

Men and women are fairly similar in the time spent with other
household adults, organization members, service providers, and
strangers.

All the men and women in this study spent some waking time in
solitude. Most men (82%) spent considerable amounts of time with their

TABLE 6.7 Gender and Marital Status Patterns in Time Spent in Obligatory Activities: Daily Average Hours and Minutes

	Men		Women	
	Married (85)	Widowed (10)	Married (56)	Widowed (81)
Paid work	1:43	:29	:47	:30
Housework	1:47	2:08	3:40	2:58
Helping	:02	:00	:13	:13
Child care	:04	:02	:04	:08
Personal care	2:18	2:20	2:12	2:09
Sleep	9:01	8:51	8:57	9:08
Total	14:55	13:50	15:53	15:06

spouses while less than half of the women had a marital partner with whom to spend time. Nearly all the respondents spent time with friends and relatives. Significantly more women than men interacted with friends and relatives during the four days observed.

About half of the men and over half of the women spent some time with strangers, acquaintances, in large crowds, or with others during the four days. Men were more likely to spend time with colleagues than women were. Only one-sixth to one-third of the respondents spent any time with service providers, neighbors, other household adults, children in the household, and organizational members. Men and women were equally involved (or noninvolved) with these other social activities.

Men who are participants in a certain type of interaction often have different levels of interaction than women do. In this sample, men who have some interaction with a spouse spent less time with their wives than the women who have some interaction with their husbands. The men also had less interaction with friends and relatives, based on the daily averages for participants, than women did. They interacted less with organization members and service providers. Those men who did interact with children in the household and colleagues did so for longer periods than their female counterparts.

(2) Gender and age patterns. Many hours of each day are filled with marital companionship for each age group of men. For each age group of men, solitude is a significant experience but less time is devoted to solitude than to marital companionship. For each age group of women, more time is spent in solitude than in marital companionship. The oldest group of women spends little time in marital companionship. By the age of 75 and beyond, about eight and a half hours of waking time are spent in

TABLE 6.8 Time Spent in Social Interaction by Men and Women 55 and Older in 1975: Daily Average Hours and Minutes

	Daily Averages: Overall		Percentage of Participants During Four Days		Daily Averages for Participants	
	Men (106)	Women (154)	Men (106)	Women (154)	Men	Women
Spouse	5:30	2:56***	82%	40%***	6:43	7:16
Child	:42	:20*	25%	18%	2:44	1:52
Other household adult	:34	:50	22%	21%	2:35	3:59
Friends and relatives	1:59	2:50**	83%	93%**	2:23	3:03
Colleagues	1:10	:34**	44%	29%**	2:39	1:57
Organization members	:06	:08	15%	15%	:44	:53
Neighbors	:05	:10*	24%	35%*	:22	:28
Service providers	:04	:07	23%	32%	:16	:23
Stranger or acquaintances	:24	:29	50%	60%	:48	:49
Solitude	4:53	6:24***	100%	100%	4:53	6:24

*p ≤ .05; **p ≤ .01; ***p ≤ .001

TABLE 6.9   Gender and Age Patterns in Time Spent in Social Interaction: Daily Average Hours and Minutes

	Men			Women		
	55-64 (51)	65-74 (44)	75 and Older (11)	55-64 (70)	65-74 (59)	75 and Older (25)
Spouse	5:01	6:05	5:28	3:35	2:58	1:00
Child	:54	:36	:06	:36	:04	:16
Other household adult	:25	:31	1:23	:42	:60	:48
Friends and relatives	2:07	2:03	1:06	2:45	3:16	2:04
Colleagues	2:11	:17	:02	:58	:18	:06
Organization members	:04	:08	:14	:08	:10	:06
Neighbors	:06	:04	:06	:11	:09	:10
Service providers	:03	:04	:07	:05	:09	:10
Strangers or acquaintances	:26	:26	:10	:32	:31	:17
Solitude	4:51	5:01	4:27	5:53	6:11	8:24

solitude for women. The corresponding figure is about half that for men 75 and older.

For all age groups, friends and relatives remain important contacts. For both men and women, however, the oldest age group experiences about an hour less each day in interaction with friends and relatives. Involvement with children in the household is lower for each age group of men, and is lower for women 65 and older than for younger women.

Other household adults become more important in the daily lives of older men, while older women show no higher levels for this type of interaction. Both men and women have lower levels of involvement with colleagues after age 65 and both have lower involvement with strangers and acquaintances after age 75. The extent of involvement with neighbors, organization members, and service providers is fairly low and constant for men and women across the age groups.

(3) Gender and marital status. Widowed women spent four more hours than married women in solitude. Widowed men spend five and a half more hours in solitude than their married counterparts. Married men and married women spent equal amounts of time in solitude. Both men and women who were widowed spent more time with friends and relatives than men and women who were married. Marital status, however, was related to decreased interaction with children in the household and to increased interaction with others in the household for men only.

Married men and women spent more time with colleagues than widowed men and women did. A slightly greater amount of time was

TABLE 6.10 Gender and Marital Status Patterns in Time Spent in Interaction: Daily Average Hours and Minutes

	Men		Women	
	Married (85)	Widowed (10)	Married (56)	Widowed (81)
Spouse or fiancé	6:52	:00	7:41	:09
Child	:47	:32	:21	:24
Other household adult	:15	1:24	:42	:48
Friends and relatives	1:48	3:20	2:25	3:17
Colleagues	1:14	:08	:32	:26
Organization members	:07	:08	:06	:10
Neighbors	:06	:02	:08	:12
Service provider	:03	:09	:06	:08
Stranger or acquaintances	:25	:22	:34	:26
Solitude	4:00	9:30	3:58	7:45

spent with service providers for widowed people, and widowed women were slightly less involved with strangers and acquaintances. Other forms of interaction were similar across marital status for men and for women.

Themes and Variations in Daily Life

Gender

Demographic differences between older men and women and the lifelong patterns of preferences and opportunities that differentiate the lifestyles of men and women lead us to a gendered analysis of daily life in later life. Given the several bases for expecting gender patterns in daily life, it is surprising to find so many similarities. Men and women over the age of 55 have similar levels of involvement with social leisure, religious activities, entertainment, and educational activities. Older men and women are similar in the amounts of sleep, personal care, and child care in which they participate. They are quite similar in the less time-absorbing social relations: strangers and acquaintances, service providers, organization members, other household adults.

How, then, does gender pattern the daily lives of older Americans? In general, men in later life experience more leisure. The types of leisure in which men and women spend time are different.

When obligatory activities are considered, life-course patterns of men's greater involvement in the labor force and women's greater involvement in unpaid domestic labor are replicated. When domestic labor and paid labor are combined, however, these older men and women spent equal amounts of time in labor. There is another dimension of work that involves caring for others. Child care and helping adults in or out of the household are often considered women's work. This service to others is predominantly, but not exclusively, women's work among older Americans. Considering the paid labor, housework, caring for adults, and child care, it is worth noting that older Americans spent about four hours a day in these productive activities.

Social life is somewhat different for men and women. Women spent more time with neighbors, friends, and relatives while they also spent more time in solitude. Men devoted more time to martial companionship, colleagues, and offspring in the household. Overall, older men have more social contact time during daily life, due primarily to their marital interaction.

Marital Status

Many advantages accrue to married people. Health, wealth, and social life are generally more abundant for the married. Some of the advantages may be reflected in daily life, and whatever the benefits of marriage in daily life, men would be the more likely beneficiaries. The married spend more time at work, but this is most likely a function of age. The married spend less time in leisure, more time on obligatory activities, and less time with most types of social partners. The central advantage of marriage, it would seem, is in interacting with a comfortable intimate and not necessarily in a more socially desirable pattern of activities.

Widowed men and women engage in more leisure activities. Men who have lost a spouse, however, increase involvement in different leisure activities more than women do. With regard to obligatory activities, widowed men increase their household work, while women decrease the time spent on household tasks. Social involvements shift for the widowed as well. Women, and especially men, spent more time in solitude. Widowed men and women substitute friends and relatives for the absent spouse to some extent (see Altergott, 1985).

Age Differences Among Older People

Age status varies for those over 55 as well. Whether the terms *young-old, old,* and *old-old* are accepted or not, the variety of life experiences captured in the 33-year age range here can reasonably be divided into separate age grades. Though the proportion of employed adults begins to decrease before the age of 65, 65 might still be treated as a turning point because of the conventional acceptance of retirement at that age and because of the actual concentration of people retiring at that time. Likewise, people experience decrements of health and functioning before the age of 75, but it is generally accepted that risk of disability, decrements in physical functioning, and risk of demise increase around the age of 75. These are, then, times when daily life may be expected to change as well.

When differences by age status within the older population are examined, we find several similarities: social leisure remains about the same for each age group; personal care seems constant; interaction with neighbors, organization members, and service providers remains about the same. Given the increase with age in functional disabilities, the mobility limits that might be faced, and the basic needs that emerge in later life, formal sources of assistance might be somewhat more visible in the daily lives of older people. Considering all possible forms of service providers, those over 75 have no real increase in the amount of time spent with a service provider.

Some differences do occur among the three age categories considered here. Obligatory activities show a shift for the age group 65-74. A decline in work and child care and an increase in sleep seem to occur. Other subtle differences exist for the oldest group. Those over 75 have more religious and creative moments during their daily lives. They also participate in more passive leisure. Women relinquish their voluntary organization involvement in their late seventies and eighties, however. It is also only the women over 75 who show lower levels of helping other adults.

No age category of men experiences as high an average of solitude as women of even the youngest age group. But the oldest women in this study experience almost twice as much solitary time as any age group of men and over two hours more than the young-old women. Both men and women experience lower levels of interaction with friends and relatives in the oldest age category.

In summary, some gender-differentiated choices of leisure activity and men's greater amount of leisure are coupled with similarity in about half of the leisure activities across men and women, younger and older, married and widowed. Paid work and unpaid household labor are, in combination, similar for men and women, but women help other adults much more intensely than men. Obligatory activities shift with age and shift slightly for people in different marital statuses. Social interactions show quite distinct patterns for men and women, in large part due to marital status differences among men and women in later life.

There are many similarities between older men and women and all adults in American society, but older people spend more time in passive activities, TV, religious activities, and sleep, and less time in entertainment, education, paid work, and child care. Older people spend more time with their spouses, if they are married, and less time with colleagues than their younger counterparts. Most other activities and interactions were quite similar for the late-life respondents and the respondents of all ages.

Understanding Daily Life in Later Life

Beyond the pattern of behavior lies individual preferences, capacities, and choices. Beyond the readily observed daily life, there exists a set of social forces that shape and limit individual behavior. In the next steps of inquiry, both intraindividual and supraindividual conditions should be incorporated in order to improve our understanding of daily life.

Individual Propensities

Why do people do what they do? Some part of the explanation lies within. Enjoyment, choice, and capacities are part of the explanation of human behavior (Chapin, 1974). Some of the preferences and capacities are socialized and become routinized by later life. Examples in American society may include women's preference for creative leisure and men's preference for active leisure. Some *incapacities and aversions*, though those terms may be too strong, are socialized as well. Men show some evidence of an incapacity to socialize with others independent of their wives. The fact that women travel less for leisure, and indeed participate less in leisure outside the home, may be explained by complementary dependence on male companionship in order to enter the public realm. The fact that oldest women in this study had given up activities such as helping and voluntary organizations may be due to other incapacities: physical limitations, inability to negotiate a hostile or difficult environment, inability to get to the necessary location.

Individual choice might be expected to be dominant in the retirement years and, indeed, certain pleasurable activities were more likely after age 65. The number of hours older people spend in obligatory activities, however, remains quite high. Prior commitments to people and to roles limit the freedom to choose activities and interactions even among retired people. Capacities, interests, and preferences may have a great deal to do with the increased amount of religious activity, passive leisure, and TV viewing among those over 75. Or viable alternative activities and interactions may simply be unavailable to older people. The amount of choice, voluntarism, and control in the domain of daily life is not clear yet.

Some have begun to investigate the subjective aspects of daily life (Altergott and Eustis, 1981; Lawton, 1982). This direction of linking choice, preference, and, perhaps in the future, capacity and perceived opportunity to the analysis of behavior is necessary.

Opportunity and Constraints

Some part of the age pattern can be attributed to changed preferences, opportunities, and capacities. But, to a considerable extent, one's capacities and preferences are shaped by the social environment. In addition to social status, one must consider whether the daily lives of older Americans are affected by the role structure, the social environment, the historically unique demographic situation modern nations face. Finally, we could ask whether daily life is defined by policies concerning the resources and opportunities of older Americans.

Chapin's model of human behavior included much more than an analysis of individual preferences (Chapin, 1974). He also includes the structural characteristics such as level of tolerance, quality, and variety of activity available; interaction sites open to individuals with certain characteristics; and the structured availability of resources necessary to engage in certain activities and interactions. With regard to the analysis presented above, it is possible that women face barriers in attempts to participate in active leisure, or that older people lack opportunities to work because of systematic discrimination in the labor force, or that the need and desire to interact with formal service providers exists but the care system in the United States is not adequate to meet the needs of the population (see Little, 1982).

Cowgill's (1986) model of modernization and aging points to the structural restrictions older people face. His work does not imply modern societies necessarily place older people at a disadvantage; he suggests that many changes accompanying modernization have had negative consequences. Examples may be the institutionalization of retirement and the accompanying limit on economic productivity and resources. Older Americans may gain a second-class status, with all the limitations on activity and interaction low status entails. Americans value work so much, and most older people don't work. Furthermore, the particular types of productivity older people do engage in (domestic work and caring) are not highly visible or valued in American society, again reducing the social value of elders.

Riley's (1976) work on age stratification introduces several other structural features that help us understand the social behavior of the older Americans. First, each person is limited by the role structure in society that is differentiated by age (as well as by gender, race, and other criteria). Entries and exits from roles for the individual are constrained by the socially defined role structure. If retirement is normatively prescribed and structurally supported, this makes it difficult for the individual to resist the transition to retirement at the defined age. Behavior paths guide us through the life course; there may always be the option of nonconformity, innovation, and change.

This is linked to another aspect of Riley's model: social change. The constant possibilities of change and the actual transformations of role structures that have been observed in societies leave the future open. In the domain of old age, a great deal of social creation might be going on. If older men choose creative leisure, if women in later life take on new voluntary organizational roles, aren't they producing social change? Because ours is the first century that allowed men and women to feel confident they would reach old age, and perhaps spend several decades beyond the age of 65, isn't social innovation and change necessary? It is yet to be seen whether the aged will be the avant garde for the twenty-first century, showing us all ways to live our full life span, or if the aged will be constrained by the models and barriers based on ageism. But social changes will influence the older Americans lifestyles, and their lifestyles will produce social changes.

The third aspect of Riley's model that draws our attention is cohort flow. The older people observed here had certain cohort characteristics.

Those 55-64 in 1975 were born in the 1910-1920 period; the middle group was born in the 1900-1910 period; and the oldest group was born in the nineteenth century. Each cohort lived through a set of historical events and milieus that shaped them—and influenced the way they were aging. Some of the age differences may be due to cohort variations in educational level, gender role ideologies, or perhaps cohort size. The major requirement for any study of daily life in later life is to acknowledge the possibility of historical or cohort specificity in the findings. The long-term goal of understanding later life will require replication of this study across different historical periods, ages, and cohorts.

Chapin, Cowgill, and Riley are just three of many social scientists who force us to take into account national context in the analysis of social life. The factors they describe—role structure, demographic characteristics of context, opportunity structures, value systems, institutions—can be considered national in scope. None of these authors, however, took the implicit or explicit policies that define daily life into account. To imagine how policies in other nations, if adopted in the United States, would affect aging, we need to study the structure, culture, policies, and daily life experiences of older people in a variety of national contexts. To understand fully the social forces affecting patterns of activity and interaction in daily life, comparative analysis is necessary.

This chapter has provided, first of all, a brief description of one national context. Within this nation, older people were observed and careful description and analysis of their daily lives were presented. The primary analysis consisted of examining social statuses, including gender, marital status, and age, to determine the pattern of similarities and differences within the national context. Future work on daily life in later life needs to delve into the subjective experiences accompanying activities and interactions as well as incorporating social forces.

REFERENCES

Altergott, K. 1985. "Marriage, Gender, Social Relations in Late Life." Pp. 51-70 in *Social Bonds in Later Life*, edited by W. Peterson and J. Quadagno. Beverly Hills, CA: Sage.

———. and N. Eustis. 1981. "Evaluation of Everyday Life." Paper presented to the Gerontological Society Meeting.

Amann, A. 1980. *Open Care for the Elderly in Seven European Countries*. Oxford: Pergamon.

American Association of Retired Persons (AARP). 1984. *A Profile of Older Americans.* Washington, DC: Author.

Bader, J. 1986. "Socioeconomic Aspects of Aging." Pp. 51-61 in *Vision and Aging*, edited by A. Rosenbloom and M. Morgan. New York: Professional Press Books.

Barberis, M. 1981. "America's Elderly: Policy Implications." Policy Supplement to *Population Bulletin* 35(4).

Chapin, F. Stuart, Jr. 1974. *Human Activity Patterns in the City*. New York: John Wiley.

Cowgill, D. 1986. *Aging Around the World*. Belmont, CA: Wadsworth.

———. and N. Baulch. 1962. "Use of Leisure Time by Older People." *Gerontologist* 2(1):47-50.

Fischer, D. 1977. *Growing Old in America*. New York: Oxford University Press.

Gordon, C. and C. Gaitz. 1976. "Leisure and Lives: Personal Expressivity Across the Life Span." Pp. 310-41 in *Handbook of Aging and the Social Sciences*, edited by R. Binstock and E. Shanas. New York: Van Nostrand Reinhold.

Havighurst, R. 1957. "The Leisure Activities of the Middle-Aged." *American Journal of Sociology* 63:152-62.

Juster, F. T. 1985. *Time, Goods and Well-Being*. Ann Arbor, MI: Institute for Social Research.

———., P. Courant, G. Duncan, J. Robinson, and F. Stafford. 1976. *Time Use in Economic and Social Accounts*. Ann Arbor, MI: Survey Research Center.

Larson, R., J. Zuzanek, and R. Mannell. 1985. "Being Alone Versus Being with People: Disengagement in the Daily Experience of Older Adults." *Journal of Gerontology* 40(3):375-81.

Lawton, M. P. 1978. "Leisure Activities for the Aged." *Annals, AAPSS* 438(July):71-80.

———. 1982. "Environment and Other Determinants of Well-Being in Older People." Presentation to the Gerontological Society of America.

Levin, L. and W. Levin. 1980. *Ageism: Prejudice and Discrimination against the Elderly*. Belmont, CA: Wadsworth.

Little, V. C. 1982. *Open Care for the Aging*. New York: Springer.

Michelon, L. C. 1954. "The New Leisure Class." *American Journal of Sociology* 59(4):371-78.

Moss, M. and M. P. Lawton. 1982. "Time-Budgets of Older People: A Window on Four Lifestyles." *Journal of Gerontology* 32:115-23.

Palmore, E. 1981. *Social Patterns in Normal Aging: Findings from the Duke Longitudinal Study*. Durham, NC: Duke University Press.

Riley, M. W. 1976. "Age Strata in Social Systems." Pp. 189-217 in *Handbook of Aging and the Social Sciences*, edited by R. Binstock and E. Shanas. New York: Van Nostrand Reinhold.

Robinson, J. 1988. "Time-Diary Evidence About the Social Psychology of Everyday Life." Pp. 134-48 in *The Social Psychology of Time: New Perspectives*, edited by J. McGrath. Newbury Park, CA: Sage.

Rose, A. 1965. "The Subculture of the Aging: A Framework for Research in Social Gerontology." Pp. 3-16 in *Older People and Their Social World*, edited by A. Rose and W. Peterson. Philadelphia: F. A. Davis.

Schorr, A. 1980. *"Thy Father and Thy Mother": A Second Look at Filial Responsibility and Family Policy*. Social Security Publication No. 13-11953. Washington, DC: Department of Health and Human Services.

Szalai, A. 1972. *The Use of Time*. The Hague, Netherlands: Mouton.

Townsend, P. 1968. "Problems in Cross-National Study of Old People in the Family." In *Methodological Problems in Cross-National Studies in Aging*, edited by E. Shanas and T. Madge. Basel and New York.

U.S. Bureau of the Census. 1977. "Projections of the Population of the United States: 1977 to 2050." *Current Population Reports* (Series P-25, No. 704). Washington, DC: Government Printing Office.

———. 1980. *Current Population Reports* (Series P-25, No. 704). Washington, DC: Government Printing Office.

———. 1981. "Marital Status and Living Arrangements: March 1981." *Current Population Reports* (Series P-20, No. 372). Washington, DC: Government Printing Office.

———. 1986. "Money Income and Poverty Status of Families and Persons in the United States: 1985." *Current Population Reports* (Series P-60, No. 154). Washington, DC: Government Printing Office.

U.S. Senate Select Committee on Aging. 1982a. *Developments in Aging*. Vol. 1. Washington, DC: Government Printing Office.

———. 1982b. *Every Ninth American*. Washington, DC: Government Printing Office.

Villers Foundation. 1987. *On the Other Side of Easy Street*. Washington, DC: Author.

7

Life Course and the Daily Lives of Older Adults in Canada

JIRI ZUZANEK
SHEILA J. BOX

Mr. Pim is 69 years old. He lives with his wife in a single-family house. Before he retired at the age of 65, Mr. Pim worked as a supervisor for a large insurance company in Kitchener-Waterloo, Canada. He and his wife have three children, whom they see often. Mr. Pim continues to work part-time for the company from which he retired. He and his wife live comfortably on a company pension and his additional earnings. During the year preceding the survey, Mr. Pim took two vacation trips, one to Atlantic City, another to Trout Creek. He belongs to a senior citizens' club, considers himself to be in good health, and has a pet. His favorite leisure pursuits are watching TV, playing cards, golfing, and curling. He would like to travel more, engage more in photography, and learn gourmet cooking. Keeping in touch with family, friends, the neighborhood, and engaging in hobbies are extremely important for Mr. Pim. Keeping in touch with his former workmates is, on the other hand, only moderately important. Mr. Pim reported an almost perfect score (19 out of 20) on a composite scale of life satisfaction. When asked directly about his physical well-being, however, he expressed some concern.

Thursday, December 3, 1981, Mr. Pim woke at 7:30 a.m. He spent 30 minutes in personal care and at 8:00 had his breakfast. At 8:30, he drove

AUTHORS' NOTE: The authors would like to express their thanks to a number of colleagues who at different times contributed to the work on this chapter, particularly to S. James, R. Mannell, D. Lott, B. McPherson and K. Altergott.

to the club, where he spent close to 2.5 hours curling. At 11:30, he returned home, and between 12:00 and 1:00 p.m., had his lunch. After lunch, for 2.5 hours, Mr. Pim worked on an audit for his former employer. At 3:30, he took his car for repair, and around 4:30, stopped at his bank. From 5:00 until 6:00, he watched TV, from 6:00 to 7:00, he had his dinner. After dinner, he spent approximately an hour reading a newspaper, and from there on watched TV. He finished his day by watching the late edition of TV news, and at 11:30 retired for sleep.

Introduction

Politicians, social workers, and researchers in industrialized countries have been concerned for some time with the "graying" of their populations. Canada is no exception to these concerns. In 1931, the number of Canadians aged 65 and over was estimated at 576,000 or 5.6% of the total population. In 1951, this number was 1,086,000 or 7.8% of the total population. In 1981, there were 2,361,000 older Canadians aged 65 or 9.7% of the population. By 2001, their number is expected to reach 3.4 million, and by the year 2031, for every three persons of working age, there will be one person aged 65 or older. The median age of the population in the largest Canadian province, Ontario, is expected to increase from around 30 in the early 1980s to 39 by the year 2006 (Special Senate Committee on Retirement Policies, 1979; Statistics Canada, 1984).

These demographic trends raise several questions. What are the behavioral and psychological correlates of the process of aging? How well are the growing numbers of older adults coping with the challenges of a new life situation? How is the "graying" of our societies going to affect demand for various social, financial, consumer, and recreational resources and services?

To answer some of these questions, we need, first of all, to understand clearly the behavioral aspects of aging. Yet, while researchers assemble large amounts of partial information, attempts to examine and summarize these findings in a systematic fashion are few (see McPherson, 1984). In fact, it has been suggested by various authors that the literature on aging is still full of unproven assumptions and outright myths.

Moss (1979), in a paper examining the uses of time by the elderly in the United States, pointed to several myths associated with the daily lives of the aged. According to one of these myths, "Older people have nothing but leisure to fill their days" (Moss, 1979, p. 5). Yet in the study reported by Moss, 31.5% of the older adults' days were spent in obligatory activities.

According to another myth, all older people "are pretty much the same—often sickly, dependent, lonely and inactive" (Moss, 1979, p. 6). Yet empirical evidence collected by Moss points to considerable subgroup variance in the lives of older adults.

Another myth, according to Moss, is that old people do not spend as much time sleeping as younger people. Data collected by Moss, however, suggest that the elderly spend approximately the same amount of time sleeping as the rest of the population.

One can add a few more myths to this list. In the article "Leisure and the Elderly," Parker (1973, p. 53) makes the following statement: "Comparing the life of the retired man with the middle-aged one, we are made aware of how much of his former activity is lost, and how little extra seems to be put in its place." Yet time-budget research suggests that older people effectively fill their time with, perhaps more "passive" but subjectively satisfying, leisure activities.

According to yet another myth (see Dobbin, 1980), older people are at a loss as to how to handle their growing amounts of free time. Yet when one of the authors began administering a time-budget survey among older adults in the Kitchener-Waterloo area, a major problem he encountered was setting up time for the initial interview. Potential respondents appeared rather busy, engaged in and committed to numerous social and free time activities.

Data Sources, Problem Statement

The following chapter was born out of a need to examine critically empirical evidence about the behavioral effects of the aging process. In the past, studies that examined the daily lives of the elderly from a theoretical perspective often relied on generalized measures of activity and rarely examined the full spectrum of leisure participation or daily uses of time. General time-budget and leisure participation studies, on the other hand, while providing a much more detailed account of the daily lives and leisure participation of the surveyed population, usually lacked theoretical interest in the problems of old age.

The following analysis makes an attempt to utilize relatively detailed behavioral data collected as a part of time-budget and leisure participation surveys to examine systematically the changing patterns of daily and leisure lives of the older adults as a function of life cycle, progression of age, and gender. It also examines the relationship between respondents' uses of time and leisure participation, on the one hand, and their subjective well-being, on the other.

Data from four surveys are used to examine the uses of time and patterns of leisure participation among older Canadians (65+). These studies are the 1975 Survey of Participation in Selected Leisure Activities, conducted by Statistics Canada (N = 36,408); the 1981 Time Use Pilot Study, conducted by Statistics Canada (N = 2686; 312 aged 65+); the Survey of the Uses of Time Among Older Adults conducted in 1981-1982 in the Kitchener-Waterloo area (N = 117), and the Study of Leisure and Cultural Participation of Urban Canadians, conducted in 1984 in the Kitchener-Waterloo-Brantford area (N = 303). The two surveys in the Kitchener-Waterloo area were administered by the Research Group on Leisure and Cultural Development of the University of Waterloo (principal investigator-J. Zuzanek).

The chapter will address four interrelated questions:

(1) How does the transition from preretirement to retirement affect the uses of time and leisure participation?
(2) To what extent are the uses of time and rates of leisure participation of older adults affected by the progression of age, or transition from what is sometimes called the "young-old" age to the "old-old" age?
(3) What are the gender differences and/or similarities in the uses of time and rates of leisure participation among older adults?
(4) How do uses of time and participation in leisure activities among older adults correlate with levels of perceived life satisfaction?

Review of Literature

The patterns of daily lives of older adults have traditionally been examined by researchers from four perspectives: (1) the "life-cycle" perspective, that is, as a function of retirement; (2) the progression of age perspective, focusing on differences in the daily lives of "young-old" versus "old-old" adults; (3) the "gender differences" or "gender bifurcation" perspective (see Komarovsky, 1940), examining male-female differences in the daily lives of older adults; (4) the "activity/subjective well-being" perspective, centering on the relationship between the levels of activity and subjectively perceived well-being.

**Changes in the Daily Lives of
Older Adults as a
Function of Life Cycle**

According to Neugarten and Peterson (1957), transition from one life-cycle stage to another is defined by the succession of family cycle, career line, health and physical vigor, and psychological attributes and responsibilities. Individuals, according to Neugarten and Hagestad (1976, p. 44), anticipate that certain events will occur at certain times, and internalize a social clock that tells them when and how to act. "Age norms act as prods and breaks upon behavior."

For Frenkel-Brunswik (1968), life cycle is a succession of life stages characterized by a varying number of behavioral dimensions. Kuhlen (1968) and Gordon and Gaitz (1979) define *life cycle* as a progression of changing motivational structures (expansion motives versus security motives) and psychological orientations (acceptance and stability versus integration and survival). Zuzanek (1979) interprets life cycle as a functional constellation of four major biological and sociological determinants: biological age, marital status, presence of children in the household, and career or employment status.

All of these authors view old age and retirement as a discontinuation of several important social roles (gainful employment, active parent), accompanied by a complex behavioral and attitudinal adjustment, and associated with changing levels of physical vigor, declining numbers of social engagements, and changing social-psychological orientations.

According to some authors (Cumming and Henry, 1961; Frenkel-Brunswik, 1968), adjustment to old age consists essentially of a voluntary acceptance and psychological rationalization of a gradual withdrawal from a variety of middle-age roles and social behaviors.

Another group of authors—Videbock and Knox (1965), Reichard, Livson, and Peterson (1968), Maddox (1968), and Palmore (1968)—view successful adjustment to retirement as an attempt to maintain activity patterns developed during middle age, resulting in behavioral continuity rather than disengagement.

A third group of authors—Cavan (1962), Dumazedier and Ripert (1983), and Shanas et al. (1968)—regard successful adjustment to retirement as a process of developing new (substitute) roles, including the role of a competent leisure consumer.

Finally, there are those authors—Havighurst, Neugarten, and Tobin (1968)—who argue that all of the above models of adjustment may be present in old age, but to a varying degree in different subpopulations, at different stages of retirement, among respondents with diverse "personality" characteristics. Moreover, according to Havighurst, Neugarten, and Tobin (1968, p. 172):

> There appear to be two sets of values operating *simultaneously*, if not within the same individual then within the group . . .: On the one hand, the desire to stay active in order to maintain a sense of self-worth; on the other hand, the desire to withdraw from social commitments and to pursue a more leisurely and more contemplative way of life. Neither the activity theory nor the disengagement theory of optimum aging takes sufficient account of this quality in value patterns [emphasis added].

Methodologically, studies examining changing patterns of daily life and leisure participation among elderly can be divided into two large groups: (1) time-budget studies examining the varying durations of time (hours, minutes per day) spent in different daily and leisure activities; (2) studies of the rates of participation in selected leisure activities, which use respondents' recall to establish patterns of participation in a variety of leisure pursuits over a longer period of time, usually a year or a month.

Chapin (1974), Robinson (1984, 1985), Hill (1985), Juster (1985), and Palmore et al. (1985) in the United States; Zuzanek and Stewart (1983), McPherson (1984), and Box (1984) in Canada; Huet et al. (1978) in France; and Knulst (1977) in the Netherlands used *time-budget* data to examine changes in the daily lives of older adults as a function of life cycle. In spite of the fact that data reported by these authors were collected at different times, in different geographical places, using dissimilar research instruments, they established several common trends in the elderly's use of time.

The amount of time spent in market work declines dramatically after retirement. The amount of time spent in household obligations and shopping increases for both men and women, but particularly for men. More time is spent after retirement in sleeping, personal care, eating at home, and free time activities.

Of free time activities, the following expand the most: watching TV, reading newspapers and magazines (in particular, among men), hobbies (particularly among women), social leisure, relaxation, rest, and religious activities. On the other hand, the total amount of time spent by older adults in active sport and attending sporting events and outings declines after retirement.

Changes in the *rates of leisure participation*, associated with retirement, have been examined by Havighurst, Neugarten, and Tobin (1968), Palmore (1968), Lewinsohn and McPhillamy (1974), Maddox and Douglass (1974), Peppers (1976), Gray (1979), and Gordon and Gaitz (1979) in the United States; Zuzanek (1978, 1979) in Canada; and the Research Division of the French Ministry of Culture (Service des Etudes et Recherches, 1982) in France, to mention but a few.

According to most authors, involvement in structured leisure activities declines with age. Gordon and Gaitz (1979, p. 326) state: "Our data show that the older respondent, the lower the general level of activity." Other authors, however, argue that "there is a clear tendency for the aged to persist with the same relative levels of activities and attitudes as they grow older" (Palmore, 1968, p. 262), and that the "rocking chair" stereotype of the elderly is not supported by empirical evidence (Peppers, 1976). Yet another group of authors—Zuzanek (1978), Gray (1979), and Gordon and Gaitz (1979)—suggest that the slope at which participation declines in various activities may differ from one activity to another.

In general, time-budget and leisure participation studies of the elderly suggest the following:

(1) The transition to retirement is characterized by a radical reallocation of time between major groups of daily activities, with free time, sleeping, and housework being the principal "beneficiaries" of the reduced involvement in paid work.

(2) Paradoxically, although older adults possess greater amounts of free time, their rates of participation in leisure activities, and the number of leisure activities they engaged in, decline after retirement.

(3) The slope of the decline in leisure participation varies for different groups of activities, and is affected by a number of social and psychological factors, including respondents' age and their previous "activity disposition."

(4) Leisure activities marked by a substantial decline of participation after retirement include sports, sport spectatorship, culture and the arts, outings, moviegoing, and outdoor recreation. Activities affected little or not affected at all by the process of aging include visiting friends; reading magazines, newspapers, and books; listening to the radio; watching TV; playing cards; hobbies; driving for pleasure; and physically less demanding forms of outdoor activities such as walking.

(5) The composition of leisure activities, typical of various subpopulations, does not radically change with age (Videbock and Knox, 1965). There appears to be a certain life-style persistency, resulting in the maintenance

by older adults of similar patterns of leisure participation over prolonged periods of time.

Uses of Time and Leisure Participation of the Elderly in Postretirement: The "Young-Old" Versus the "Old-Old"

Neugarten (1974), in her paper "Age Groups in American Society and the Young-Old," suggests that a new division between the "young-old" and the "old-old" has emerged in North America. The "young-old," according to Neugarten, have emerged because of

increasing longevity, but more particularly because of the drop in age of retirement. The young-old, drawn mainly from those aged 55 to 75, is a group who are relatively healthy and vigorous, relatively comfortable in economic terms, and relatively free from the traditional responsibilities of both work and parenthood. Better educated than earlier cohorts of the same age, politically active, and with large amounts of free time available, this age group seeks ways of self-fulfillment and community service [Neugarten, 1974, p. 46].

Other authors—Spieth (1965), Riegel et al. (1967), and Maddox and Douglass (1974)—also favor a distinction between the two groups of older adults, based on their progressing age. Havighurst et al. (1968) suggest, for example, that "disengagement" from many social activities occurs in the "old-old" age, while "continuity" is more typical of the "young-old" age.

Empirical evidence about the changing uses of time and leisure participation, as a function of advanced age, is scanty and not altogether conclusive.

According to the *time-budget* analyses of Gronmo (1982), McPherson (1984), Nakanishi (1981), and others, advanced age among older adults carries with it greater amounts of time spent in maintenance tasks, as well as greater amounts of free time spent in essentially passive leisure pursuits (mass media).

Studies of *leisure participation*—Havighurst and Albrecht (1953), Dobbin (1980), Ontario Recreational Survey (Tourism and Outdoor Recreation Planning Study, 1978), Pratiques Culturelles des Francais (Service des Etudes et Recherches, 1982)—all indicate that levels of participation in most leisure activities decline dramatically after the age of 75, and particularly after 80.

According to Havighurst and Albrecht (1953), the mean number of frequently engaged in leisure activities declines from 5.3 in the age group 70-74, to 4.5 in the age group 75-80, and 3.4 after the age of 80. The Ontario Recreation Survey (Tourism and Outdoor Recreation Planning Study, 1978), indicates that, after the age of 71, rates of participation in 12 selected leisure activities decline considerably for all activities, with the exception of recreational driving.

According to Maddox (1968, p. 563), however, analyses of *longitudinal* rather than cross-sectional data demonstrate that "development, change and growth continue through the late years of the life-span in spite of the decrement in social, psychological and physiological functioning which typically accompanies the aging process." These and other findings have led several authors to the conclusion that the "disengagement" thesis applies no more to the "old-old" age group than it applies to the retirement situation as a whole, and that participation in leisure activities *does not* undergo radical changes after the age of 70.

Dobbin (1980, p. 48) takes a more qualified approach to this issue. His analysis of U.K. data suggests that, while participation in outdoor activities declines after the age of 75, participation in mass media consumption, reading of newspapers and magazines, hobbies, and resting does not. The analysis of the French data (Roy, 1982) also reveals that, while participation in cultural and physically active leisure subsides with age, rates of participation in mass media activities, reading newspapers and magazines, working for voluntary organizations, and "ladies' hobbies" remain stable.

In sum, there is no simple answer to the question of whether the transition from the "young-old" to the "old-old" age is marked by accelerating decline of leisure involvement or by behavioral stability. The empirical evidence on participation in structured outdoor and physically demanding activities suggests that the differences between the "young-old" and the "old-old" are both real and pronounced. It is likely that the decline in some recreational activities, such as social contacts and outdoor recreation, however, is partially compensated by greater involvement in home-centered and media activities.

Gender-Related Differences in Daily Lives and Leisure Participation of Older Adults

Cotterell (1942), Linton (1942), and Parsons (1942), in their classical studies of age and gender, argued that age variations in human behavior should always be discussed in conjunction with gender, because the two operate in an interconnected way.

Two major themes concerning the effects of age and gender on daily lives of older adults are of consequence for our following analyses. These themes are

(1) the nature and extent of male-female differences in daily behavior and leisure participation of the elderly, and
(2) possible "convergence" or "divergence" of daily behavior and leisure participation of men and women as a function of aging.

U.S., French, and Canadian *time-use* studies (Juster, 1985; Roy, 1982; Tourism and Outdoor Recreation Planning Study, 1978) demonstrate consistent gender-related differences in the uses of time by older adults. Briefly stated, women in the age group 65+, in contrast with men of the same age, report greater amounts of time spent in housework, and less free time, particularly time spent in mass media consumption. In the United States in 1981, men aged 65-97 spent 17.4 hours per week in household duties, compared to women's 26.0 hours. They reported 60.8 hours of free time per week, compared to women's 53.8 hours, and spent 25.0 hours per week watching TV, compared to women's 16.7 hours (Juster, 1985).

Studies of the elderly's *leisure participation* in the United States, Canada, the United Kingdom, Switzerland, and France also reveal considerable differences between men's and women's patterns of daily life and leisure. According to Havighurst and Albrecht (1953) and Palmore (1968), women report higher levels of overall leisure participation than men. In particular, women report higher rates of participation in such leisure activities as visiting friends and relatives, religious activities, writing letters, reading books, bingo, and the so-called ladies' hobbies (sewing, needlepoint). Men, on the other hand, report higher rates of participation in sports, the outdoors, recreational driving, gardening, newspaper and magazine reading, visiting pubs, and the so-called men's hobbies (house/auto repairs).

In sum, men in old age report more free time than women, but engage in fewer leisure activities. The repertoire of men's and women's most popular leisure pursuits seems to be strongly affected by traditional male-female role stereotypes, with men more actively engaging in mass media, sports, and outdoors, and women in social activities, culture, and hobbies.

Does Daily Behavior and Leisure
Participation of Men and Women
"Diverge" or "Converge" with Age?

The question of whether gender-related differences in human behavior and leisure participation narrow or widen with age is discussed by Havighurst (1957), Neugarten (1964), Cameron (1968), Palmore (1968), Maddox and Douglass (1974), and others.

According to Havighurst (1957), and Neugarten (1964), social differences in human behavior are accentuated with increasing age, as social constraints weaken. "Sexes become increasingly divergent with age" (Neugarten, 1964, p. 293). Other researchers (Cameron, 1968; Palmore, 1968; Maddox and Douglass, 1974), however, argue that with "death being the end point of life . . . individuals become increasingly alike, as they approach this common denominator" (Maddox and Douglass, 1974, p. 556). Bem (1975) and Sinnott (1977) argue that reduction of male-female differences in human behavior and attitudes with the progression of age is not only real but also functional. In their opinion, "androgynous" persons devoid of stereotyped forms of behavior adjust better to retirement.

Very few studies, however, have put the above-mentioned propositions to a rigorous empirical test by means of systematic analyses of time-budget and rates of participation data. One of the most interesting attempts at such an analysis was undertaken by Gronmo (1982), who used as a basis for his work the Norwegian national time-budget surveys of 1970 and 1980-1981.

According to Gronmo, there is at least one area where male-female differences tend to diminish in old age. In Norway, in 1971, the difference in the amount of time spent in housework by men and women declined from 4.7 hours per day for the 34-42 age group, to 3.6 hours for the 61-65 age group, and 2.3 hours for the 70-74 age group. Although women spent more time in household obligations than men in all life cycle groups, the "ratio of inequality," that is, women's housework time divided by men's, amounted to 3.0 in the 34-42 group compared to 1.7 in the age group 70-74 (see Gronmo, 1982, p. 11). Moreover, comparison of the 1970 data with data collected in 1980-1981 suggests that the differential gap between older men's and women's housework time narrowed rather than widened during the 10-year period separating the two surveys.

Roy (1982) reports somewhat similar findings for France. According to her analyses, the housework obligations of men almost double after retirement, while those of women increase by only 20%. As a result, the ratio of female/male inequality with respect to household obligations declines from 2.9 in the middle-aged groups to 1.7 in the age group 65+.

Differences in the rates of *leisure participation* of men and women across the life cycle are analyzed by Gordon and Gaitz (1979), Zborowski (1962), George, Fillenbaum, and Palmore (1984), and others. According to Gordon and Gaitz, levels of leisure participation decline across the life cycle at an approximately similar pace for both men and women, with few exceptions such as home entertainment, where men's and women's rates of participation converge in retirement, and participation in active sport, where male's and female's rates of participation "diverge" toward the end of the life cycle.

Palmore's (1968) data suggest that the differential span between men's and women's participation widens in retirement in such areas as hobbies and visiting friends but narrows in areas such as self-care and religious activities.

In general, existing survey evidence does not lend itself to unequivocal support of either the "convergence" or the "divergence" thesis with respect to the effects of aging on human daily and leisure behavior. It appears that, in some areas of human behavior, such as maintenance and household activities, gender differences decline with age. In other areas, such as amounts of discretionary time, gender differences persist (men consistently report greater amounts of free time than women). Yet, in other areas of daily life, that is, composition of free time activities and rates of participation in selected leisure activities, gender differences are more pronounced in old age than in middle-aged groups.

Leisure Participation and
Subjective Well-Being in Old Age

The relationship between leisure participation and life satisfaction, or subjectively perceived well-being, forms the *focus* of the theoretical discussion about the "disengagement," "continuity," "activity," or "substitution" theories of aging.

It is one of the tenets of "disengagement" theory that, in old age, there need not be a direct correlation between levels of activity involvement and adjustment to retirement. The "activity" theory, on the other hand, states that continuing participation in activities typical of the middle age assures maintenance of psychologically acceptable life-styles and results in higher levels of adjustment in the old age. According to Havighurst and Albrecht (1953): "The American formula for happiness in old age is . . . keep active." Havighurst suggests that practitioners serving older adults prefer the "activity theory" because it corresponds with their belief that

> people should maintain the activities and attitudes of middle age as long as possible and then find substitutes for the activities they must give up; substitutes for work when they are forced to retire; substitutes for clubs and associations which they must give up; substitutes for friends and loved ones whom they lose by death [Havighurst, 1961].

Havens (1968, p. 205) concludes his study of relocated older adults by saying: "There seems to be little doubt that a low level of adjustment is associated with discontinuity and that a high level of adjustment is associated with continuity."

Larson (1978, p. 115), in a summary of U.S. research on the subjective well-being of older adults, states that the research of the relationship between social activity and life satisfaction "has yielded an array of differing findings for different measures of activity and different study populations, but, in general, shows measures of these two variables to be positively related." A positive relationship between activity levels and subjective well-being has been reported by Williams (1963), Havighurst (1961), Havighurst, Neugarten, and Tobin (1968), Neugarten, Havighurst, and Tobin (1961), and others.

Lately, some authors attempted to refine the "activity" theory by suggesting that consideration should be given not only to the number of activities engaged in by older adults, but to the meanings attributed by older adults to these activities. Ragheb and Griffith (1980) found, for example, that levels of life satisfaction are better predicted by the levels of satisfaction with leisure activities than simply by the rates of leisure participation.

It has also been suggested that participation in some leisure activities correlates with perceived life satisfaction more strongly than participation in others. According to Larson (1978), apart from general measures of activity, the visitation of friends and neighbors (although not necessarily relatives) is strongly associated with subjective well-being. According to Graney (1975), perceived happiness correlates positively with visiting friends, and participation in associations, but not necessarily with watching TV or reading.

Few authors have questioned the validity of the aforementioned findings. Wilensky (1961), and Cutler (1973), however, call attention to the fact that there may be a self-selection of the "sane, the adjusted, the healthy and happy" into clubs, associations, and other organized or structured leisure activities (Wilensky, 1961). Likewise, the premises of the "activity" theory cannot be easily reconciled with the fact that older adults of advanced age (75+), while reporting lower levels of leisure participation, do not report lower levels of life-satisfaction (see Dobbin, 1980, p. 98). In general, it appears that life satisfaction of older adults is less affected by the rates of leisure participation than by the person's perception whether these rates are commensurate with his or her age and the meanings that he or she associate with this participation.

Effects of Retirement on the Life-Styles of the Elderly: Survey Findings

As a result of retirement, older Canadians gain approximately 38 extra hours of disposable time per week. How does having all this additional time affect their lives? How do the elderly distribute it between various daily activities?

A methodological note is due at this point. The data used in the following analyses are cross-sectional rather than longitudinal. As such, they do not reflect changing uses of time by one age cohort moving through different life-cycle stages, but rather differences between age groups born at different times and socialized under varying historical, social, economic, and political conditions. Therefore, when comparing the uses of time or rates of leisure participation of the aged with those of the 45-64 years old, one should, strictly speaking, talk of "differences" rather than of "changes," "increases," or "declines." Yet some cross-sectional differences reflect life-cycle change as well (see Braungart and Braungart, 1986). For example, differences between mass media consumption habits of the elderly and their 45- to 60-year-old counterparts to some extent reflect differences between their *own* uses of time today as compared to when they were younger (Statistics Canada, 1981; Zuzanek, 1981-82). It is within these limited confines that we will occasionally interpret age differences in daily and leisure behavior as an indication of life-cycle changes and a "proxy" for missing longitudinal data.

Uses of Time and Leisure Participation
Before and After Retirement

The *National Time Use Pilot Study* (Statistics Canada, 1981) indicates that older adults' withdrawal from the labor force results in a substantial restructuring of their daily lives. Contrary to the public opinion, the newly gained disposable time is not all converted into free time, but rather distributed across all major groups of daily activities. The elderly not only have more free time, but they also sleep more, spend more time in personal hygiene, devote more time to family care, eating, shopping, housework, and errands (Table 7.1).

Free time is neither the sole nor (in relative terms) the biggest beneficiary of the additional disposable time freed by retirement. Older Canadians aged 65+ report having 18 more hours of free time per week than their 45- to 64-year-old counterparts, a difference of 46%. Yet, in relative terms, housework and shopping "expand" after retirement more than free time. Older Canadians spend 28 hours per week in housework, shopping, and errands, compared to 17.4 hours spent by the 45-64 age group (employed), a difference of 60%! The amount of time spent by older adults in cooking and food preparation is almost 80% higher than in the 45-64 age group.

Activities other than free time and housework expand after retirement more modestly. The amount of time devoted to eating is 30% greater in the 65+ age group than in the 45-64 age group (82 minutes per day compared to 64 minutes). The length of the daily sleep and naps is 8.8 hours for the retirees, compared to 8.0 hours before retirement, a difference of 10%.

As a result of these trends, the proportionate composition of the retirees' daily activities differs considerably from that of the gainfully employed. Employed respondents in the 45-64 age group spend 24% of their total weekly time in work for pay, and 10.3% in household/family obligations—that is, a total of 34.3% in obligatory and semiobligatory "instrumental" activities. They spend 42.1% of the total weekly time in personal needs (sleep, personal hygiene, eating), and 22.2% in free time or discretionary activities. After retirement, only 1.8% of the total weekly time is spent in gainful employment, and 16.5% in household/family obligations—that is, a total of 18.3% spent in obligatory and semiobligatory instrumental activities; 47.5% of elderly's weekly time is spent in personal needs, and 32.4% in discretionary activities.

The access to a greater overall amount of free time has as its

TABLE 7.1   Uses of Time by Employed and Retired Population in Canada: *National Time Use Pilot Study,* 1981 (minutes per day)

	Full-Time employed 45-60	Retired 65+	Sign
Work	344.2	25.3	*
Housework	93.1	151.3	*
cooking	39.7	71.0	*
laundry	6.0	11.7	
house upkeep	36.7	58.8	*
records, bills, and so on	2.3	2.4	
Shopping and errands	36.1	53.3	*
Care of children and other family members	19.6	33.3	
Personal services and care	60.5	72.4	
Eating at home	64.3	83.0	*
Sleeping	481.1	528.3	*
Free time	319.3	467.2	*
mass media	111.6	171.0	*
reading books	12.5	26.6	*
reading newspapers and magazines	24.9	27.6	
culture, spectatorship	22.4	19.9	
clubs, organizations	13.9	9.9	
social leisure	62.6	90.0	*
hobbies	15.1	50.4	*
physical leisure, outdoors, sports	27.0	32.5	
religion	6.4	8.2	
personal communications	25.2	24.8	
Other activities	21.8	25.9	

*Significant at .05 level.

consequence allocation of more time to almost all free time activities. According to the *National Time Use Pilot Study* (Table 7.1), older Canadians spent in 1981 close to 20 hours in mass media consumption (mostly watching TV), compared to 13 hours before retirement, a difference of 53%. Time spent in hobbies amounts among older adults to 5.9 hours per week, compared to 1.8 hours before retirement, a difference of 234%! Time spent by older adults in social leisure amounts to 10.5 hours per week, compared to 7.3 hours before retirement, a difference of 44%. On the other hand, the amount of time spent in physically active leisure is only by 20% higher among older adults than among their employed counterparts, aged 45-64 (32 minutes per day compared to 27 minutes). Time spent in cultural outings is actually lower for older Canadians than for those 45-64 years old (employed)—that is, 10 minutes per day after retirement compared to 14 minutes before it.

Proportionately, employed respondents aged 45-64 spend 35% of their total free time in mass media consumption; 19.6% in social leisure activities; 11.6% in reading books and periodicals; 8.5% participating in physically active leisure; 7.0% in cultural outings; 4.7% in hobbies; and 13.7% in other leisure activities. After retirement, 36.6% of all free time is spent in mass media consumption; 19.3% in social leisure activities; 11.6% in reading books and periodicals; 10.8% in hobbies; 7.0% in physically active leisure; 4.2% in cultural outings; and 10.5% in other leisure activities.

The surveys of leisure participation provide a somewhat different picture of the effects of retirement on the daily and leisure lives of the elderly than the time-budget surveys. The survey of Canadians' participation in selected leisure activities conducted in 1975 by Statistics Canada (Table 7.2), and the 1984 survey of leisure and cultural participation in the Kitchener-Waterloo-Brantford area (Table 7.3), suggest that older adults report lower rates of participation than their younger employed counterparts in nearly all leisure activities.

According to the Leisure Study—Canada 1975, the composite index of leisure participation in 25 selected leisure activities is 10.5 points on a 100-point scale for retired men and 12.7 points for retired women compared to 14.6 and 18.3 points for the 55-64 age group (Table 7.2). According to the Kitchener-Waterloo-Brantford survey, the composite index of participation in 55 selected leisure activities is 59.4 points, on a 100-point scale, for those aged d 35-45; 49.0 points for those aged 45-64; and 40.2 points for the elderly aged 65+. Table 7.3 indicates that participation "declines" with age particularly strongly in physically active leisure pursuits, sporting activities, outings, and certain forms of social leisure.

In general, time-budget surveys and surveys of leisure participation suggest the following: (1) Apart from personal needs, free time activities become, after retirement, the single largest group of daily activities, accounting for almost one-third of the total daily time. (2) Retirement does not mean a complete withdrawal from work or obligatory activities. Some of the time freed from gainful employment by retirement is substituted by work and family obligations at home. (3)

TABLE 7.2   Life-Cycle Variations in Levels of Leisure Participation:
Survey of Participation in Selected Leisure Activities, 1975
(factor composite index of leisure participation; 0-100)

	Men	Women	Female Homemakers
Student, single, 19-24 years	34.9	36.4	
Full-time employed, single, 19-24 years	24.7	30.5	
Full-time employed or not in labor force, married 19-24 years	22.2	27.6	21.8
Full-time employed, homemakers, married, 25-34 years	20.8	22.4	22.1
Full-time employed, homemakers, married, 35-44 years	16.8	21.3	22.3
Full-time employed, homemakers, married, 45-54 years	15.2	17.1	17.5
Full-time employed, homemakers married, 55-64 years	14.6	18.3	16.2
Retired/not in labor force, married, 65 years and over	10.5	12.7	13.4
Retired/not in labor force, widowed, 65 years and over	10.9	12.3	12.6

NOTE: The factor composite index of leisure involvement was constructed as a weighted score of participation in 25 selected leisure activities.

Home-centered and more passive free time activities such as mass media consumption and hobbies occupy a proportionately greater share of free time after retirement than before it. (4) Older adults engage in fewer structured leisure pursuits and report lower rates of participation in a great majority of leisure activities than middle-aged respondents. The study of the daily and leisure lives of the elderly reveals that many of the changes caused by retirement are accentuated by the subsequent process of aging, that is, *transition from the "young-old" to the "old-old" age*.

Table 7.4 indicates that there are discernible differences between the uses of time by the elderly under the age of 70 and after 71. Briefly stated, as the older adults become "older," they spend less time in housework and shopping. On the other hand, the amount of time that they devote to personal needs and free time activities "increases." Older adults, aged 71+, spend 16.4 hours per week in household obligations and shopping, compared to 21 hours spent by respondents aged 70 or under—a "reduction" of 21%. Of housework activities, the ones that "shrink" the most in the "old-old" age are housecleaning and nonfood shopping. Cooking and grocery shopping, on the other hand, are less affected by

TABLE 7.3   Participation in Selected Leisure Activities by Age: Kitchener-Waterloo Area, 1984 (percentage)[a]

| Activity | Age Group | | | |
	< 45	45-60	65+	Sign
Jogging/calisthenics	72.0	49.3	37.8	**
Walking (recreational)	94.3	89.0	89.2	N.S.
Swimming	87.0	67.1	54.1	**
Skating, skiing	73.6	41.1	18.9	**
Racquet sports	59.1	27.4	13.5	**
Golfing	57.5	38.4	32.4	**
Curling	40.9	26.0	24.3	**
Bowling	66.3	43.8	18.9	**
Team sports	56.5	27.4	13.5	**
Fishing/hunting	65.8	46.6	35.1	**
Visit national/provincial park	72.0	64.4	37.8	**
Work for community/ethnic groups	58.5	42.5	43.2	*
Work for church groups	58.0	56.2	56.8	N.S.
Go to movies	78.8	56.2	54.1	**
Go to sporting events	54.9	38.4	29.7	*
Go to fair/festival	77.2	49.2	45.9	**
Visit public library	79.3	65.8	64.9	*
Take general interest/art courses	57.0	37.0	16.2	**
Play musical instrument/sing	62.2	47.9	32.4	**
Painting, sculpturing, pottery	46.1	32.9	21.6	**
Gardening	81.3	83.6	86.5	N.S.
Dine out	95.3	94.5	81.1	**
Bingo	47.2	42.5	27.0	N.S.
Cards, board games	89.6	89.0	67.6	**
Pinball, pool, shuffleboard	59.1	38.4	18.9	**
Composite index of participation (0-100)	59.4	49.0	40.2	**

a. Percentage of respondents who participated in an activity at least once during the year preceding the survey.
*Significant at .05 level.
**Significant at .005 level.

TABLE 7.4   Uses of Time by the "Young-Old" and "Old-Old" Adults in Kitchener-Waterloo Area, 1981-1982 (minutes per day)

	< 70	70+	Sign
Work	15.7	15.3	
Travel	33.2	27.4	
Housework	133.7	108.1	
cooking	58.0	53.2	
laundry	13.2	8.3	
house upkeep	51.4	39.8	
records, bills, and so on	8.3	5.0	
Shopping for food	15.4	15.6	
Shopping for nonfood	30.8	16.5	*
Care of children/grandchildren	4.4	1.2	
Personal care	59.9	69.2	
Sleep	517.2	537.4	
Eating at home	94.6	97.5	
Free time	535.1	551.8	
seniors' clubs	4.4	15.3	
other clubs & organizations	6.1	2.4	
religious activities, attending church	21.3	27.8	
physically active leisure (walk, sports, exercise)	34.9	19.4	
hobbies	40.2	28.6	
social leisure (dine out, visiting, table games)	117.9	99.9	
mass media (TV and radio)	203.8	268.8	**
watching TV	182.6	238.6	**
reading books	44.6	28.2	
reading newspapers and magazines	31.3	38.3	
telephone and letters	20.1	22.4	
other free time	10.5	0.7	

*Significant at .05 level.
**Significant at .005 level.

the progression of age. Retirees aged 71+ spend 82 hours per week in personal needs, compared to 78 hours for the 65-70 age group. The amount of daily sleep increases from 8.6 hours for the 65-70 years old to 9.0 hours for those aged 71+.

The amount of free time reported by the 71+ age group is 67 hours per week, compared to 63 hours for the "younger" elderly (–70). Among free time activities, social leisure, hobbies, and particularly physically active leisure "lose out," while time spent attending senior clubs and watching TV increases in both absolute and relative terms.

Data on the elderly's leisure participation demonstrate that, with the advancement of age, their rates of participation in most leisure activities decline rather steeply. According to Table 7.5, the composite index of leisure participation in selected leisure activities is 41.3 points for those aged 71+, compared to 45.5 points for those aged 65-70, a difference of 10%. Older adults in the 71+ age group report lower rates of participation in virtually all surveyed leisure activities, particularly the physically active and "out of home" ones, such as swimming, going to beaches, walking, window-shopping, listening to records and tapes, visiting library, attending concerts, and traveling overseas. Participation in home-centered social and mass media activities is, on the other hand, less affected by the advancement of age.

In general, the analysis of the changing uses of time and leisure participation *after and during* retirement reveals several interesting trends:

(1) The amount of free time available to older adults increases after retirement, first at the expense of paid work, and later (at a considerably slower rate) at the expense of housework and shopping time. The share of free time activities as a part of the total daily time increases from 22.2% before retirement to almost 40% in the late postretirement years.

(2) The proportionate share of personal needs (sleep, personal hygiene, eating) also "increases" after retirement, although not at the same rate as free time. Personal needs occupy 49.0% of the total daily time of the elderly aged 71+, as compared to 42.1% for the employed respondents aged 45-64 and 46.7% for those aged 65-70.

(3) Household and family obligations increase as a result of retirement. It appears that some of the time previously spent in paid work is now spent working at home. With the older adults' advancement in age, however, the absolute and relative amount of time spent in housework (particularly housecleaning) and shopping (in particular, nonfood) declines.

(4) Among free time activities, home-centered and passive activities, such as hobbies and mass media consumption, increase their share of free time. With the progression of age, further regrouping of free time activities occurs. The share of mass media consumption as a part of free time continues to grow (47% of the total free time in the 71+ age group), while the share of social leisure activities, hobbies, outings, and particularly physically active leisure gradually declines.

(5) Surveys of leisure participation indicate that the rates of participation in most leisure activities decline during retirement. The spectrum of leisure participation (number of activities pursued by older adults) narrows considerably after 65, and particularly after 71. Relatively few leisure activities such as watching TV, reading books, participation in senior

TABLE 7.5   Leisure Participation of Older Adults Aged ≤ 70 and 70+: Kitchener-Waterloo Area, 1981-1982 (percentage)[a]

	≤ 70	70+	Sign
Watching TV	97.9	100.0	
Listening to radio	95.8	88.9	
Listening to records, tapes, or cassettes	83.3	66.7	
Reading newspapers	100.0	96.3	
Reading magazines	93.8	74.1	
Reading books—fiction	72.9	53.7	
Attending social club or meeting	77.1	64.8	
Working for a community or church group	54.2	46.3	
Going to church	87.5	81.5	
General interest courses	2.9	2.0	
Visit library	62.5	44.4	
Visiting a fair, festival, exhibition	52.1	53.7	
Visiting a historical site	54.2	46.3	
Visiting a general or science museum	20.8	22.2	
Visiting an art gallery	33.3	40.7	
Attending live theater	54.2	37.0	
Attending a concert	52.1	48.1	
Going to movies	33.3	27.8	
Going to a sporting event	20.8	22.2	
Dining out	95.8	98.1	
Going to a bar/pub	20.8	24.1	
Going dancing	41.7	31.5	
Visiting friends/relatives	100.0	100.0	
Entertaining at home	95.8	92.6	
Socializing with children/grandchildren	81.3	83.3	
Playing cards	81.3	75.9	
Betting, lottery	64.6	68.5	
Pool, snooker	8.3	22.2	
Bingo	35.4	31.5	
Crosswords	31.3	37.0	
Chess, checkers	22.9	14.8	
Darts	16.7	14.8	
Computer games	8.3	7.4	

(continued)

TABLE 7.5 continued

	≤ 70	70+	Sign
Walking	97.9	85.2	*
Playing with pets	43.8	38.9	
Calisthenics	41.7	31.5	
Swimming	35.4	16.7	*
Fitness classes	16.7	16.7	
Going to the beach	60.4	40.7	*
Recreational driving	68.8	72.2	
Visiting national/provincial parks	50.0	40.7	
Visiting private cottage	43.8	40.7	
Boating, sailing	35.4	24.1	
Fishing	16.7	16.7	
Bowling	22.9	25.9	
Golfing	18.8	9.3	
Curling	8.3	5.6	
Gardening	43.8	46.3	
Home/auto repair—hobby	22.9	14.8	
Photography, home movies	37.5	38.9	
Plant care	75.0	53.7	*
Sewing, needlepoint	56.3	48.1	
Gourmet cooking	22.9	24.1	
Collectioneering	27.1	24.1	
Playing musical instrument	10.4	14.8	
Sculpture, painting	6.3	7.4	
Window shopping	83.3	64.8	*
Sightseeing	70.8	75.9	
Traveling overseas	14.6	3.7	
Composite index of leisure participation (0-100)	45.5	41.3	*

a. Percentage of respondents who participated in an activity at least once during the year preceding the survey.
*Significant at .05 level.
**Significant at .005 level.

citizens' club activities, and recreational walking do not show a marked decline in the reported rates of participation.

(6) The advancement of the elderly's age accentuates the paradox of retirement, namely, that while the elderly have more free time, they report lower rates of participation in nearly all leisure activities. This is,

of course, only a seeming paradox. Its explanation is simple: Older adults engage in fewer activities, but they spend considerably more time in each one of these activities, particularly mass media consumption. Simply stated, older adults spend more time in fewer leisure pursuits.

Till Leisure Us Part . . .?

Time-budget surveys and studies of leisure participation suggest that retirement affects differently the uses of time by men and women. Gender differences are particularly pronounced in two areas: uses of time for housework and free time activities.

According to the time-budget survey of older adults in the Kitchener-Waterloo area (Table 7.6), women in retirement spend approximately 21 hours per week in housework and shopping, compared to men's 14 hours, a difference of 50%. Of this time, women spend 8.8 hours per week in cooking and food preparation, compared to men's 3.0 hours, a difference of 191%! Women in the 65+ age group spend 1.6 hours per week in laundry, compared to men's 40 minutes—that is, 2.5 times more—and 3 hours in nonfood shopping, compared to men's 2 hours— that is, 1.5 times more. House upkeep, grocery shopping, and various forms of paperwork (paying bills, keeping records), are, on the other hand, distributed more evenly.

There are, as well, considerable gender differences in the amounts and, in particular, the distribution of free time among the elderly. The amount of free time available to men aged 65+ is 70 hours per week, compared to 62 hours for women of the same age group, a difference of 13%. Older men spend 35 hours per week in mass media consumption, compared to women's 23 hours, a difference of 51%. They spend close to 6 hours per week in newspaper and magazine reading, compared to women's 3 hours, a difference of 92%. Men's participation in physically active leisure amounts to 4.8 hours per week, compared to women's 2.1 hours, a difference of 128%! Women, on the other hand, spend more time than men in social leisure activities and hobbies. According to the Kitchener-Waterloo time-budget survey of the elderly, women aged 65+ spend 14.2 hours per week in social leisure activities (visiting friends, having visitors, dining out), compared to men's 10.3 hours, a difference of 38%. They spend 5.3 hours per week in hobbies, compared to men's 2.2 hours—a difference of 40%—and 3.5 hours talking to friends and relatives on the telephone or writing letters, compared to men's 0.8 hours—a difference of 345%!

Surveys of elderly's *leisure participation* suggest that women parti-

TABLE 7.6   Housework, Shopping, and Free Time of Older Adults in Kitchener-Waterloo Area, 1981-1982: Gender Differences (minutes per day)

	Men	Women	Sign
Housework	82.9	141.1	**
cooking	26.0	75.6	**
laundry	5.6	13.9	**
house upkeep	43.0	43.5	
records, bills, and so on	7.0	5.4	
Shopping for food	19.6	12.5	
Shopping for nonfood	16.8	25.8	
Free time	603.9	536.6	**
seniors' clubs	11.3	8.1	
other clubs & organizations	6.1	3.9	
religious activities, attending church	24.0	27.9	
physically active leisure (walk, sports, exercise)	40.8	17.9	
hobbies	19.1	45.8	**
social leisure (dining out, visiting, games)	88.3	122.1	*
mass media (TV and radio)	299.7	198.1	
watching TV	261.3	179.8	**
reading books	30.4	35.5	
reading newspapers and magazines	50.9	26.5	**
telephone and letters	6.7	29.8	**
other free time	32.7	30.6	

*Significant at .05 level.
**Significant at .005 level.

cipate in approximately the same number of activities as men. Activities in which the two genders participate vary considerably, however.

According to the Kitchener-Waterloo survey of older adults (1981-1982), men's leisure involvement measured on a composite index of leisure participation amounted to 38.6 points on a 100-point scale, compared to women's 40.6 points (Table 7.7). Of the 60 leisure activities that formed the composite index, women reported higher rates of participation in 11 activities: reading books and magazines; visiting the library; working for a community or church group; visiting an art gallery; going to live theater or a concert; sewing, needlepoint; plant care; bingo (significant at .05 level). Men reported higher rates of participation in 6 activities: golfing, curling, fishing, home/auto repairs, gardening, pool/snooker (significant at the .05 level).

As indicated earlier, the question that intrigues many researchers is as

TABLE 7.7   Leisure Participation of Older Adults in Kitchener-Waterloo
Area, 1981-1982 (percentage)[a]

	Men	Women	Total	Sign
Watching TV	93.2	90.4	91.5	
Listening to radio	86.4	84.9	85.5	
Listening to records, tapes, or cassettes	61.4	69.6	66.7	
Reading newspapers	90.9	90.4	90.6	*
Reading magazines	65.9	83.6	76.9	**
Reading books—fiction	40.9	67.1	57.3	**
Participation in clubs or associations	59.1	65.8	63.2	
Working for community or church group	36.4	50.7	45.3	**
Going to church	70.5	80.8	76.9	
General interest courses	0.0	6.8	4.3	*
Visit library	34.1	58.9	49.6	**
Visiting a fair, festival, exhibition	47.7	46.6	47.0	
Visiting a historical site	50.0	42.5	45.3	
Visiting a general or science museum	13.6	23.3	19.7	
Visiting an art gallery	22.7	41.1	34.2	**
Attending live theater	27.3	49.3	41.0	**
Attending a concert	34.1	53.4	46.2	**
Going to movies	20.5	30.1	26.5	
Going to a sporting event	27.3	13.7	18.8	*
Dining out	90.9	89.0	89.7	
Going to a bar/pub	27.3	16.4	20.5	
Going dancing	38.6	31.5	34.2	
Visiting friends/relatives	93.2	91.8	92.3	
Entertaining at home	88.6	86.3	87.2	
Socializing with children/grandchildren	79.5	72.6	75.2	
Playing cards	70.5	71.2	70.9	
Betting, lottery	63.6	56.2	59.0	
Pool, snooker	27.3	5.5	13.7	**
Bingo	11.4	41.1	29.9	**
Crosswords	25.0	35.6	31.6	
Chess, checkers	18.2	16.4	17.1	
Darts	18.2	11.0	13.7	
Computer games	6.8	6.8	6.8	

(continued)

TABLE 7.7 continued

	Men	Women	Total	Sign
Walking	81.8	86.3	84.6	
Playing with pets	45.5	34.2	38.5	
Calisthenics	31.8	35.6	34.2	
Swimming	25.0	23.3	23.9	
Fitness classes	25.0	23.3	23.9	
Going to the beach	9.1	17.8	14.5	
Recreational driving	63.6	65.8	65.0	
Visiting national/provincial parks	34.1	45.2	41.0	
Visiting private cottage	43.2	32.9	36.8	
Boating, sailing	22.7	27.4	25.6	
Fishing	29.5	9.6	17.1	**
Bowling	27.3	20.5	23.1	**
Golfing	22.7	5.5	12.0	**
Curling	13.6	1.4	6.0	**
Gardening	63.6	30.1	42.7	**
Home/auto repair—hobby	34.1	5.5	16.2	**
Photography, home movies	36.4	32.9	34.2	
Plant care	34.1	74.0	59.0	**
Sewing, needlepoint	13.6	68.5	47.9	**
Gourmet cooking	20.5	23.3	22.2	
Collectioneering	22.7	23.3	23.1	
Playing musical instrument	6.8	13.7	11.1	
Sculpture, painting	2.3	9.6	6.8	
Window shopping	65.9	71.2	69.2	
Sightseeing	72.7	63.0	66.7	
Traveling overseas	9.1	8.2	8.5	
Composite index of leisure participation (1-100)	38.3	40.5	39.7	

a. Percentage of respondents who participated in an activity at least once during the year preceding the survey.
  *Significant at .05 level.
**Significant at .005 level.

follows: Does the gender gap in the daily and leisure lives of men and women widen or narrow with age? Are men and women becoming behaviorally more alike or more different in the old age compared to previous stages of their life? Analysis of the data collected as a part of the 1981 *National Time Use Pilot Study* and Leisure Study—Canada 1975 suggests that the answer to this question should be a qualified one.

According to the *National Time Use Pilot Study*, in the 45-64 age group (employed), women spend 70% more time than men in housework and shopping. After retirement, they spend "only" 20% more time than men in these same activities (Table 7.8). This "narrowing" of the male-female differences after retirement can be explained by the fact that, after retirement, men "increase" their involvement in household obligations by 70%, while women increase it only by 25%. As a result, men's and women's behavior in old age appears to "converge" rather than "diverge."

The reverse seems to be true of free time activities. According to the *National Time Use Pilot Study*, men report having more free time than women both before and after retirement. While the difference is 5% before retirement, it is 11% after retirement. After retirement, men spend 48% more time in mass media consumption than women, while the difference is only 30% in the 45-64 age group (employed). The amount of time spent by retired women in hobbies is almost six times greater than the amount reported by retired men. In the 45-64 age group (employed), the difference is less than twofold. In general, differences in the use of free time appear to widen rather than narrow with age, although this trend does not apply to all free time activities (social leisure, reading books, and physically active leisure are some of the exceptions).

In sum:

(1) Gender differences in the daily lives of older adults are pronounced in the domain of housework and in the use of free time.

(2) In general, women in old age sleep longer than men; they spend more time in household obligations, but have less free time. Men spend more of their free time in mass media consumption, newspaper and magazine reading, and physically active leisure. Women, on the other hand, spend more time than men (both in absolute and relative terms) in social contacts of all kinds and hobbies.

(3) Older men and women engage in an approximately similar number of leisure activities. The makeup of these activities, or the leisure repertoire, of men and women, however, is different. Men, generally, report higher rates of participation in physical, sporting, and do-it-yourself activities. Women report higher rates of participation in social, cultural, religious, and community activities, as well as hobbies. These findings lend some support to the notion that women's leisure repertoire is more expressive and social than the males', while the males' leisure repertoire is marked

TABLE 7.8 Uses of Time by Middle-Aged and Older Adults in Canada, Controlled for Gender and Employment Status: National Time Use Pilot Survey, 1981 (minutes per day)

	Men		Women			Significant at .05 Level*
	Full-Time Employed 45-65	Retired 65+	Full-Time Employed 45-65	Homemakers 45-65	65+	
Work	358.1	21.6	315.2	17.7	16.1	1, 3/2, 4, 5
Housework	74.3	134.5	132.3	237.0	169.1	1/2, 3, 4, 5
Shopping and errands	32.5	48.1	43.5	55.9	50.9	4/1, 2, 3, 5
Care of children and other family members	15.9	25.0	27.4	30.1	20.6	
Personal services and care	54.6	53.9	73.0	56.1	69.0	
Eating at home	65.8	92.5	61.2	80.6	77.8	2/1, 3; 3/2, 4
Sleeping	482.7	519.8	477.7	529.9	559.2	1, 3/4, 5
Free time	334.0	516.9	316.1	436.1	464.1	1/2, 4, 5
mass media	120.5	241.3	93.0	135.7	163.3	3/2, 4, 5
reading books	10.7	31.2	16.5	7.6	24.5	2/1, 3, 4, 5
reading newspapers and magazines	26.6	44.7	21.3	15.1	25.1	
hobbies	12.0	11.0	21.4	67.2	64.2	2/3, 4, 5
physical leisure, sports, outdoors	32.5	48.1	43.5	55.9	50.9	
social leisure	57.2	71.1	73.9	84.5	75.6	4, 5/1, 2, 3
Other activities	22.1	27.7	0.0	0.6	13.2	

NOTE: Travel related to work, shopping, and free time are included into respective categories. Daily totals may not add up to 1440 minutes due to rounding.

*Numbers in this column identify subpopulations for which differences in the uses of time are significant at .05 level: 1 = full-time employed men, aged 45-64; 2 = retired men, 65+; 3 = full-time employed women, aged 45-64; 4 = female homemakers, 45-64; 5 = women, 65+. 1/2 signifies that the difference between the uses of time by full-time employed men, 45-64, and full-time employed women, 45-64 is significant.

even after retirement by competitiveness (sports) and instrumentality (do-it-yourself activities).

(4) There is no simple answer to the question of whether men's and women's daily lives "converge" or "diverge" with age. It appears, however, that, in general, men and women in old age are more akin than in the middle stages of their lives in the domain of obligatory activities such as housework, but further apart from each other in the discretionary domain of their lives, that is, in the uses of free time and leisure participation. In housework—united! In leisure—divided!

Life Satisfaction, Free Time, and Leisure Participation

The time-budget survey of older adults in the Kitchener-Waterloo area allows us to examine in some detail relationships between elderly's life satisfaction, measured by the Life Satisfaction Index (LSI) of Neugarten, Havighurst, and Tobin (1961), their uses of time, and the rates of their participation in selected leisure activities (Table 7.9). This analysis indicates that there are few significant relationships between the *amount of time* older adults spend in various daily and free time activities and perceived levels of their life satisfaction. On the other hand, correlations between levels of perceived life satisfaction and the *rates of* respondents' *participation* in leisure activities are almost without exception highly significant.

According to Table 7.9, there are no significant relationships between the level of perceived life satisfaction and the amount of time spent by older adults in either housework or free time activities. Having more free time does not make older adults happier. Nor do greater amounts of housework necessarily reduce elderly's life satisfaction (although conceivably this may be the case for older men). For women, longer hours of sleep and a greater amount of time spent in hobbies are associated with lower levels of life satisfaction (significant at .05 level). This can, of course, be caused by the fact that, in old age, longer hours of sleep and greater amounts of time spent in hobbies are often associated with greater infirmity.

The positive correlation between women's involvement in social leisure activities and LSI ($r = .17$; $p = 068$) corresponds with the findings of other researchers. The nonsignificant negative correlation between life satisfaction and the amount of time spent in social leisure by *men*, however, is not readily explicable. While the underlying reasons for the difference between men and women are not clear, it is tempting to

TABLE 7.9   Correlations Between Perceived Life Satisfaction, Uses of Time, and Leisure Participation of Older Adults in Kitchener-Waterloo Area, 1980-1981 (Pearson's "r")

Leisure Participation and Uses of Time	Men "r"	p	Women "r"	p	Total Sample "r"	p
Measures of leisure *participation:*						
Spectrum (composite index, 0-100)	.57	*	.69	*	.63	*
clubs and organizations	.34	*	.52	*	.43	*
culture/education	.39	*	.47	*	.39	*
physically active leisure	.30	*	.51	*	.41	*
outdoor recreation	.19		.42	*	.34	*
social leisure	.66	*	.61	*	.63	*
hobbies	−.04		.24	*	.10	
fitness	.41	*	.38	*	.39	*
travel	.42	*	.55	*	.51	*
Measures of the uses of *time:*						
free time	.02		.05		.07	
housework	−.09		.05		−.04	
sleeping	.07		−.22	*	−.09	
mass media	.06		.05		.10	
clubs and organizations	−.08		.12		.05	
religious activities	.04		−.08		−.05	
physically active leisure	.13		−.06		.07	
social leisure	−.11		.17		.05	
hobbies	−.16		−.27	*	−.26	*
reading newspapers and magazines	.04		.01		.06	
reading books	.11		−.13		−.05	

*Significant at .05 level.

speculate that social leisure activities are much more organically interwoven with the lives of older women than older men. For older men, social leisure activities are often—much the same way as watching TV—an attempt to fill a void, a compensation for the absence of supportive behavioral structures that they relied upon in their pre-retirement life (work). For women, on the other hand, social leisure activities represent a more natural continuation and extension of their life-styles.

The correlations between the LSI and older adults' rates of participation in selected leisure activities are mostly positive and significant. The correlation between the Life Satisfaction Index and the composite measure of leisure participation (number and diversity of leisure activities pursued by older adults) is .63, significant at .005 level. Correlations are also strong between the LSI and participation in most leisure activities, with the exception of hobbies. The correlations between the LSI, on the one hand, and participation in physically active leisure, fitness exercise, and outdoor recreation, on the other, are respectively: .41, .39, and .34 (all significant at the .005 level). The correlations between the LSI and rates of participation in voluntary activities (clubs, organizations) and cultural outings are .43 and .39 (significant at .005 level). The correlations between the LSI, social leisure activities, and traveling overseas are particularly strong, that is, .63 for social leisure and .51 for traveling overseas (both significant at the .005 level). In general, it appears that the greater the number of leisure activities older adults engage in, and the greater their participation in structured leisure pursuits, the happier they are.

How is one to reconcile the seemingly contradictory finding that life satisfaction correlates positively with leisure participation but does not significantly correlate with the amounts of free time available to the elderly? What do these findings tell us about the lives of the older adults? The answer to these questions has a methodological and a substantive aspect to it.

Methodologically, leisure participation data are more "specific" and more susceptible to subjective interpretation or "normative editing" than the time-budget data. Data on leisure participation are based on "long-term" rather than "immediate" recall. The question in the studies of leisure participation usually reads: "Have you participated in a given activity at least once during the *last year?*" The time-budget questionnaire, on the other hand, typically asks: "Have you done it *yesterday?*" As a result, reporting on what people do is more objective in time-budget surveys than in the surveys of leisure participation. To some extent, leisure participation data tell us not only what a person actually did but also what he or she would like to have done. Because leisure participation data are more heavily loaded with subjective connotations, it should not be surprising that they correlate more strongly than time-budget data with the measurements of a subjectively perceived level of life satisfaction.

Substantively, time-budget measures provide us with information about the amount of discretionary or "opportunity" time. Data on leisure participation provide us, on the other hand, with an understanding of how this opportunity time is filled with specific structured leisure activities. If one were to use Csikszentmihalyi's (1975) notions of "action opportunities" and "action capabilities," time-budget data would correspond more closely with the notion of "action opportunities," while data on leisure participation, to a certain degree, reflect upon "action capabilities," that is, respondents' skills, competencies, and abilities to fill and structure their free time. It has been reported by other researchers that greater amounts of "opportunity" time do not necessarily correlate with higher levels of life satisfaction. In fact, beyond a certain point, the reverse seems to be true (Robinson, 1977). According to Csikszentmihalyi (1975), satisfying "flow" or autotelic experiences are characterized by a match between action opportunities (challenges) and action capabilities (skills). If one were to apply this perspective to the daily lives of older adults, one is to expect that the levels of retirees' life satisfaction *ought to be* more strongly affected by the ability to structure their time (engage in a greater number of structured leisure activities), than by the amount of free time at their disposal, which is "given" and nonnegotiable.

In sum, our findings support the gerontologists' maxim that to be happy one has to be active. Having more free time does not automatically translate into greater happiness. Being able to fill this time with activities and to structure it in a meaningful and diversified way does! Acquiring a satisfying life-style in retirement presupposes an ability to structure one's time.

Summary and Discussion

Analysis of the daily lives and leisure participation of older Canadians from a life-cycle perspective indicates that, in general, the elderly spend more time than the employed population in all activities, save paid work. The increases are particularly pronounced at first in housework and free time, later primarily in free time. In Canada, similar to other countries, growing amounts of free time among older adults are accompanied by the narrowing of the elderly's leisure repertoire. Older adults spend more time in fewer leisure activities.

The question of whether changes in the daily lives of older adults are best described in terms of the "disengagement" or "continuity" theories is difficult to resolve. Time-budget and leisure participation data suggest that changes in the daily lives of older adults can be better described by the notion of "*restructuration*" of their daily behavior, or behavioral "trade-offs" and "substitutions" than by that of "withdrawal" or "continuity."

Advanced age reduces older adults' participation in most leisure activities, particularly physically active ones. The difference between the composite index of leisure participation for those aged 71 and more, and those under 70 years of age, however, is only 4 points on a 100-point scale. It seems that, at least in the case of healthy older adults, advanced age carries with it gradual and controlled restructuring of older adults' daily lives rather than a radical withdrawal from, or discontinuation of, activity participation.

Free time of older women is dominated to a greater extent than free time of older men by expressive and social activities. Men's free time appears "dichotomized" between passive mass media consumption, on the one hand, and competitive and instrumental leisure pursuits, on the other (sports, house/auto repairs, and so on). This suggests that, behaviorally, women may be more at ease with the challenges of retirement than men. Levels of perceived life satisfaction reported by older men and women, however, are almost identical. This invokes caution in assessing comparative levels of males' and females' adjustment in old age.

Life-cycle analysis of male-female differences in the uses of time and leisure participation suggests that, as a result of aging, gender differences narrow in housework activities but widen in the domain of free time. Age appears to close the gap in obligatory activities, but widens differences in the area of leisure pursuits.

The Kitchener-Waterloo survey of older adults indicates that there is a strong correlation between life satisfaction and rates of leisure participation, but little correlation between life satisfaction and the older adults' uses of time. The life satisfaction of older adults is affected to a greater extent by their leisure interests and competencies than by the amounts of free time. This may be attributed to the fact that measures of leisure participation contain a certain element of status defense and status conferral. They reflect not only on what people do, but how they perceive themselves or how they would like to be perceived by others and thus reflect upon respondents' self-assessment.

Two concluding remarks ought to be made at this point:

As we have said earlier, time-budget data and measures of participation in a broad spectrum of leisure pursuits were rarely employed to study systematically changing patterns of daily lives and leisure behavior of older adults. Yet many trends in aging are *"activity specific."* Decline of participation in certain groups of activities is often accompanied by an increase in others. Studies of leisure participation, using large lists of individual leisure activities, and time-budget data, provide particularly useful tools for the analysis of the daily lives of older adults viewed as a process of "restructuring" and a system of "trade-offs." They allow us to examine the impact of aging on human behavior from the perspective of gradual *"behavioral restructuration"* rather than unilateral "withdrawal" or "continuation."

Substantively, analyses in this chapter support research findings of those authors who challenged some perpetual myths about the older adults' lives. Older adults in our studies were neither lonely nor miserable; they were not at a loss as to what to do with their time. They pursued a variety of activities and derived their satisfaction from being able to live up to the challenges of retirement. In some way, they seemed to be less confused than the researchers. They knew that they can control and enhance, but not stop or reverse their lives.

REFERENCES

Baley, J. A. 1955. "Recreation and the Aging Process." *Research Quarterly* 26(1):1-7.

Bem, S. 1975. "Sex Role Adaptability: One Consequence of Psychological Androgyny." *Journal of Personality and Social Psychology* 31(4):634-43.

Box, S. 1984. "Leisure and the Life Cycle." Honours B.A. thesis, Department of Recreation and Leisure Studies, University of Waterloo.

Braungart, R. G. and M. M. Braungart. 1986. "Life-Course and Generational Politics." *Annual Review of Sociology* 12:205-31.

Cameron, P. 1968. "Masculinity-Femininity in the Aged." *Journal of Gerontology* 10(23):63-70.

Cavan, R. S. 1962. "Self and Role in Adjustment During Old Age." In *Human Behavior and Social Process*, edited by A. M. Rose. Boston: Houghton Mifflin.

Chapin, F. S., Jr. 1974. *Human Activity Patterns in the City.* New York: John Wiley.

Cowgill, D. O. and N. Baulch. 1961. "The Use of Leisure Time by Older People." *Gerontologist* 2(1):47-50.

Csikszentmihalyi, M. 1975. *Beyond Boredom and Anxiety.* San Francisco: Jossey-Bass.

Cumming, E. and W. H. Henry. 1961. *Growing Old: The Process of Disengagement.* New York: Basic Books.

Cutler, S. J. 1973. "Voluntary Association Participation and Life Satisfaction: A Cautionary Research Note." *Journal of Gerontology* 28:96-100.

Dobbin, I. 1980. *Retirement and Leisure*. Salford: University of Salford, Center of Leisure Studies.

Dumazedier, J. and L. Ripert. 1983. "Retirement and Leisure." *International Social Science Journal* 15:438-47.

Frenkel-Brunswik, E. 1968. "Adjustments and Reorientation in the Course of the Life Span." In *Middle Age and Aging*, edited by B. L. Neugarten. Chicago: University of Chicago Press.

George, L., G. Fillenbaum, and E. Palmore. 1984. "Sex Differences in the Antecedents and Consequences of Retirement." *Journal of Gerontology* 39(3):342-49.

Gordon, C. and C. Gaitz. 1979. "Leisure and Lives: Personal Expression Across the Life Span." In *Handbook of Aging and the Social Sciences*, edited by R. H. Binstock and E. Shanas. New York: Van Nostrand Reinhold.

Graney, M. J. 1975. "Happiness and Social Participation in Aging." *Journal of Gerontology* 30(6):701-6.

Gray, H. R. 1979. "Effect of Aging on Outdoor Recreation Activity and Attitudes." *The Third Nationwide Outdoor Recreation Plan* (Survey Technical Report 4). Washington, DC: Government Printing Office.

Gronmo, S. 1982. "Sexual Differences in Household Work: Patterns of Time Use Change in Norway." Paper presented to the 10th World Congress of Sociology, Mexico City.

Havens, B. J. 1968. "An Investigation of Activity Patterns and Adjustment in an Aging Population." *Gerontologist* 8(3):201-6.

Havighurst, R. J. 1957. "The Social Competence of Middle Aged People." *Genetic Psychology Monographs* 56:297-375.

———. 1961. "Successful Aging." *Gerontologist* 1:8-13.

———. and R. Albrecht. 1953. *Older People*. New York: Longman, Green.

Havighurst, R. J., B. L. Neugarten, and S. S. Tobin. 1968. "Disengagement and Patterns of Aging." In *Middle Age and Aging*, edited by B. L. Neugarten. Chicago: University of Chicago Press.

Hill, M. 1985. "Patterns of Time Use." In *Time, Goods and Well-Being*, edited by F. T. Juster and F. P. Stafford. Ann Arbor: University of Michigan, Institute for Social Research.

Huet, H. T., Y. Lemel, and C. Roy. 1978. "Les emplois du temps des citadins, Resultats provisoires de l'enquete 1974-1975." Paris: Institut National de la Statistique et des Etudes Economiques.

Juster, F. T. 1985. "A Note on Recent Changes in Time Use." In *Time, Goods and Well-Being*, edited by F. T. Juster and F. P. Stafford. Ann Arbor: University of Michigan, Institute for Social Research.

Komarovsky, M. 1940. *The Unemployed Man and His Family*. New York: Dryden.

Lalive d'Epinay, C. et al. 1983. *Vieilleses*. Saint-Saphorine: Editions Georgi.

Knulst, W. P. 1977. *En week tijd*. Staatsuitgeverij—Gravenhage: Sociaal en Cultureel Plan Bureau.

Kuhlen, R. G. 1968. "Developmental Changes in Motivation During the Adult Years." In *Middle Age and Aging*, edited by B. L. Neugarten. Chicago: University of Chicago Press.

Larson, R. 1978. "Thirty Years of Research on the Subjective Well-Being of Older Americans." *Journal of Gerontology* 33(1):109-25.

Lewinsohn, P. M. and D. J. McPhillamy. 1974. "The Relationship Between Age and Engagement in Pleasant Activities." *Journal of Gerontology* 29(3):290-94.

Linton, R. 1942. "Age and Sex Categories." *American Sociological Review* 7:589-603.

Maddox, G. L. 1965. "Fact and Artifact: Evidence Bearing on Disengagement Theory from the Duke Geriatric Project." *Human Development* 8:117-30.

————. 1968. "Persistence of Life Style Among the Elderly: A Longitudinal Study of Patterns of Social Activity in Relation to Life Satisfaction." In *Middle Age and Aging*, edited by B. L. Neugarten. Chicago: University of Chicago Press.

————. and E. B. Douglass. 1974. "Aging and Individual Differences: A Longitudinal Analysis of Social, Psychological and Physiological Indicators." *Journal of Gerontology* 29(5):555-63.

McPherson, B. 1984. "The Meaning and Use of Time Across the Life-Cycle." Keynote address presented at the Canadian Association of Gerontology, Vancouver.

Moss, M. S. 1979. "Meaningfulness of Time Use by Elderly." Paper presented to the National Parks and Recreation Congress, New Orleans.

Nakanishi, N. 1981. "How Do People Spend Their Time Survey." Report on the 1980 survey. Tokyo: Studies of Broadcasting.

Neugarten, B. L. 1964. "A Developmental View of Adult Personality." In *Relations of Development and Aging*, edited by J. E. Birren. Springfield, IL: Charles C Thomas.

————. 1974. "Age Groups in American Society and the Rise of Young-Old." *Annals of the American Academy of Political and Social Science* 415:187-98.

————. and G. O. Hagestad. 1976. "Age and Life Course." In *Handbook of Aging and the Social Sciences*, edited by R. H. Binstock and E. Shanas. New York: Van Nostrand Reinhold.

Neugarten, B. L., R. Havighurst, and S. Tobin. 1961. "The Measurement of Life Satisfaction." *Journal of Gerontology* 16(2):134-43.

Neugarten, B. L. and W. A. Peterson. 1957. "A Study of the American Age-Grade System." *Proceedings of the Fourth Congress of the International Association of Gerontology* 3:497-502.

Office of Economic Policy. 1985. *Ontario Population Projections 1984-2006*. Toronto: Ministry of Treasury and Economics.

Opinion Research Corporation. 1957. *The Public Appraises Movies: A Survey for Motion Picture Association of America*. Vol. 2. Princeton, NJ: Author.

Palmore, E. B. 1968. "The Effects of Aging on Activities and Attitudes." *Gerontologist* 8(3):259-63.

————., B. Burchett, G. Fillenbaum, L. George, and L. Wallman. 1985. *Retirement: Causes and Consequences*. New York: Springer.

Parker, S. 1973. "Leisure and the Elderly." *Society and Leisure* 5(4):49-61.

Parsons, T. 1942. "Age and Sex in the Social Structure of the United States." *American Sociological Review* 7:604-16.

Peppers, L. G. 1976. "Patterns of Leisure and Adjustment to Retirement." *Gerontologist* 16(5):441-46.

Phillips, B. 1957. "A Role Theory Approach to Adjustment in Old Age." *American Sociological Review* 22:212-17.

Ragheb, M. and C. Griffith. 1980. "The Contribution of Leisure Participation and Leisure Satisfaction to the Life Satisfaction of Older Persons." Paper presented at SPRE Research Symposium, Phoenix.

Reichard, S., F. Livson, and P. G. Peterson. 1968. "Adjustment in Retirement." In *Middle Age and Aging*, edited by B. L. Neugarten. Chicago: University of Chicago Press.

Riegel, K., R. Riegel, and G. Meyer. 1967. "Socio-Psychological Factors of Aging: A Cohort-Sequential Analysis." *Human Development* 10:27-56.

Robinson, J. 1984. "Weighted Mean Hours per Week by Age: 87 Activities and 10 Subtotals." Unpublished manuscript.

————. 1985. "Changes in Time Use: An Historical Overview." In *Time, Goods and Well-Being*, edited by F. T. Juster and F. P. Stafford. Ann Arbor: University of Michigan, Institute for Social Research.

Rosow, I. 1961. "Retirement Housing and Social Integration." *Gerontologist* 1(2):85-91.

Roy, C. 1982. "Place des activites culturelles dans la vie quotidienne des Francais." Paris: INSEE.

Schliewen, R. E. 1977. "A Leisure Study: Canada 1975." Ottawa: Comstat Services.

Service des Etudes et Recherches. 1982. "Pratiques Culturelles des Francais." Paris: Ministere de la Culture.

Shanas, E., P. Townsend, D. Wedderburn, J. Friis, P. Hilhoj, and J. Stehower. 1968. *Older People in Three Industrial Societies.* New York: Atherton.

Sinnott, J. D. 1977. "Sex-Role Inconstancy, Biology and Successful Aging." *Gerontologist* 17:459-63.

Special Senate Committee on Retirement Policies. 1979. *Retirement Without Tears.* Ottawa, Canada: Author.

Spieth, W. 1965. "Slowness of Task Performance and Cardiovascular Disease." In *Behavior, Aging and the Nervous System: Biological Determinants of Speed of Behavior and Its Changes with Age*, edited by A. T. Welford and J. E. Birren. Springfield, IL: Charles C Thomas.

Spreitzer, E. and E. E. Snyder. 1974. "Correlates of Life Satisfaction Among the Aged." *Journal of Gerontology* 29(4):454-58.

Statistics Canada. 1973. *A Leisure Study: Canada 1972.* Ottawa: Department of the Secretary of State, Arts and Culture Branch.

————. 1975. *Survey of Participation in Selected Leisure Activities.* Ottawa: Author.

————. 1981. *National Time Use Pilot Study.* Ottawa: Author.

————. 1984. *The Elderly in Canada.* Ottawa: Author.

Tourism and Outdoor Recreation Planning Study. 1974. *Ontario Recreation Survey Progress.* Vol. 2. Toronto: Queen's Park.

————. 1978. *Ontario Recreation Survey Tourism and Recreational Behaviour of Ontario Residents.* Vol. 4. Toronto: Queen's Park.

Videbock, R. and A. B. Knox. 1965. "Alternative Participatory Responses to Aging." In *Older People and Their World*, edited by A. M. Rose and W. A. Peterson. Philadelphia: F. A. Davis.

Wilensky, H. 1961. "Life Cycle, Work Situation and Participation in Formal Associations." In *Aging and Leisure: A Research Perspective into the Meaningful Use of Time*, edited by R. W. Kleemeier. New York: Oxford University Press.

Williams, R. H. 1963. "Styles of Life and Successful Aging." In *Process of Aging*, edited by W. Donahue, R. Williams, and C. Tibbitts. New York: Atherton.

Zborowski, M. 1962. "Aging and Recreation." *Journal of Gerontology* 17(3):302-9.

Zuzanek, J. 1978. "Social Differences in Leisure Behavior: Measurement and Interpretation." *Leisure Sciences* 1(3):271-93.

————. 1979. "Leisure and Cultural Participation as a Function of Life-Cycle." Paper presented at the annual meeting of the Canadian Sociology and Anthropology Association, Saskatoon.

————. 1981-1982. *Survey of Uses of Time Among Older Adults.* Unpublished survey.

————. 1984. *Study of Leisure and Cultural Participation of Urban Canadians.* Unpublished survey.

————. 1985. "Time-Budget Research: Methodological Problems and Perspectives." Paper presented at the conference "Time as a Human Resource," Saskatoon.

————. and T. Stewart. 1983. "Mass Media and Art Participation: Quantitative Dimensions and Life-Cycle Variations." Report submitted to the Department of Communications, Ottawa.

8

Sociodemographic Factors and Variations in the Allocation of Time in Later Life

Aged Japanese Canadians

K. VICTOR UJIMOTO

There is a growing body of literature on activity patterns and general well-being of the aged (Hoyt et al., 1980; Herzog and Rodgers, 1981; McClelland, 1982; Seleen, 1982; Moss and Lawton, 1982; Soumerai and Avorn, 1983; Windley and Scheidt, 1983; Hooker and Ventis, 1984; Golant, 1984; Altergott, 1985). Very little attention, however, has been given to differences in the patterns of daily activities by aged ethnic minorities. Furthermore, with the exception of the Moss and Lawton (1982) and Altergott (1985) studies, the methodology employed to obtain data on various activities did not take into account the frequency and duration of activities. In this chapter, we will examine selected aspects of daily life of a particular ethnic minority, the aged Japanese Canadians, to see if there are any generational and occupational status differences in the allocation of time to various activities. In order to secure our answers, we will utilize time-budget data obtained from a

AUTHOR'S NOTE: An earlier version of this chapter was presented at the 13th International Congress of Gerontology, New York, July 12-17, 1985. Research and travel support provided by the Social Sciences and Humanities Research Council of Canada (SSHRC), Grant No. 492-81-0006, and the Gerontology Research Centre, University of Guelph, are gratefully acknowledged.

sample of Japanese Canadians who were 65 years of age and over and who resided in both urban and rural areas.

Unlike many other ethnic minorities, aged Japanese Canadians have an extremely unique history. For illustrative purpose, consider the life of Takako Hayashi, who migrated to Canada as a bride when she was only 19 years old. She was educated and socialized in Japan during a period in which Confucian moral ideals were still very strongly emphasized, and thus the dominant cultural values of traditional Japan remained with her throughout her life in Canada. These values, which stressed loyalty, diligence, *gaman* (forbearance), and *enryo* (restraint), enabled Takako to survive the uprooting and incarceration during World War II. Her entire life was devoted to her family of seven children and so she never left home to work elsewhere for money. There was no need to as she was interned to an agricultural relocation project in southern Alberta. Before internment, Takako and her husband operated a prosperous grocery store in Vancouver. It had meant long hours of work; however, it was not as strenuous as the sugar beet farm work that required long hours of toil and labor from dawn until dusk, year after year, where prosperity on the farm was decided by the weather and not by the amount of labor. There was very little one could do about the weather. Internment and relocation did not provide any choice: deportation or repatriation to Japan or interior agricultural or road camps. Canadian citizenship didn't mean very much if one's racial background was the same as that of the enemy. Takako's only consolation was that her family stayed together, unlike many other families that were separated and dispatched to different make work projects across Canada.

There was very little variation in the way of life from year to year. A change in occupation from shopkeeper to farmer required a long period of self-learning, a period of trial and error. Sugar beet crops had to be fertilized and sprayed with insecticides. An incorrect mixture of chemicals or too strong a fertilizer meant crop loss and a further wait until the following year before being able to correct one's mistake. Eventually, when it was time for Takako's eldest son to consider enrollment in a high school, a decision was made to move to an urban center where better educational facilities were available. The sugar beet farm was now very prosperous and the weather had been extremely cooperative in recent years, however, education for her children was sacrificed during the internment years and now it was time to compensate for those lost years.

Leaving the farm, Takako became a full-time housewife and immersed herself in the traditional Japanese house-mother's role. This role continued for over 25 years until all of her seven children completed high school and eventually left home to continue on their own careers. For the *Issei*, or first generation of Japanese immigrants, this general pattern of devotion to the family or to the family occupation is a very common one in which social interaction with others in the community was minimal because of various circumstances. First, it was extremely difficult to converse in English. Unlike today, there were no English as second language facilities. Second, external discrimination and prejudice forced the Japanese to form their own social networks within their own communities as a means of survival. Third, the geographic dispersal of the Japanese further meant that the sense of community and social interaction were extremely limited to special occasions only.

Today, these Issei are now retired, and, therefore, an interesting question arises as to whether or not there are any discernible differences in what they do in time and in space as compared to the *Nisei*, or second generation Japanese Canadian, aged given the vastly different sociodemographic characteristics of the Canadian born and educated. This is an important question to consider as there are relatively few studies that recognize the intergenerational differences in ethnic minority groups. In order to obtain the data for the study, we utilized a time-budget methodology, which provided a record of activities by the aged respondents over a one-week period. In addition, a questionnaire was employed to obtain sociodemographic data as well as information on the various types of jobs held prior to retirement. Finally, the Michalos Satisfaction Instrument was self-administered to ascertain the general well-being of the aged Japanese Canadian respondents.

Time-Budget Methodology in Research on Aging

An excellent overview of the growing literature on time-budget methodology in gerontological research is provided by Little (1984). Little reports that most studies that she reviewed were limited to a 24-hour period. It is recognized by most time-budget methodologists that activity data obtained for only a single 24-hour period is neither representative nor sufficient; however, because of the extreme cooperation and patience required and the subsequent costs involved in data coding and analysis, time-budget studies are often limited to a single day. In the study, respondents were asked to record at regular intervals throughout the day the various primary and secondary activities on the time-budget sheets provided. Because of the variations in daily activities depending on the day of the week, the respondents were asked to complete their time-budget sheets for each day for a whole week.

Typically, time-budget records commenced at midnight and the respondents recorded their primary activity, where it took place, with whom, and if applicable, the secondary activity as well. For example, preparing a meal may be a primary activity and listening to the radio while preparing the meal the secondary activity. The time-budget form employed in the study was a slightly modified version of the form developed by Robinson (1977) in that the time recording technique developed by Leroy and Deliege (1978) was incorporated. This refinement enabled the aged respondents to record the beginning and end of each activity easily. In order to minimize loss of information due to recall difficulties, respondents were encouraged to fill in their time-budget forms as often as possible throughout the day.

There are several distinct advantages in utilizing the time-budget methodology for research on aging. First, in addition to the information on the temporal distribution of daily and weekly human activities, a time-budget methodology provides further information on each of the activities such as the duration, frequency, location, social networks involved, and the sequence of events. Second, because the daily expenditure of time for all primary activities must add up to 24 hours or 1440 minutes, it provides a means through which a comparative analysis of time expenditure for various activities can be made. Changes in the allocation of time over a given period for selective activities may provide valuable information for social policy analysts in developing future policies concerning the aged. For example, the allocation of time to a given activity such as sleeping may differ by age groups as well as by ethnocultural groups. Furthermore, there may be differences in when such an activity may occur, either at sporadic moments throughout the day or as a single nighttime activity. Finally, with time-budget data, the possibility exists for analyzing the allocation of time to various activities in relation to the well-being or subjective state of the individual. An activity may be perceived to be satisfying to an individual—however, which aspects of the activity made it satisfying? Was it the location of the activity or was it the social context in which the activity occurred? As noted by Szalai (1984), the distinction between the main or primary and concomitant activities are at the discretion of the individual; however, the frequency, duration, location of the activity, and the social context or with whom the activity took place will enable us to differentiate between satisfying and nonsatisfying activities.

Sociodemographic Characteristics of Respondents

The present study is based on a sample of Japanese Canadians (N = 374) who were 65 years of age or over and who resided in four major Canadian cities and four relatively rural communities in the Okanagan Valley of British Columbia. Table 8.1 illustrates the distribution of the respondents in the various cities. For historic reasons, a meaningful study of aged Japanese Canadians must take into account the differences in the regional sociodemographic characteristics of Japanese Canadians. On February 24, 1942, Order-in-Council P.C. 1486 was passed by the Canadian government, which empowered the minister of justice "to control the movements of all persons of Japanese origin in certain "protected areas" (Adachi, 1976). The ultimate result was the uprooting and forced removal of all Japanese Canadians from the so-called protected coastal areas of British Columbia. The Canadian order only followed what had already occurred on February 19, 1942, in the United States through Executive Order 9066, which had empowered the War Department to remove Japanese Americans from the Pacific coast (Daniels, 1971).

The government evacuation order dispersed Japanese Canadians across Canada. Although it affected all Japanese Canadians, the severity of the impact on individuals varied. For those in the educational system, it meant a complete disruption of their future aspirations. In those instances in which the men were assigned to labor camps and interior work projects, women and children were left behind "to fend for themselves" (Adachi, 1976). Those who were sent to farm projects in Alberta, Saskatchewan, and Manitoba, however, were usually evacuated as a family. Often, social network ties based on Japanese prefectural origin facilitated the migration and adjustment processes. The more enterprising and entrepreneurial of the group migrated to eastern Canada. Therefore, given the diversity in occupational and social mobility factors associated with Japanese Canadian resettlement patterns, it will be of interest to see if there are any discernible

TABLE 8.1 Aged Japanese Canadians in Various Cities by Sex (N = 383)

City	Sex	
	M (N = 218)	F (N = 165)
	%	%
Montreal	6.0	12.1
Toronto	33.0	40.6
Winnipeg	12.8	12.1
Vancouver	26.6	17.6
Okanagan	21.6	17.6
	100	100

differences in postretirement activities of aged Japanese Canadians.

In order to capture some of this diversity, the sample of respondents was selected from both urban and rural Japanese Canadian communities. One of the most remarkable features of a Japanese Canadian community is the meticulous record of senior citizens that is maintained by the *Issei* (first-generation) community leaders. This enabled us to secure a random sample quite easily for each of the communities selected for the study. A very brief overview of the sociocultural and demographic profile of the sample will now be provided so that a much better appreciation of the time-budget data on the allocation of time to various activities can be obtained.

The aged Japanese Canadian respondents who resided in the farming communities in the Okanagan Valley of British Columbia tended to retain a high degree of traditional cultural values as compared to their urban counterparts. For example, 71.6% of the Okanagan Valley respondents stressed discipline and perseverance as important factors that contributed to their successful aging and well-being. In contrast, discipline and perseverance was noted by only 13.3% of the Montreal respondents, 21.5% of the Winnipeg respondents, and 23.8% of the Vancouver respondents. The retention of traditional values, at least on the discipline and perseverance dimensions, is highly related to the realities of the work environment.

The level of education possessed by the sample of aged Japanese Canadians is illustrated in Table 8.2. From Table 8.2, it can be seen that the overall level of education of both the *Issei* (first or immigrant generation) and *Nisei* (second generation or Canadian born) is relatively high compared to the *Kika Nisei* (or those who were repatriated to Japan and who returned to Canada after the termination of World War II). If we examine the level of education and the number of moves made during and after their internment, it is of interest to note that a relatively high proportion of the respondents who had moved at least four to seven times were clustered in the elementary to junior high school levels. Those who were able to secure at least high school or higher-level education tended to have moved only three times or less. The data also revealed that, as far as educational attainment to the senior matric[1] level was concerned, there was very little difference between male and female respondents. A slightly higher proportion of male respondents than female respondents had a college or university education, however.

Finally, if we examine the level of education as shown in Table 8.2 with reference to internment locations, a relatively high percentage of those respondents who reported no education or less than a junior high school level of education were interned in Hastings Park, B.C., interior road camps, labor camps in Angler and Petawawa, Ontario, and various sugar beet projects in Alberta and Manitoba. Those who were able to obtain a high school, senior matric, or university education were mostly in independent relocation and no internment categories.

Participation in Daily Activities

As noted earlier, we are interested in examining the variations in daily life activities by generational and occupational status differences of aged Japanese Canadians. For the research, the time-budget data collected over a whole week produced a plethora of data and, therefore, we must be selective in our present data analysis. We will limit the discussion to only three types of activity categories, namely, obligatory, discretionary, and discretionary social activities.

The generational variations in the allocation of time to obligatory activities are illustrated in Table 8.3. Because of various daily circumstances, variations in the allocation of time even for obligatory activities are likely to occur and, therefore, the data, which are based on the mean number of hours per week spent on the various activities by the *Issei*, *Nisei*, and *Kika-Nisei*, provide a more representative picture of their activities.

While at first glance it may appear that the allocation of time for obligatory activities is very similar, a closer examination of the data will reveal some interesting differences. The *Issei* tend to spend more time than the *Nisei* (Canadian born) and *Kika-Nisei* (repatriated Canadian born) on such obligatory activities as sleeping, washing up and getting

TABLE 8.2   Level of Education of Aged Japanese Canadians by
Generation (N = 379)

| Level of Education | Generation | | |
	Issei (237) %	Nisei (114) %	Kika-Nisei (27) %
None	18.2	5.2	37.0
1-6 years	30.8	31.6	40.7
7-10 years	38.4	37.7	7.4
11-12 years	9.7	13.2	0
Senior matric	.8	4.4	7.4
College	1.3	1.8	3.7
University	.4	6.1	3.7
Other	.4	0	0
	100	100	100

dressed, breakfast and dinner, toilet and personal hygiene, preparing lunch, washing dishes, medication, and for shower or bath. In contrast, the *Nisei* allocated more time than the *Issei* and *Kika-Nisei* to preparing breakfast and dinner, housekeeping, ironing, shopping, looking after their financial affairs, and on visits to medical centers or to doctor's offices. These differences in the allocation of time tend to reflect both age and health considerations as indicated by the observation that the *Nisei* are more engaged in those activities involving movement or active energy. If this is indeed the case, will this same general pattern hold for discretionary activities as well?

The allocation of time to discretionary activities is provided in Table 8.4. The discretionary activities shown in Table 8.4 follow closely those discretionary activities reported in an earlier study on aged ethnic minorities in France by Ujimoto (1985). From Table 8.4, it can be observed that, with the exception of the allocation of time for daily exercise and visiting the library, the mean number of hours per week spent on sedentary activities by the *Issei* far exceeded that by the *Nisei* and *Kika-Nisei*. The *Issei* spent more time on watching videotapes, listening to radio or stereo, listening to the radio and reading or knitting, listening to records or tapes while reading, writing letters, and taking a nap or resting. The *Nisei* spent more time than did the *Issei* and *Kika-Nisei* on eating out, baking, and traveling, which supports the earlier observations that the *Nisei* tend to be engaged in those activities involving movement and active energy. The *Kika-Nisei* spent the most

TABLE 8.3   Mean Hours Per Week Spent on Obligatory Activities by *Issei, Nisei,* and *Kika-Nisei*

Obligatory Activities	*Issei* (N = 218) Hours	*Nisei* (N = 109) Hours	*Kika-Nisei* (N = 27) Hours
Sleep	55.30	54.76	52.49
Wash up/dress	2.12	2.02	1.75
Prepare breakfast	1.59	1.65	1.14
Breakfast	3.70	3.42	3.44
Wash dishes	.82	.86	.34
Toilet/personal hygiene	5.71	3.81	3.46
Hairdresser/manicure	.28	.39	.40
Barber	.07	.10	.24
Housekeeping	3.35	4.17	2.77
Laundry	.56	.60	.65
Iron	.20	.36	.30
Shop	3.47	3.84	3.84
Prepare lunch	1.35	1.20	.79
Lunch	4.20	3.91	4.50
Wash dishes	.69	.66	.34
Prepare dinner	3.15	3.34	1.70
Dinner	5.77	5.51	5.21
Wash dishes	1.27	1.17	.50
Financial affairs	.19	.50	.39
Visit medical center	.28	.44	.32
Medication	.46	.33	0
Shower/bath	3.51	3.37	2.84
Prepare to sleep	.27	.27	.49

time on such sedentary activities as reading, watching television, and on coffee or tea breaks.

Although there are numerous social and social network activities that can be examined here, we will limit the analysis to the visiting and phoning social network activities. The data are shown in Table 8.5. It can be seen from Table 8.5 that there is a very close similarity in the *Issei* and *Nisei* allocation of time for both visiting and phoning friends. The data reveal, however, that the *Issei* spent more time with relatives who visit them, and also in both phoning and receiving telephone calls from their relatives. This appears to be one good indication of filial network ties. As noted by Sugiman and Nishio (1983), and Osako and Liu (1986), filial piety is one of the many traditional Japanese values that emphasized loyalty to one's parents. Aspects of filial behavior are manifested through social and financial support provided by children to

TABLE 8.4   Mean Hours Per Week Spent on Discretionary Activities by *Issei, Nisei,* and *Kika-Nisei*

Discretionary Activities	*Issei* (N = 218) Hours	*Nisei* (N = 109) Hours	*Kika-Nisei* (N = 27) Hours
Coffee/tea break	2.17	2.29	2.52
Exercise	1.09	.80	.92
Reading	6.37	6.90	7.87
Television	12.20	13.87	18.61
Video	2.21	1.06	1.69
Radio/stereo	1.24	1.12	.81
Radio & reading	.14	.13	.07
Radio & knitting	.76	.67	.19
Record/tape listening & reading	.26	.17	.07
Nap	1.20	.74	.82
Rest	3.26	1.34	1.55
Eat out	.30	.40	.14
Write letters	1.22	.88	1.13
Change to go out	.08	.20	.27
Travel	3.61	4.58	4.94
Visit library	6.46	3.75	.13
Baking	.59	.94	.47

their aged parents. The highest mean hours per week spent in visiting relatives was by the *Kika-Nisei,* which is another indication of the strong kinship ties maintained by the *Kika-Nisei.* This is not surprising if one considers the fact that the *Kika-Nisei* were socialized and educated in Japan during their most formative years, and thus they are most likely to retain certain Japanese traditional values such as *kansha,* or the feeling of gratitude, and *giri,* or moral obligations and responsibility to others.

It was noted earlier in the discussion that the level of education of both the *Issei* and *Nisei* was relatively high compared to that of the *Kika-Nisei.* It was also noted in Table 8.2 that the highest percentage of postsecondary education was held by the *Nisei.* These facts should be kept in the back of our minds when we examine the relationship between the occupational status of the respondents prior to retirement and their allocation of time to various activities. Because of the small sample size in both the professional and the proprietary occupational categories, we have combined these two categories into a single category for the analysis. For similar reasons, we have also combined the clerical and skilled occupational categories together. The data for the allocation of

TABLE 8.5   Mean Hours Per Week Spent on Discretionary Social
Activities by *Issei, Nisei,* and *Kika-Nisei*

Discretionary Social Activities	*Issei* (N = 218) Hours	*Nisei* (N = 109) Hours	*Kika-Nisei* (N = 27) Hours
Visit friends	1.39	1.37	.87
Visit relatives	1.47	1.15	1.90
Visit from friends	1.25	1.34	1.00
Visit from relatives	.93	.81	.29
Phone friends	.57	.57	.48
Phone relatives	.17	.15	.12
Phone call from friends	.26	.33	.32
Phone call from relatives	.12	.11	.09

time to obligatory activities by occupational status of the respondents
prior to their retirement are provided in Table 8.6.

One way in which we can analyze the data in Table 8.6 is to select the
occupational status category that indicates the highest mean hours per
week allocated to each of the obligatory activities. The pattern that
emerges in Table 8.6 is that the unskilled tended to spend the highest
mean hours per week on such obligatory activities as washing up and
getting dressed, breakfast and dinner, toilet and personal hygiene,
washing dishes after dinner, and in taking a shower or bath. The
semiskilled respondents spent the highest mean hours per week on such
obligatory activities as preparing breakfast, housekeeping, laundry,
shopping, lunch, preparing dinner, and on visits to a medical center.
Respondents in the professional and proprietary occupational groups
indicated the highest mean hours per week for sleeping, going to the
barber, lunch, looking after their financial affairs, medication, and in
preparing for sleep. The clerical/skilled group of respondents did not
have a single obligatory activity in which they indicated the highest
mean hours per week.

If we compare the data shown in Table 8.6 to that provided in Table
8.3, it can be seen that a very similar pattern is reflected by the mean
hours per week spent on the various activities by the *Issei* and *Kika-Nisei.* This is hardly surprising given that a very high proportion of the
Issei (36.4%) and *Kika-Nisei* (22.2%) respondents were in the unskilled
occupational category. Similarly, 56% of the *Kika-Nisei* and 45% of the
Issei were in the semiskilled occupational category.

TABLE 8.6 Mean Hours Per Week Spent on Obligatory Activities by Occupational Status Prior to Retirement

Obligatory Activities	Professional/Proprietory (N = 43) Hours	Clerical/Skilled (N = 44) Hours	Semi-skilled (N = 163) Hours	Unskilled (N = 105) Hours
Sleep	57.73	53.29	54.59	56.28
Wash up/dress	1.98	1.99	2.04	2.17
Prepare breakfast	1.28	1.49	1.68	1.58
Breakfast	3.54	3.35	3.50	3.86
Wash dishes	.59	.45	.88	.87
Toilet/personal hygiene	4.70	4.15	4.38	6.26
Hairdresser/manicure	.23	.44	.45	.11
Barber	.15	.02	.10	.09
Housekeeping	2.98	3.75	4.00	3.06
Laundry	.45	.56	.80	.30
Iron	.16	.12	.37	.18
Shop	3.18	3.82	3.88	3.29
Prepare lunch	.85	.81	1.47	1.29
Lunch	4.50	3.88	3.89	4.47
Wash dishes	.60	.40	.66	.79
Prepare dinner	1.83	2.59	3.48	3.26
Dinner	5.68	5.43	5.45	6.01
Wash dishes	.73	1.08	1.34	1.18
Financial affairs	.57	.39	.35	.09
Visit medical center	.34	.36	.38	.23
Medication	.52	.31	.30	.49
Shower/bath	3.23	3.16	3.41	3.61
Prepare to sleep	.34	.31	.31	.21

The mirror image provided in the comparison of the data in Table 8.3 and Table 8.6 is not so pronounced when we examine the mean hours spent on discretionary activities in relation to one's occupational status prior to retirement. Those in the unskilled and semiskilled occupational categories spent the highest mean hours per week on coffee and tea breaks, daily exercises, watching video, listening to the radio and knitting, taking a nap, resting, writing letters, and visiting a library. This allocation of time to discretionary activities by various occupational status is illustrated in Table 8.7.

In contrast to the data presented in Table 8.6, it is of interest to note that, for discretionary activities, those respondents in the clerical/skilled occupational category had the highest mean hours per week for several activities such as reading, watching television, listening to the radio or stereo, listening to the radio and reading, listening to records or tapes and reading, eating out, changing to go out, and in traveling. For discretionary activities, those in the professional/proprietary occupational category did not have a single discretionary activity in which they had the highest mean hours spent per week. A vastly different picture emerges, however, when we examine the data for discretionary social activities. This is shown in Table 8.8.

From the data provided in Table 8.8, it can be observed that the highest mean hours spent per week on discretionary social activities are by those in the professional/proprietary occupational category. These discretionary social activities include visiting relatives, having friends or relatives visit, phoning friends, and receiving phone calls from friends. For discretionary social activities, those in the unskilled occupational category did not have a single activity in which they had the highest mean hours per week.

Summary and Conclusion

Our examination of the weekly mean amounts of time for obligatory, discretionary, and discretionary social activities in terms of generational and occupational status differences of aged Japanese Canadians yielded several interesting findings. The allocation of time for obligatory activities with respect to generational differences indicated that the Issei tended to spend more time on sedentary activities. While this observation may be a reflection of both age and health considerations associated with the *Issei* respondents who are much older than the *Nisei* and

TABLE 8.7 Mean Hours Per Week Spent on Discretionary Activities by Occupational Status Prior to Retirement

Discretionary Activities	Professional/Proprietory (N = 43) Hours	Clerical/Skilled (N = 44) Hours	Semi-skilled (N = 163) Hours	Unskilled (N = 105) Hours
Coffee/tea break	1.91	2.10	1.85	3.02
Exercise	.80	.98	.84	1.27
Reading	7.43	8.41	6.48	5.88
Television	11.87	15.44	13.70	12.11
Video	1.48	.94	1.44	2.89
Radio/stereo	1.17	1.72	.99	1.23
Radio & reading	.05	.20	.11	.18
Radio & knitting	.32	.13	1.11	.43
Record/tape listening & reading	.15	.31	.16	.30
Nap	1.05	.69	.87	1.41
Rest	2.34	2.15	2.34	3.06
Eat out	.34	.43	.39	.17
Write letters	.73	.64	1.30	1.14
Change to go out	.09	.26	.16	.06
Travel	4.05	5.42	4.15	3.15
Visit library	3.28	3.23	5.21	6.66
Baking	.45	.44	1.09	.30

TABLE 8.8 Mean Hours Per Week Spent on Discretionary Social Activities by Occupational Status Prior to Retirement

Discretionary Social Activities	Professional/Proprietory (N = 43) Hours	Clerical/Skilled (N = 44) Hours	Semi-skilled (N = 163) Hours	Unskilled (N = 105) Hours
Visit friends	.99	1.89	1.39	1.17
Visit relatives	1.54	1.36	1.47	1.25
Visit from friends	2.16	.91	1.18	1.16
Visit from relatives	1.08	.32	.87	.91
Phone friends	.85	.28	.69	.37
Phone relatives	.10	.09	.24	.11
Phone call from friends	.45	.13	.32	.23
Phone call from relatives	.11	.06	.16	.08

Kika-Nisei, it was also noted that the *Issei* spent more time on daily exercise than did the *Nisei* or *Kika-Nisei*.

In order to account for this observation, the following explanation is provided. The aged *Issei* themselves may have recognized the sedentary nature of their daily lives, and, therefore, they made a conscious effort to engage in some daily exercise. If such is indeed the case, then we must exercise some caution in how we code the data. For the *Issei*, daily exercise may be perceived as an obligatory and necessary function. In contrast, the active nature of daily life for the *Nisei* and *Kika-Nisei* may not make it necessary for them to engage in any special daily exercise, and hence such activity will receive less priority. In this latter case, exercise as an activity can be perceived as a discretionary activity.

The nature of the brief discussion above illustrates the need to examine all available time-budget data for the week before making any conclusive statements. Our present discussion is based on a limited set of daily activities that obviously did not include recreational or leisure activities. Here again, data coding problems can emerge because recreational activities such as tennis, bowling, jogging, and even going for a walk may be considered as an important or required component of one's overall health or exercise program. In this regard, future studies should ask the respondents to indicate those recreational activities that they consider to be a part of their overall exercise program and not just for leisure or relaxation.

Another observation to be noted with reference to obligatory activities concerns the mean hours per week spent on visiting a medical center or a doctor's office. While it has been observed that the sedentary nature of *Issei* activities probably reflected both their age and their health considerations, this observation is supported only by the fact that the *Issei* spent the highest mean hours per week on medication. The data shown in Table 8.3, however, indicate that the *Issei* spent the least amount of time per week visiting a medical center or a doctor's office. One reason for this stems from the fact that the *Issei* are not fluent in English and this acts as a barrier to effective communication. As a result, there is some reluctance to visit a doctor unless accompanied by an interpreter, usually one's son or daughter, who is able to convey the intended message to the family doctor.

An evaluation of the amount of time spent by the *Issei* at a medical center or at a doctor's office may not be a very good indicator of their health status. The role of the retention of traditional Japanese values will also have to be examined. It will be recalled the *Issei* were socialized in Japan according to a strict Confucian philosophy (Osako and Liu, 1986). Furthermore, as noted by Sugiman and Nishio (1983), the *Issei* were also socialized according to certain traditional Japanese values such as *enryo*, or modesty. Encompassed within the norm of *enryo* are other behavioral codes such as reserve, reticence, self-effacement, self-reliance, humility, hesitation, and denigration. There is one other extremely important behavioral code that has a significant bearing on the present discussion and that is the concept of *gaman*. Kobata (1979) defines *gaman* as forbearance or the tendency to suppress emotions, to bear pain or suffer in silence. Therefore, a combination of these behavioral codes interact to influence the *Issei* ways of thinking and behaving. Consequently, there is some hesitancy on the part of the *Issei* when it comes to visiting a doctor's office and a tendency to bear pain or suffer in silence and to seek relief from known medication or herbal remedies.

Filial concerns for the well-being of the aged *Issei* appear to be manifested quite strongly in the data (Table 8.5) as indicated by the mean hours per week spent with visiting relatives or on phoning relatives. This pattern of social interaction with relatives parallels Ishizuka's (1978) observation that the aged Japanese Americans consistently turned to their family members when requiring various types of assistance.

When we examine the time-budget data for selected obligatory, discretionary, and discretionary social activities in terms of the respondent's occupational status prior to retirement, there is a very close similarity to the time allocation pattern that we had observed earlier when we examined the generational differences in the allocation of time to various activities. Although this similarity can stem from the very high correspondence in occupational status with generational differences, it remains for a multivariate analysis of the complete time-budget data in order to secure a more accurate and meaningful relationship of the various factors involved.

NOTE

1. In the Canadian school system, senior matric is the 13th grade in high school and equivalent to the first year of University.

REFERENCES

Adachi, Ken. 1976. *The Enemy That Never Was: A History of the Japanese Canadians.* Toronto: McClelland and Stewart.

Altergott, Karen. 1985. "Marriage Gender and Social Relations in Late Life." Pp. 51-70 in *Social Bonds in Later Life*, edited by Warren A. Peterson and Jill Quadagno. Beverly Hills, CA: Sage.

Daniels, Roger. 1971. *Concentration Camps USA: Japanese Americans and World War II.* New York: Holt, Rinehart & Winston.

Golant, Stephen M. 1984. "Factors Influencing the Nighttime Activity of Old Persons in Their Community." *Journal of Gerontology* 39:485-91.

Herzog, Anna Regula and Willard L. Rodgers. 1981. "The Structure of Subjective Well-Being in Different Age Groups." *Journal of Gerontology* 36:472-79.

Hooker, Karen and Deborah G. Ventis. 1984. "Work Ethic, Daily Activities, and Retirement Satisfaction." *Journal of Gerontology* 39:478-84.

Hoyt, Danny R., Marvin A. Kaiser, George R. Peters, and Nicholas Babchuk. 1980. "Life Satisfaction and Activity Theory: A Multidimensional Approach." *Journal of Gerontology* 35:935-41.

Ishizuka, Karen C. 1978. *The Elder Japanese.* San Diego, CA: Campanile Press.

Kobata, Fran. 1979. "The Influence of Culture on Family Relations: The Asian American Experience." Pp. 94-106 in *Aging Parents*, edited by Pauline K. Ragan. Los Angeles: University of California Press.

Leroy, X. and D. Deliege. 1978. "Time Budget of the Belgian Physician Nowadays and in Future." Paper presented at the 9th World Congress of Sociology, Uppsala, Sweden.

Little, Virginia C. 1984. "An Overview of Research Using the Time-Budget Methodology to Study Age-related Behaviour." *Aging and Society* 4:3-20.

McClelland, Kent A. 1982. "Self-Conception and Life Satisfaction: Integrating Aged Subculture and Activity Theory." *Journal of Gerontology* 37:723-32.

Moss, Miriam S. and M. Powell Lawton. 1982. "Time Budgets of Older People: A Window on Four Lifestyles." *Journal of Gerontology* 37:115-23.

Osako, Masako M. and William T. Liu. 1986. "Intergenerational Relations and the Aged Among Japanese Americans." *Research on Aging* 8:128-55.

Robinson, John P. 1977. *Changes in Americans' Use of Time: 1965-1975.* Cleveland: Cleveland State University, Communications Research Center.

Seleen, Diane R. 1982. "The Congruence Between Actual and Desired Use of Time by Older Adults: A Predictor of Life Satisfaction." *Gerontologist* 22:95-99.

Soumerai, Stephen B. and Jerry Avorn. 1983. "Perceived Health, Life Satisfaction, Activity in Urban Elderly: A Controlled Study of the Impact of Part-Time Work." *Journal of Gerontology* 38:356-62.

Sugiman, Pamela and H. K. Nishio. 1983. "Socialization and Cultural Duality Among Aging Japanese Canadians." *Canadian Ethnic Studies* 15:17-35.

Szalai, Alexander. 1984. "The Concept of Time Budget Research." Pp. 17-34 in *Time Budget Research: An ISSC Workbook in Comparative Analysis,* edited by Andrew S. Harvey et al. Frankfurt: Campus Verlag.

Ujimoto, K. Victor. 1985. "The Allocation of Time to Social and Leisure Activities as Social Indicators for the Integration of Aged Ethnic Minorities." *Social Indicators Research* 17:253-66.

Windley, Faul G. and Rick J. Scheidt. 1983. "Service Utilization and Activity Partici-
    pation Among Psychologically Vulnerable and Well Elderly in Rural Small Towns."
    Gerontologist 23:283-87.

9

Daily Life in
Later Life in the
Changing Japanese Context

SHUICHI WADA

A Day in the
Life of a Japanese Couple

Mr. A is 66 years of age, and is now employed by a rather small business corporation as a part-time manager. He is assigned to work at his office three days a week. He started his occupational career, just after graduating from college, on the accounting staff in a business department in a big corporation, and became a section head in the corporation. He left the corporation at the age of 58 due to mandatory retirement, and he was advised by the manager to work at the current corporation. Mrs. A is 62 years of age; she has followed the way of life of her generation and has had no paid job. Her major focus in life has been domestic problems, and even today family problems are her primary concern.

They have two sons (39 and 33 years old) and a daughter (30), all of whom graduated from college. The eldest son's family is living in a house that is built in the same yard as Mr. and Mrs. A's house. The younger son and the daughter are living in distant towns. Mr. and Mrs. A and the eldest son's family have, in an economic sense, mutually independent life-styles, but they consider themselves a single, big extended family. The members of the two families not only have very intimate human relationships but also share domestic tasks. It is, for example, Mr. and Mrs. A's (especially Mrs. A's) task to take care of the eldest son's little children when he and his wife, who is a teacher in high school, are away at work. The eldest son and his wife regard it as their task to support their old parents emotionally and to take care of them in the case of long-term or short-term illness.

Today, because Mr. A is free from his work, he used his time by tending dwarf trees in the morning, and he had a few guests over to play "Go." Until he was around 60 years old, he often played golf on holidays, but he feels too tired these days to visit a rather distant golf course. When the eldest son's little children came home from their schools, he played with them, too. It was Mrs. A who enjoyed the children's company. This is because Mrs. A had had nothing but domestic chores while her husband had his hobbies. She sometimes complains, but she regards it natural for women of her generation not to have hobbies.

At night, it is very usual for Mr. and Mrs. A to spend their time watching TV. Because they have a couple of TV sets, it is not at all a problem that they have quite different orientations to TV programs. The little children sometimes visit them and play some indoor games with them, but their mother prefers them not to do so. Grandparents are often overindulgent to grandchildren. Even little boys and girls are, in current Japan, expected to study hard to pass entrance examinations (to high school, college, and so on). In addition to academic study, they have many daily tasks to accomplish, such as piano lessons.

Instead of the children tonight, the eldest son and his wife visited Mr. and Mrs. A. In the conversation, the son's wife, who was trained in psychology at college, recommended that Mr. A and Mrs. A join some organization in the community to have fun with a wider range of persons. She thinks it is necessary for any person, especially an elderly one, not to confine themselves to family life. Mr. and Mrs. A, however, hesitated to join such associations. Neither of them has had such experience outside of family or occupation. This tendency is quite common for their generation today.

Daily Life in Later Years

Two topics that reflect the unique aspects of Japanese society are the family life of the elderly seen from the perspective of intergenerational relationships and exchanges, and occupational life in the later life stage in relation to the retirement process.

The sociocultural background of the family lives and occupational lives of elderly Japanese is going to change drastically, as is the demographic structure of the entire Japanese population. These changes are going to modify both the life-style and the life consciousness of the older members of Japanese society. A sketch of Japanese life in the later years and a description of changing demographic structure provide background for understanding the family, work life, and life-style of Japanese elders.

We will, first, take a look at the Japanese people's allocation of time in later life to various activities on weekdays and Sunday.[1] While Tables 9.1 and 9.2 make comparisons between the years 1970 and 1980, between the sexes, among age strata, and between weekdays and Sunday, we will focus only on differences between men and women.

The time allocation comparison shows us that the division of roles between the sexes, with the occupational role for men and the domestic role for women, was marked in 1970 and remained so in 1980. In the case of men, 8 hours on the average were allocated to paid work on weekdays by those in their fifties and 6 hours and 36 minutes by men in their sixties in 1970. In 1980, 7 hours and 23 minutes were allocated to work for wages by men in their fifties, 4 hours and 58 minutes in the age strata of the sixties, and 2 hours and 43 minutes in the strata of the seventies or over. The time spent on unpaid housework by men never exceeded one and a half hours. The longest time spent on housework was one hour and 14 minutes in the age strata of the sixties on Sundays in 1980.

On the other hand, the longest time expended for work for wages for women was 4 hours and 34 minutes spent by women in their fifties on weekdays in 1970, and the second longest allocation was 3 hours 56 minutes in the age strata of the fifties on weekdays in 1980. In all other cases, the women spent less than 3 hours on paid work. Women, however, spent much more time on unpaid weekday housework: 4 hours and 54 minutes by women in their fifties, and 5 hours and 20 minutes in their sixties in 1970, and in 1980: 5 hours and 10 minutes in their fifties, 5 hours and 12 minutes in their sixties, and 3 hours and 38 minutes in their seventies or over.

The figures clearly show that Japanese men expend almost twice as much time on paid work as women do, while women spend three to five times as much time on housework as men do. This indicates that considerable differentiation by sex in role distribution is still present

TABLE 9.1   Japanese Males' Daily Time Allocation in the Middle and Later Life Stages by Sex, Age Strata, and Day, 1970 and 1980 (unit hours:minutes)

| | 1970 | | | | | | 1980 | | | | | |
| | 50-59[a] | | 60-69 | | 70 & over[d] | | 50-59 | | 60-69 | | 70 & over | |
Activity	W[b]	S	W	S	W	S	W	S	W	S	W	S
N[c]	320	198	241	159	—	—	1938	1740	1236	1084	724	644
Sleep	7:55	8:30	8:18	8:51	—	—	8:01	8:51	8:28	9:00	9:24	9:38
Eating	1:35	1:37	1:37	1:39	—	—	1:36	1:41	1:40	1:43	1:43	1:39
Personal care	:59	:59	:58	:57	—	—	1:03	:57	1:02	:57	:57	:57
Paid work	8:00	5:08	6:36	4:05	—	—	7:23	3:00	4:58	2:34	2:34	1:14
Education[e]	:00	:01	:00	:00	—	—	:01	:00	:00	:00	:00	:00
Housework	:31	:57	:56	1:07	—	—	:29	1:05	:59	1:14	1:06	1:06
Social intercourse[f]	:46	:58	:38	1:04	—	—	:34	1:21	:40	1:13	:42	1:12
Rest[g]	:40	:44	:50	1:02	—	—	:42	:45	:58	:54	1:18	1:20
Hobbies & leisure	:19	1:11	:32	1:12	—	—	:27	1:21	:44	1:08	:56	1:13
Transportation	:43	:27	:32	:20	—	—	1:06	:42	:46	:30	:29	:25
Reading[h]	:37	:42	:37	:37	—	—	:49	:55	:55	:51	:52	:57
Radio	:17	:14	:26	:29	—	—	:35	:30	:29	:26	:28	:24
TV	3:10	4:14	3:39	4:00	—	—	3:14	4:39	4:06	5:14	4:57	5:06

SOURCE: NHK (1970, 1980).

a. Age strata (*e.g., 50- to 59-year-olds).
b. W: weekdays; S: Sunday.
c. Shows the number of pertinent activities.
d. No data available for 70 and older in 1970.
e. Education: both at school and other places.
f. Social intercourse: both with friends and acquaintances.
g. Rest: both for relaxation and medical treatment.
h. Reading: includes newspapers, magazines, and books.

TABLE 9.2 Japanese Females' Daily Time Allocation in the Middle and Later Life Stages by Sex, Age Strata, and Day, 1970 and 1980 (unit hours:minutes)

	1970 50-59[a]		1970 60-69		1970 70 & over[d]		1980 50-59		1980 60-69		1980 70 & over	
Activity	W[b]	S	W	S	W	S	W	S	W	S	W	S
N[c]	340	235	235	182	—	—	2030	2034	1388	1251	869	785
Sleep	7:40	8:00	8:09	8:45	—	—	7:31	8:12	8:09	8:40	9:13	9:38
Eating	1:38	1:38	1:40	1:45	—	—	1:42	1:44	1:41	1:47	1:40	1:46
Personal care	:57	:57	:55	:49	—	—	1:01	1:03	:58	:57	:55	:56
Paid work	4:34	2:46	2:51	2:38	—	—	3:56	1:48	2:14	1:19	1:13	:37
Education[e]	:01	:00	:00	:00	—	—	:01	:00	:00	:00	:00	:00
Housework	4:54	5:22	5:20	4:17	—	—	5:10	5:20	5:12	4:36	3:38	3:29
Social intercourse[f]	:43	1:20	:51	1:13	—	—	:40	1:16	:48	1:26	:59	1:05
Rest[g]	:34	:38	:54	:43	—	—	:35	:32	:51	:45	1:43	1:33
Hobbies & leisure	:16	:29	:18	:32	—	—	:31	:46	:37	:44	:32	:39
Transportation	:22	:16	:12	:10	—	—	:33	:33	:22	:24	:14	:14
Reading[h]	:21	:17	:17	:09	—	—	:27	:24	:25	:22	:19	:19
Radio	:27	:10	:12	:12	—	—	:35	:25	:21	:12	:20	:15
TV	3:57	4:20	4:25	4:37	—	—	4:31	4:40	5:06	4:54	5:03	5:02

SOURCE: NHK (1970, 1980).

a. Age strata (*e.g., 50- to 59-year-olds).
b. W: weekdays; S: Sunday.
c. Shows the number of pertinent activities.
d. No data available for 70 and older in 1970.
e. Education: both at school and other places.
f. Social intercourse: both with friends and acquaintances.
g. Rest: both for relaxation and medical treatment.
h. Reading: includes newspapers, magazines, and books.

within the middle and elderly generations.[2]

Looking at 1980, a comparison of men's and women's social intercourse, or interaction with nonfamily members, shows that, while a tendency for women to spend a longer time than men of the same age for this category of activity could be seen, the difference between the sexes is not large. Both men and women today have almost the same frequency and density of social intercourse.

Second, the comparison between the age groups on social intercourse shows that the time spent on this activity is longer for the older age strata than for the younger one for both men and women. Even today middle-aged Japanese are not good at the cultivation of human relationships outside of occupational or family life. Elderly people have more free time than middle-aged people.

Third, a comparison between the years 1970 and 1980 does not show a marked difference in either sex or age strata. The time span of ten years is not long enough to change people's life-style in a society.

Finally, let us examine the amount of time spent watching TV. The time allocated to TV increased greatly between 1970 and 1980 for both men and women in each age stratum. This tendency could be interpreted as due to technological advances in such mass media, such as an increase in the variety of broadcasts and the remarkable decrease in the cost of ownership. On the other hand, however, it shows that it is TV that predominately attracts people's interest in later life. The image of those elderly people who are watching TV for a long time in a day is not a healthy one. It could be accompanied by the experience of loneliness.

Family Life

Table 9.3 shows the ratio of those elderly people who are living with their spouse, married son, married daughter, child's spouse, unmarried children, and/or grandchildren, and also indicates the ratio of elderly who are living alone in Japan, Thailand, the United States, the United Kingdom, and France.[3] The table reveals that the dominant pattern of family life for the elderly in the United States, the United Kingdom, and France is to live with a spouse or to live alone. In Thailand, it is typical to live with a married daughter or son. The dominant pattern in Japan is to live with a married son and grandchildren. In other words, the prevailing household types in the later life stage are the conjugal family or single-member household in European or American society, but it is the extended family household in Japan and Thailand.

TABLE 9.3   Household Composition of the Elderly (percentages)

Living with	Japan	Thailand	United States	United Kingdom	France
Spouse	65.4	51.1	47.0	49.1	55.8
Married son	41.0	25.3	0.9	0.5	3.5
Married daughter	9.2	37.8	2.5	1.9	5.6
Child's spouse	34.0	49.2	1.6	0.7	3.5
Unmarried children	18.7	33.0	9.0	5.1	10.6
Grandchildren	41.0	62.6	3.8	1.1	5.8
Alone	5.7	4.7	41.3	41.6	30.0

SOURCE: Prime Minister's Office (1982, p. 7).
NOTE: Multiple answers.

The Japanese family system for people in the later life stage is, however, different from that in Thailand. The guiding principle in Japan is that a married son lives with his old parents. In Japan, 41% of the elderly live with a married son and 9.2% with a married daughter, but there seems to be little preference to a son and daughter in Thailand, where 25.3% of the elderly live with a married son and 37.8% with a married daughter. That is, the Japanese family descends on a unilateral male line, but the Thai family descends on a bilateral line.

Many of the elderly people in Japan are not only in fact living with married children and grandchildren, but also regard it as desirable to live together with younger generations. The Prime Minister's Office survey of the elderly (1982) also shows that 59% of the total subjects in Japan and 59% in Thailand were of the opinion that "it is best for the whole family (old parents, their children and grandchildren, etc.) to live together." On the contrary, in the United States, the United Kingdom, and France, this opinion was held by only 6.5%, 6.1%, and 11.6%, respectively, of respondents. The opinion that "it is best for the younger and older members of the family to meet occasionally for meals and a chat" was held by many respondents in these three countries.

Work-Oriented Life and Retirement

The 13 categories of behavior in Tables 9.1 and 9.2 could be grouped into three clusters: behaviors gratifying basic human needs ("sleep," "eating," "personal care," and "rest"); those strongly correlated with social role ("paid work," "education," and "housework"); and behaviors engaged in for pleasure ("social intercourse," "hobbies and leisure," "reading," "radio," and "TV").[4] A third distinguishing characteristic of the life-style of the Japanese elderly can be found in time allocation among these three categories of behavior. That is, when we compare the second category of behavior, role activity, and the third category, a kind of pastime, we notice that the elderly in Japan still use more of their time for the second category of behavior than for the third one (except for watching TV).

The proportion of people 65 or older in the labor force is very high in Japan relative to other industrialized countries. According to the Economic Planning Agency (1984, p. 167), the ratio of participation in the labor force in the age strata of 65 years or older is 19.1% in the United States, 7.4% in the United Kingdom, 8.2% in France, and 14.3% in the age strata of 65 to 69 years and 5.5% in the strata of 70 years or older in England, but it is 41.0% in Japan. This macro-structure of engagement in the labor force in Japan is sustained by the individual elderly person's high job motivation. Many Japanese elderly were and still are eager to remain in the labor force in later life regardless of their socioeconomic status.

The Prime Minister's Office (1982) compared figures on the distribution of opinions of the elderly on retirement age in each sex and in each of five countries. The figures indicate a similar opinion about the ideal retirement age in each country except Japan. The ideal retirement age is about 60 years in Thailand, the United Kingdom, and France, and about 65 years in the United States. In Japan, opinions are split between two ages (men placed the ideal retirement age at about 65 or about 70, and women at about 60 or about 65). The difference between men and women suggests the existence of sex roles; and the fact that a retirement age of 70 is supported by about 30% of all male subjects could be interpreted as proof of Japanese elderly people's high motivation for their jobs.

Social Life

Table 9.4 highlights some features of Japanese elderly people's social activities. First, compared to other countries, very few Japanese elderly people frequently engage in religious activities. Only 10.9% of Japanese males "often" or "sometimes" engage in religious activities, and only 14.9% of females. In Thailand, the comparable figures are 84.2% and 88.8%; in the United States, 59.3% and 67.0%; in the United Kingdom,

TABLE 9.4 Participation in Activities by the Elderly in Five Countries by Sex (percentages)

	Japan		Thailand		United States		United Kingdom		France	
	Male	Female	Male	Female	Male	Female	Male	Female	Male	Female
Political activities	8.8	3.0	74.3	53.4	23.7	20.1	7.3	4.9	4.8	1.2
Religious activities	10.9	14.9	84.2	88.8	59.3	67.0	26.1	45.3	18.5	36.3
Evening courses	7.7	4.7	13.0	5.7	16.9	20.8	2.4	5.2	1.3	.6
Social gatherings	6.9	5.4	26.2	18.5	63.4	71.3	43.0	43.7	37.3	31.9
Clubs/hobby groups	8.7	16.5	11.6	5.3	40.3	46.8	35.2	32.5	20.5	17.2
Participative sports	10.1	4.5	8.8	3.5	27.7	13.9	16.8	3.6	11.5	5.7
Community volunteer activities	21.1	8.1	28.3	13.7	28.9	30.1	12.0	14.1	17.3	15.5
Group activities (at day centers and so on)	21.9	27.3	7.9	4.0	31.0	33.8	7.1	11.3	22.3	23.3

SOURCE: Prime Minister's Office (1982); formulated by reconstruction of cross-tabulations of Appendix 3.
NOTICE: The figures show the percentage of people who chose "Often" or "Sometimes." Political activities in Thailand includes voting and membership into Villagee Scouts, a political organization found in each village.

26.1% and 45.3%; and in France, 18.5% and 36.3%.

Second, very few Japanese elderly attend social gatherings either, with only 6.9% of men and 5.4% of women often or sometimes attending social gatherings. In Thailand, the figures are 26.2% and 18.5%; in the United States, 63.4% and 71.3%; in the United Kingdom, 43.0% and 43.7%; and in France, 37.3% and 31.9%.

Third, few elderly Japanese play sports: men, 10.1%, and women, 4.5%. The figures are also low in Thailand: 8.8% and 3.5%, but in the United States, the figures are 40.3% and 46.8%; in the United Kingdom, 35.2% and 32.5%; in France, 20.5% and 17.2%.

Some of the characteristics of the Japanese people's later life could be summarized as follows: first, sex differences in social roles should not be neglected, because a major part of men's later life includes their occupational life, and the life of women cannot be discussed without reference to their family life. Second, many elderly Japanese are indifferent to religion, and are not involved in social activities in general.

Current and Future Demographic Change in Japan

The aging of the total population is making a steady and rapid advance in Japan. In *Future Populations Projections* for Japan published by the Institute of Population Problems, Ministry of Health and Welfare, Japan, the following changes in the Japanese population structure are predicted:

a) Total Population

 The total population in Japan was 116.92 million, and it is projected to reach 122.83 million in 1990, 128.12 million in 2000, and to peak in 2008 at 130.36 million. The total population will steadily decrease for 60 years after the peak, and will then stabilize at around 118.40 million.

b) Age Structure of Total Population

 The aging of the population will progress quite rapidly. The percentage of the aged population (65 years old or over) will be 15.6% in 1990, 19.8% in 2000, and reach a peak of 21.8%. The percentage will decrease after the peak for some time, and will increase again to a second peak of 22.2% in 2043.

On the other hand, the percentage of the youth population (under 15 years old), which was 23.6% in 1980, will decrease to 17.1% by 1996. After that, it will range between 16% and 19%.

The youth population has always outnumbered the aged population in the Japanese population, but in 2009, in which the percentage of the youth population will be 18.4% and that of the aged population, 18.7%, the relationship will be inverted.

The percentage of the working-age population, which will increase from 67.4% in 1980 to 90.0% in 1990, will decrease after the peak in 1990 to be 61.5% in 2025 and 59.3% in 2040. The dependency ratio was 48.4% in 1980, and will first bottom out at 42.8% in 1990, and then increase to 68.6% in 2040, only to again decrease and subsequently stabilize at 61% in the 2070s [Institute of Population Problems, 1985].

The demographic change could be characterized as a change in the shapes of population pyramids, from a bell in 1980 to a rectangle in 2025. This foretells that the change will be very rapid and drastic, and it also tells us that the size of the generation under 30 years old will remain relatively stable between the years 1980 and 2025, while the size of the older generations (older than 50 years old) will increase by a sizable margin. That is, it shows us that the structural change in the Japanese population will stem from the increase of the elderly generation, not from a decrease of the younger generation, and that the increase of elderly people will be produced by the aging of the generation that was born between 1945 and 1950.[5]

The scale and degree of the demographic population change in Japan can be interpreted from Table 9.5. Table 9.5 shows a predicted population structure in the year of 2025 for 13 nations. In 2025, there will be 6 nations of the 13 in which the percentage of the age strata of 65 years or older is 20% or higher. Japan will be one of those nations. The others are Luxembourg, Switzerland, Italy, Sweden, and the Federal Republic of Germany. In all 6 nations, one-fifth of the total population will be made up of the elderly. Aging indexes that show the number of people aged 65 years old or over versus 100 people age 15 years old and under are shown on the right-hand side of Table 9.5. Japan is found to have the fifth highest aging index (123.5), following upon Luxembourg (137.2), Switzerland (131.7), Italy (125.5), and Sweden (124.4). Japan, as well as some European nations, will be a "matured society" in the twenty-first century.

TABLE 9.5 Age Structure Projected for 2025 of Major Nations (percentages)

Nations	Percentage of Age Strata			Young Dependency Ratio	Aged Dependency Ratio	Dependency Ratio	Aging Index
	0-14	15-64	65+				
Japan	17.2	61.5	21.3	62.7	28.1	34.6	123.5
Australia	20.1	64.2	15.7	55.8	31.4	24.5	78.1
Brazil	30.4	62.3	7.3	60.6	48.8	11.7	24.0
Canada	17.6	65.7	16.7	52.3	26.9	25.4	94.9
France	18.4	63.1	18.6	58.6	29.1	29.5	101.1
Federal Republic of Germany	17.6	62.5	20.0	60.1	28.2	32.0	113.6
India	23.1	69.4	7.5	44.0	33.2	10.8	32.5
Italy	16.5	62.9	20.7	59.0	26.2	32.9	125.5
Luxembourg	16.4	61.1	22.5	63.7	26.9	36.8	137.2
Sweden	16.8	62.3	20.9	60.6	26.9	33.6	124.4
Switzerland	16.7	61.3	22.0	63.0	27.2	35.8	131.7
United Kingdom	17.6	63.8	18.6	56.8	27.6	29.2	105.7
United States	20.7	63.5	15.8	57.6	32.6	25.0	76.3

SOURCE: Institute of Population Problems (1985, p. 111).

The Family Life Cycle, the Family System, and Intergenerational Relationships

Changes in the Family Life Cycle and in Frequency of Family Types

The demographic change projected in the previous section is fueled by both the decrease in fertility and the prolonging of the span of individual life,[6] and these forces modify the family life cycle as well as the demographic structure. These changes in life cycles, in turn, are changing Japanese women's life-style. Kumagai (1984, p. 202) summarized the change in Japanese people's life cycle and life-style with this comment: "The overall pattern of the family career of Japanese women today closely resembles that of their American and Canadian counterparts."

A comparison has been made of three generations of couples' family life cycle: a younger couple with the husband born in 1948 and the wife born in 1952; a couple from the generation of the young couple's parents; and another couple of the generation of their grandparents (Economic Planning Agency, 1984, p. 12). First, the span of the stage devoted to child rearing decreased from the grandparents' generation through the parents' generation to the younger couple's generation. Second, other two stages—the stage prior to marriage and the post-child rearing (or later life) stage—have lengthened remarkably. The length of the post-child-rearing stage of the youngest generation is interpreted to have almost expanded to 20 years. Because the generation's average life expectancy for both sexes is over 80 years, almost one-fourth of the entire life of this generation will be during this later life stage.

According to the Japanese census, the number of conjugal family households and single-member households is gradually increasing, while the number of extended family households is decreasing. In 1920, conjugal families accounted for 54% of all households, single-member households accounted for 7%, and 31% of all households were extended families, with other types constituting 8%. In 1980, however, the conjugal type increased to 63% of all households, the single-member type increased to 16%, and the extended family type decreased to 20.7%.

While these changes in frequency of family types are concerned with households in general, changes have also touched the elderly people's household (Economic Planning Agency, 1982), as can be seen in a comparison of the years of 1960 and 1980. In 1960, 87.3% of all households containing people 65 years old or over were made up of an elderly person or elderly couple living with their children and grandchildren. Only 7.0% of households of the elderly consisted of only an elderly couple, and only 5.7% of the elderly lived alone or in another type of household. In 1980, those elderly people who lived with their adult children and/or other relatives had decreased to 70% of all households of the elderly, while the number of households comprising just an elderly couple increased to 18%.

Changes in the frequency of various family types are predicted to continue. Table 9.6 shows both measured and projected ratios of each type of household in the whole Japanese society. The percentage of extended families has constantly decreased and is also predicted to decrease in the future. That is, 23.0% of households were extended families in 1970, 20.3% in 1975, and 18.8% in 1980, and extended families are predicted to decrease to 17.8% in 1985, 15.5% in 2000, and 15.1% in 2015. It would seem clear that the decrease in the extended family is accompanied by a decrease in the percentage of the elderly who live with their adult children and/or grandchildren. That is, the trend toward a later life stage spent in a conjugal household or single-member household rather than in an extended family will accelerate in the future.

These changes in the frequency of family types suggest that the traditional family system that was sustained by the descent of the family in a direct line has been destroyed.

**Orientation Toward Independent
Life for the Elderly**

The above discussion shows that increased life expectancy has prolonged the length of the later life stage by as much as 20 years, but on the other hand, the type of household of the elderly is moving from the extended family to the conjugal household or single-member household. A new life-style for the later life stage should be developed for the Japanese elderly people to help them "successfully age" under these new circumstances. What new way of life suggests itself for the later life stage? While a new life-style has not yet been established, I think that one new wave can be found today in middle-aged and elderly people's life-style and life consciousness: an attitude toward family life in the later life stage that could be called an orientation toward "a way of life independent from younger generation" (Wada, 1984).

TABLE 9.6   Percentage of Households by Family Pattern

Types of Household	Measured			Projected		
	1970	1975	1980	1985	2000	2015
Couple only or with children	57.1	58.1	57.4	56.1	52.3	47.5
Single parent with children	6.4	5.8	6.0	6.4	7.6	8.6
Extended family	23.0	20.3	18.8	17.8	15.5	15.1
Single	10.8	13.5	15.8	18.0	23.1	27.8
Others	2.8	2.3	2.0	1.8	1.2	1.0

SOURCE: Economic Planning Agency (1982, p. 74).

Traditionally, in Japanese society, the elderly lived with adult children and grandchildren in an extended family. The major reason for that was that the elderly parents were able to obtain financial support, personal care, gratification of emotional needs, and so forth only within the family. In Japan today, as in other industrialized countries, a social support system for the elderly citizen (social security, health insurance, pensions, and so on) has been institutionalized, and, therefore, the necessity for elderly people to be dependent on adult children has decreased. The need remains, however, for the elderly to live with adult children and/or grandchildren for emotional gratification.

It has been said that the frequency and quality of intergenerational exchange varies considerably by whether it occurs inside the family among those living together or outside the family among those living apart. We also know that frequent and intimate exchanges between elderly parents and their children is a very important factor in promoting the life satisfaction of the elderly.

Compared to peers in other industrialized societies, Japanese elderly people still frequently wish to turn to their adult children and/or grandchildren. But when we examine their opinions in a longitudinal way, we notice a change in their opinion. Table 9.7 shows the change in the elderly's desire to live with the younger generation. Each figure in the table shows the percentage of those who were eager to live with younger generations. Although it is consistently found that the percentage of those who were eager to live intergenerationally increases when we go up the age strata, a comparison between 1969 and 1980 reveals a decrease of the figure in each age strata of both sexes. For males between 60 and 64 years of age, the figure changed from 69.5% in 1969 to 55.4% in 1980; for men of 65 to 69, it changed from 77.7% to 55.5%; and at the oldest strata, it declined from 79.6% to 56.1%. For females, the ratios decreased from

TABLE 9.7   Ratio of the Elderly Who Wish to Live Together with Their Children and/or Grandchildren, by Sex and Age Grade (percentages)

	1969	1980
Male:		
60-64 years old	69.5	55.4
65-69	77.7	55.5
70 and over	79.6	56.1
Female:		
60-64 years old	79.8	56.1
65-69	84.3	61.5
70 and over	89.2	70.0

SOURCE: Wada (1984b); used by permission. Materials from Prime Minister's Office (1969) for the data on 1969, and Prime Minister's Office (1982) for the data on 1980.

NOTE: The figures in the table show the ratio of those who answered "Yes" to the question "Do you desire to live (to continue living) with your children?" in 1969, and those who chose "It is best to live with my children and grandchildren" to the question "What do you think about interaction with children and grandchildren in your later life?" in 1980.

79.8% to 56.1%, from 84.3% to 61.5%, and from 89.2% to 70.0% (Wada, 1984).

Wada (1984) interpreted the meaning of this decline in the ratio of Japanese elderly people who desire to live with younger generations as an anticipatory self-defense against the younger generation's new way of life. It is the younger generation (in particular, young women) who are reluctant to live with elderly parents, primarily because of worrisome conflict between the generations. The elderly people, who are aware of this increasing reluctance, defend their own life by means of changing their attitude toward the pattern of intergenerational exchange.

Occupational Life and the Retirement Process

The Traditional Employment and Retirement System and Changes Therein

Retirement can be generalized as a social process. According to Atchley (1980, p. 163), retirement is "a process that involves withdrawing from a job and taking up the role of retired person." Retirement, being a process, includes several steps from the starting stage to the ending stage.

The initiating factors of the retirement process can be either voluntary, for self-chosen retirement, or compulsory, when retirement is enforced by some kind of institutionalized power. Many Japanese employees are pushed, even against their will, into the retirement process due to the mandatory retirement system called *Teinen Taishoku*. Each corporation has its own system of *Teinen Taishoku*, and its employees are obliged to leave their former occupations and/or positions at a predetermined age.[7] Because *Teinen Taishoku* compels employees to leave their organization, but says nothing about "taking up the role of retired person," there are not a few who, after *Teinen Taishoku*, still work at paid jobs, either by finding new employment in another corporation (whether as full-timers or as part-timers) or by beginning a business of their own.[8]

In the traditional style of personnel management in Japanese corporations, *Teinen Taishoku*, the seniority wage system, and the lifelong system of employment formed a trinity, and they compensated each other to ensure loyalty and high morale among the employees and assist recruiting for the organization. It might be possible to say that this trinity in the traditional Japanese system of personnel management was one of the factors that spurred Japan's remarkable economic progress after World War II.[9] This traditional system is now going to be modified. The system only works well if a young age such as 55 or 56 is the standard age of *Teinen Taishoku* because otherwise it is not suitable for developing employment opportunities for the elderly.

Because the aging of the labor force is now steadily progressing, supplying the matured labor force with the chance to find jobs is one of the most serious social problems. Tsuda (1985) analyzes the future Japanese labor force and mentions that the movement of two groups, those of 55 to 64 years of age and those of 15 to 24 years of age, should be noted. Because the percentage of 55- to 64-year-olds will continue to increase until about 2000, and the proportion of 15- to 24-year-olds, which decreased in the 1970s, will increase again until about 1990, under low economic growth, jobs for the two groups may need to be developed to avoid increased unemployment.

These changes in the labor force are being given serious consideration, and the traditional system of personnel management is already being reformulated in each organization. For example, according to a survey of business corporations, reform of the seniority system in wages has been instituted in 44% of all corporations, and weaknesses in the system are now under investigation for the purpose of reform in 33% of corporations surveyed (Nagamachi, 1985, p. 78, figure 2).

Work, Retirement, and Social
Integration in the Later Life Stage

When we discuss the psychosocial influences of the retirement process on individual's later life in a Japanese sociocultural context, we cannot neglect the fact that there exists a clear difference in level of life satisfaction between those who have already left behind their working role and those who are still active in jobs at the age of 70 or younger (Wada, 1983, 1985). Understanding the reason for this difference in morale also seems to clarify the reason for the elderly's high motivation for paid employment.

Because people in general work in order to earn income to sustain their own and their family's everyday life, the elderly's participation in the labor force can be explained from the economic perspective: They are working to support themselves financially. Tsuda (1985) supports the financial explanation by showing that the higher the rank of pension payment climbs, the lower the ratio of the elderly engaged in paid work.[10]

Although this relation between the amount of pension and the employment ratio cannot be denied, it also should be noted that, even in the highest rank of pension (210,000 yen or more per month), 49.8% of 60- to 64-year-old males and 44.6% of 65- to 69-year-old-males are still employed.[11] That is, if the elderly are working just to earn income, the employment rate at the highest rank of pension should be much less than this. Could this not suggest that something in addition to economic necessity motivates the elderly's strong desire and tendency to remain employed even in the later life stage?[12]

Figure 9.1 shows the ratio of elderly people who expressed preference for an active working role and those who preferred an easy life of retirement from a working role ("No Answer" is omitted, so that the figures total less than 100%), categorized by attitude toward human relations (a) and toward social activities (b). In regard to human relations, the subjects are grouped into (A1) those who prefer having intimate relations with as many friends as possible, and (A2) those who prefer living free from care about human relations. In regard to social activities, subjects are grouped into (B1) those who prefer active engagement in social activities, and (B2) those who prefer enjoying personal hobbies.

Bar A in Figure 9.1 shows that among those who prefer having intimate relations with as many friends as possible, 80% prefer an active

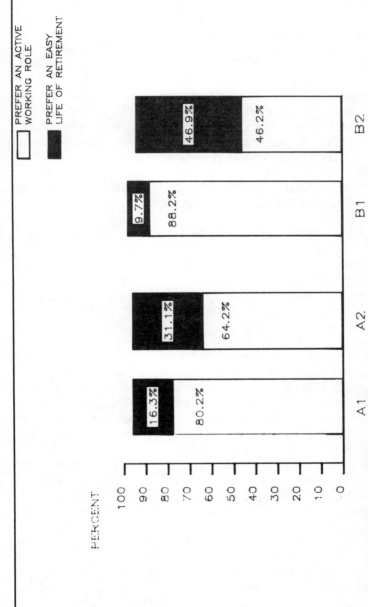

PERCENT

PREFER AN ACTIVE
WORKING ROLE

PREFER AN EASY
LIFE OF RETIREMENT

SOURCE: Wada (1985a, p. 235); used by permission.
NOTE: A1—prefer many friends; A2—prefer few friends; B1—prefer social activities; B2—prefer personal hobbies.

Figure 9.1 Attitude of the Elderly Toward a Working Role in Later Life

223

working role. Among those who prefer living free from care about human relations, 65% prefer an active working role. Bar B reveals that 88% of those who prefer social activities also prefer an active working life, and 46% of those who prefer enjoying personal hobbies also prefer an active working life. In this breakdown by preference for human relations and by social activities, those elderly who are included in A1 or B1 are assumed to be more active in human relations or social activities. These results suggest that elderly people who prefer to retain a life of active engagement in a working role are more highly represented among those who prefer having intimate relations with as many friends as possible and among those with an active interest in social activities. This might lead us to conclude that the elderly's motivation to continue working is highly related with their social integration. That is, it might be pointed out that having a job would make it easier for an elderly person to join in social life.

In industrialized societies, occupation is the most fundamental medium through which individuals are integrated into the social system. The later stage of life is, however, considered an exception to the rule, and people in this stage are sometimes even regarded, at least in an affluent society, as a leisure class. In many industrialized societies, the systems of social security and public pensions have enabled the elderly to be free from paid employment to lead a life untroubled by economic problems.

Japan is today one of the affluent societies, and the elderly are supported by public pensions, which seem to have dismissed the people's anxiety about economic life. Many elderly Japanese are still very eager to continue paid employment, however, not for economic reasons but as a means of social involvement. The lives of many are sustained only by the two areas of occupational life and family life, not by community life. Men tend to develop their networks of human relationships not through community life, but through occupational life. Women with young children communicate and establish a network in the community, but the network is not maintained once the children have grown up.

According to the time allocation patterns of the Japanese people shown in Tables 9.1 and 9.2, it is true that the time budgeted for paid work is gradually decreasing. This might suggest that the focus of the life-style of the elderly in regard to occupational life is going to shift from work to something else. What is the something else? According to Tables 9.1 and 9.2, it is just watching TV. The challenge for Japanese elderly people now is to develop a way to spend time other than in work (Wada, 1985).

Summary and Conclusion

In this chapter, two facets of the later life stage in Japanese society were examined in terms of new trends: family life (especially inter-generational relations within the family), and retirement and occupational life. Sociocultural changes are leading to a decrease in the proportion of extended family households and a corresponding increase in households composed of a single elderly person or an elderly couple. The elderly are thus going to pick up an orientation toward the independent later life stage from their adult children and/or grand-children. Both the strong desire of Japanese women for permanent jobs outside the family and the younger generation's reluctant attitude toward traditional family life will help popularize the choice of an independent later life stage for the Japanese elderly.

The ratio of the matured labor force is gradually increasing in all Japanese corporations, and these organizations are starting to cope with this population shift by adopting new personnel management policies that are not necessarily based on the traditions of the seniority system of wages and lifelong employment. Despite these changes, many elderly people, especially elderly men, still desire to remain employed even in their later life stage. Judging from the higher life satisfaction and higher integration into the social network found among those who are still active in a working role, having a job in the later life stage has the special function of allowing the elderly to maintain human exchanges through the working role.

Because paid employment is such a convenient way for the elderly to gain a network of human relationships, their interest in employment cannot be expected to fade away in the near future. When the elderly population accounts for a certain percentage of the total population, and employment opportunities must be shared between generations and between sexes, however, some kind of new later stage life-style in which activities other than work are valued should be developed in the twenty-first century.

Some characteristics of elderly people's way of life in modern Japan can be summarized. First, the traditional pattern of men working outside the family and women remaining inside the family is still influential. Both men and women spend a long, and increasing, amount of time watching TV daily. One of the reasons for this may be that neither is good at developing human relationships and social activities outside family and occupational life. The time spent on personal hobbies is not sizable, because a large part of the current elderly people have not developed hobbies. According to the traditional way of thinking in Japan, nothing is valued but official work in the case of men and domestic work in the case of women. The pressures of present circumstances are certain to change the experiences of later life for future generations of Japanese men and women.

NOTES

1. A national survey of people's time allocation on weekdays, Saturday, and Sunday has been done by NHK (Hihon Hoso Kyokai; the Japanese National Broadcasting Corporation) every five years since 1960. The design of every survey is as follows: (1) The major items are the kinds, time, and duration of all of the behaviors in which the subjects engaged from 0:00 a.m. to 12:00 p.m. (2) The method is self-report. (3) Subjects include all Japanese citizens over 9 years old. (4) Sampling is based on a stratified multistage design.

2. It is true that the differentiation of sex roles is, in current Japanese culture, becoming less and less valued, particularly among the younger generation. The discussion of the life-style of the current middle-aged generation or older generation, however, cannot neglect the different distribution of roles between men and women.

3. Each of the figures should be read in this example: In regard to the first figure for Japan, 65.4% of all subjects are living with a spouse whether or not they might also live with any other relatives.

4. "Transportation" does not fit neatly into these three categories, because this behavior is subordinate to some other behavior.

5. This largest generation, a baby-boom generation that was born shortly after World War II, is now reaching middle age. This will cause a swelling of the middle-aged population before the percentage of the aged population increases.

6. The average life expectancy was, in 1950, 59.57 years for men and 62.97 for women; in 1960, 65.32 and 70.19, in 1970, 69.31 and 74.66; and in 1984, 74.54 for men and 80.15 for women. The average life expectancy in the twenty-first century is projected to be over 80 years for both men and women.

7. The most common age for *Teinen Taishoku*, which was 55 or 56 until just a few years ago now tends to be 60 or older (the age of *Teinen Taishoku* for employees of the federal government is now 60).

8. Hiraoka (1983) shows, based on a survey of the retirees of four large corporations in metropolitan Tokyo, that among those who left the corporation due to mandatory retirement, only 4.5% retired completely from a working role.

9. It was very convenient for big corporations establishing the mandatory system of *Teinen Taishoku* that the labor market in Japanese society is divided into two subsystems: the market for governments and big corporations and the market for small corporations. Mandatory retirement is usually institutionalized in each organization, but the particular retirement age is determined by the management of each organization. Usually, the retirement age in government or big corporations is younger than in small corporations. Thus employees who were dismissed under *Teinen Taishoku* from the big corporations were able to find new jobs in the smaller organizations.

10. For males aged 65 to 69, the employment ratio in each rank of pension is as follows: $40,000 yen or less, 69.7%; 50,000-80,000 yen, 62.5%; 90,000-120,000 yen, 57.8%; 130,000-160,000 yen, 45.8%; 170,000-200,000 yen, 37.8%; and 210,000 yen or more, 44.6%.

11. Of females collecting a pension of 210,000 yen or more, 26.4% of those aged 60 to 64 years old are employed and 4.8% of those aged 65 to 69 are employed. While these figures are low in the case of females, even at the lowest rank of pension, employment figures stand at 43.6% and 34.0%.

12. The international comparison conducted by the Prime Minister's Office (1982) shows also that most Japanese subjects who report satisfaction with their income level also wish to continue working until the age of 65 or even 70.

REFERENCES

Aoi, Kazu and Shuichi Wada, eds. 1982. *Retirement and Occupational Life in the Middle and Later Life Stages* (in Japanese). Tokyo: University of Tokyo Press.

Atchley, Robert A. 1980. *The Social Forces in Later Life*. 3rd ed. Belmont, CA: Wadsworth.

Economic Planning Agency, Japan. 1982. *Japan in 2000: Planning a Welfare Society for Adjusting to the Aging of the Population* (in Japanese). Tokyo: Author.

————. 1984. *Toward a Vigorous Matured Society: Problems of Matured Society and Their Resolution* (in Japanese). Tokyo: Author.

Fukutake, Tadasi and Kazuo Aoi, eds. 1985. *The Structure of the Future Japanese Society and Its Problems: Planning for the 21st Century* (in Japanese). Tokyo: University of Tokyo Press.

Hiraoka, Koichi. 1983. "Occupational Change." Pp. 75-79 in *Retirement and Occupational Life in the Middle and Later Life Stages* (in Japanese), edited by K. Aoi and S. Wada. Tokyo: University of Tokyo Press.

Institute of Population Problems. 1985. *Future Populations Projections* (Institute of Population Problems Research Series, No. 234) (in Japanese). Japan: Ministry of Health and Welfare.

Kumagai, Fumie. 1984. "The Life Cycle of the Japanese Family." *Journal of Marriage and the Family* 46:191-204.

Nagamachi, Mitsuo. 1985. "Problems Concerning Middle-Aged and Mature Workers in Corporation." Pp. 74-84 of *The Yearbook of Aging 1985* (in Japanese), edited by Zenkoku Koureika-Shakai Kenkyuu Kyokai. Tokyo: Shinjidaisha.

NHK (Nihon Hoso Kyokai; National Broadcasting Corporation). 1970. *A National Survey on Time Allocation in Everyday Life* (in Japanese). Tokyo: Author.

————. 1980. *A National Survey on Time Allocation in Everyday Life* (in Japanese). Tokyo: Author.

Prime Minister's Office, Japan. 1969. *A Report on an Opinion Poll on Later Life* (in Japanese). Tokyo: Author.

————. 1982. *The Life and Life Consciousness of the Elderly: A Report on an International Comparative Survey* (in Japanese). Tokyo: Author.

Tsuda, Masumi. 1985. "The Labor Force in the Matured Society." Pp. 61-73 of *Yearbook of Aging '85* (in Japanese), edited by Zenkoku Koreika-Shakai Kenkyu Kyokai. Tokyo: Shin-Jidaisha.

Wada, Shuichi. 1981. "Occupational Mobility as a Condition of Later Life Adjustment."
Paper presented at the 12th International Congress of Gerontology, Hamburg.
————. 1983a. "The Psychosocial Conditions of the Pension Earner's Life Satisfaction."
Retirement and the Occupational Life in Middle and Later Life Stage (in Japanese),
edited by K. Aoi and S. Wada. Tokyo: University of Tokyo Press.
————. 1983b. "The Anxiety of Middle-Aged and Mature Workers in Corporations." In
A Report of an International Symposium on Demographic Change. Tokyo.
————. 1984a. "The Influences of Being Employed or Retired on Pension Earners' Lives"
(in Japanese). *Social Gerontology* 19:88-102.
————. 1984b. "Changed in Elderly People's Life Consciousness" (in Japanese). *Jurisuto
Sogo Tokushu* 36:88-93 (Tokyo: Yuhikaku Publishing Co.)
————. 1985a. "A Structural Effect of Later Life on People's Satisfaction." In *The
Structure of the Future Japanese Society and Its Problems: Planning for the 21st
Century* (in Japanese), edited by Tadasi Fukutake and Kazuo Aoi. Tokyo: University
of Tokyo Press.
————. 1985b. "The Structure of Anxiety Amidst Current Rapid Population Structure
Change in Japan." Pp. 343-51 in *Yearbook of Aging 1985* (in Japanese), edited by
Zenkoku Koreika-Shakai Kenkyu Kyokai. Tokyo: Shin-Jidaisha.
Zenkoku Koreika-Shakai Kenkyu Kyokai, ed. 1985. *Yearbook of Aging 1985.* Tokyo:
Shin-Jidaisha.

10

National Context and
Daily Life in Later Life

KAREN ALTERGOTT
STEPHEN DUNCAN

Daily Life in Later Life

The daily life perspective in this volume bridges many levels of social reality. The meaningful activities and interactions of ordinary people as they go about their daily lives are linked to the national context in which they live. The central question that can be examined by comparing the daily lives of older people in Canada, Great Britain, Hungary, Japan, the Netherlands, Sweden, and the United States is: How does national context modify the daily lives of older people in modernized societies? Authors in this volume articulated the forces operating at the national level to modify daily life. These include demographic trends, cultural patterns, policies of the nation, role structures for older people, and historical events as well as social changes. This book would be incomplete without a comparative analysis of the contexts of aging the seven nations represent.

In this chapter, we provide several types of overviews. First, we summarize the national analyses of daily life in later life, with special attention to common patterns and meaningful divergence from common patterns. Second, the demographic, cultural, and policy environments are reviewed as possible explanations for differences in daily life patterns. Finally, through the analyses of daily life and national context, we propose a multilevel framework for understanding daily life in later life.

Work and Retirement

Each author dealt with the fact that retirement is a phenomenon of later life. Abrams points out the age stratification of work quite dramatically by taking a slice of time, 9:00 a.m., and examining how many people 65 and older are at work (2%) compared to people 45-64 (42%). This illustrates a trend in each country for paid labor force activity to decline for older people. Americans show a decline in paid work by the late sixties. Still, 10% of women and 20% of men are found in the paid labor force after age 65. Sweden and the Netherlands have the lowest levels of paid labor force participation by older people.

There are two exceptions to the pattern of steep decline in paid work: Hungary and Japan. In Hungary, the pensioning age is rather early and people are both physically able to continue to work and anticipating a long enough life. Pensions are low and only modestly adjusted each year for increases in cost of living, therefore, economic well-being declines with age. Additional labor is seen as necessary to ensure current and future economic well-being. Older people frequently participate in agricultural production on household plots, in private dwelling construction, and in repair work. These productive activities outside the salaried world of work are essential for older Hungarians.

In Japan, there is a decline in work time from the fifties to the sixties for men but there is a great desire to remain economically productive. About 40% of Japanese men aged 65 and older are working. The explanation for Japan's pattern is complex. The earlier system combined mandatory retirement from some positions with corporate responsibility for locating another position for those retired. That system, which never covered everyone, is withering. The newer public pension system is moving toward maturity. As pensions become adequate, older people may leave the labor force. The availability of part-time work for older people is another factor. But the desire to work in Japan is associated with both economic needs and cultural norms sanctioning unproductive activity.

In each society considered, men are more likely to participate in paid labor and, if participating, they spend more time working.

The fact that most older people are not in the labor force makes the analysis of daily life in later life most interesting. What do people do with the time supposedly freed from paid labor?

Unpaid Productivity

Across the nations considered here, domestic work in modern societies is predominantly women's work. The exact ratios vary from one nation to another. The difference among older people is greatest in Japan, where women spend three to five times as many hours per day in housework (4-5 hours per day), and is also high in the Netherlands, where most men spend less than 5 hours a week on housework and most women spend more than 15 hours a week on housework during retirement. In the Netherlands, some retirees increase their housework, others decrease, and others remain involved at a stable level. Women in later life were more likely to increase household duties than men were. The gender difference in domestic labor may be lowest in Sweden, where home help provided by organizations replaces some domestic labor of household members. In Hungary, more time is spent on domestic tasks in retirement, but some of these tasks may actually produce goods for the market. This form of unpaid productive activity seems to have a high level of voluntarism, based on the variable pattern of changes and stability in amounts of time spent in domestic work.

The amount of time devoted to helping other adults in and out of the household varied from country to country. In the Netherlands, few participated in helping other adults. But in the United States, about two-fifths of women 55 or older spent some time helping either adults in the household or others outside of the household. Across the four days considered, an average of two hours was devoted to this activity. The relatively privatized care system in the United States may explain this high level of involvement in helping others. Declines in helping occur only after age 75 for this sample. It is this type of unpaid labor that makes the total work load of women greater in late life than the total work load of men in the United States.

Though rarely considered a productive activity, self-care is something that needs to be done and is often done by paid labor for those who cannot care for themselves. Thus some of the basic activities of daily life are productive. Self-maintenance includes personal health care, hygiene, and meeting physiological needs. Sleep and eating are self-care as well, however, increases in these two activities may indicate social circumstances or preferences rather than physiological need. For each national context in which self-care was assessed, these basic activities took up around half of each 24-hour day. There were few differences by gender. Several authors noted that older people spend somewhat more time sleeping, resting, and eating meals (Andorka, Zuzanek and Andersson) than younger people.

Leisure Activities

Older people have more free time in their daily lives. The amount of time freed from obligatory activities, paid, and unpaid labor is not as great as might be expected. The increment of time older people have ranges from four hours more free time in the United Kingdom (compared to nonretired) and three extra hours a day in Sweden (compared to younger age groups) to two and a half hours a day in Canada (compared to nonretired individuals) to nearly two hours a day for those 65 and older (compared to those 55-64) in the United States. As Zuzanek notes, however, the time is allocated across existing obligatory and leisure activities. While this means that daily life is restructured, there is not the radically different life-style often associated with retirement stages of life.

Abrams and Andersson note another commonality: later life is homebound. In the United Kingdom, one-third of respondents hadn't gone out during the previous weekend. Knipscheer showed that going out declined significantly, and Zuzanek noted a decrement in out-of-home leisure activity after age 70. Abrams and Andorka attribute the change in out-of-household activity to economic factors. Not being able to afford leisure such as meals out, movies, sporting events, and entertainment is demonstrated by Abrams through expenditure patterns in the United Kingdom. In Hungary, the low-cost cultural activities were shown to increase in salience for older people, while the higher cost out-of-home cultural activities were rare. The reduced household income older people have may explain the decline in leisure outside of the home. On the other hand, Knipscheer suggests that the lack of a car, presence or absence of a social partner, and the fear of leaving home in the evening may keep people home. He notes that married people go out more often. Also, older people wish to go out more often than they do, indicating that the privatization experienced is not entirely voluntary.

When at home, the dominant leisure activity in modern nations seems to be television viewing. This form of leisure involves 40% of all leisure time among Swedish elders, almost three hours a day in Canada, and an increasing proportion of time among older people in Japan. It is dominant as a form of leisure for all age groups in all countries considered, but is generally more time-consuming among older people than among younger people. Several authors lament this focus of daily life. Abrams noted an irony: the programming designed for older people drove them away from the TV. Perhaps the media planners fail to understand this significant segment of the viewing audience. Wada is most critical of the increasing absorption in television by Japanese elders, suggesting that the challenge for the future is finding other ways to use time freed from labor. Japanese elders engage in little social leisure, organizational activities, or active leisure. It is this lack of variety that Wada notes, but it is found in other countries as well.

Andersson adds to the critical analysis of daily life by reminding us that activities do not necessarily reflect preferences or satisfaction with daily life. His analysis of desired activities finds that the desire for more leisure activity is highest among working elders and lowest among disabled elders. Those with a great deal of free time may still be barred from participating in favored activities because of ability limitations, lack of opportunities, or lack of preparation for a leisure life-style. He notes that one-seventh of free time involves doing "nothing in particular" for those 65 and older. Finally, a critical question remains to be answered for those homebound elderly receiving services. What, in the isolation of their home, is a positive, valued, beneficial, and enjoyable use of the free time they have?

Differences across nations were noted in leisure activities. Religious activity was not analyzed for every nation. Nearly half of older Americans participate in religious activities and, across four days, the participants spend two hours in religious activities. This represents a high level of participation relative to other countries. For instance, in Japan, few elders participate in religious activities.

Within each nation, the leisure patterns vary somewhat. Gender was an important basis of differentiation in leisure roles. The concentration of creative leisure for women and active, passive, television viewing, travel for leisure, and amount of leisure for men in the United States is accompanied by gender similarities in the amounts of social leisure, religious participation, voluntary organization participation, entertainment, and educational activities.

In Sweden, men, especially married men, go for walks more frequently than women do. Zuzanek found greater convergence in housework and divergence in leisure pursuits among older Canadian men and women. Knipscheer found that older men receive fewer visits and older women receive more, compared to their younger counterparts. Women visit others more, especially if they are not married. Andorka notes that only women use the freed time of later life to visit friends and relatives more; men actually decrease this use of time. Wada also notes that women spend more time in social interaction, though the difference is small. Most of the gender differences are related to social leisure, with women clearly participating more. In general, men and women have different leisure life-styles.

Differences among the aged based on decade of life are fewer and less dramatic than the gender differences already discussed. The group 75 and older is different in that they experience more self-care, sleep, and free time in most countries. Those 75 and older are most likely to participate in planned senior citizen activities in the Netherlands and elsewhere. In Hungary, time in conversation is increased for this oldest group. In Japan also, more time is allocated to social leisure by those over 70. On the other hand, Altergott and others point out that women's solitude increased enormously among the oldest group, and is high even though social interaction is also high. This is due to the predominant marital status among women in the older group. Through widowhood, women lose an intimate who is only partly compensated for by the increase in interaction with others. Widowhood, as Knipscheer points out, is the most consequential transition experienced in later life in terms of daily life activities.

Variations on the themes of daily life were found for groups within each society. A generational difference was found for ethnic minorities in Canada, with the first generation preserving values and practices of Japan more than the second generation. This affects daily life. First-generation Japanese Canadians are more sedentary; second generation are more outgoing and devote more time to productive leisure and traveling; repatriated Japanese Canadians spend more time reading, watching TV, and taking coffee or tea breaks.

In every nation, educational, occupational, and resource differences exist among the aged that could affect daily life. Several authors call our attention to class differences. Ujimoto points out that the generation differences he noticed could be due to concomitant class, educational, and occupational differences. Unskilled laborers devote more time to personal care, semiskilled laborers devote more time to domestic tasks, and professional and managerial workers spend the most time in sleep, obtaining services, and leisure when these occupational groups face retirement.

The analysis of leisure activities was most extensive in this comparative volume. The common assumption that the later years constitute complete leisure and the parallel assertion that the aged represent a new leisure class were clearly refuted. The amount of free time is only somewhat greater in later years. The uses of time are modestly, not radically, restructured. In addition, specific limits on the use of free time for leisure pursuits were noted by the authors, including economic constraints (see Abrams), health constraints (see Abrams and Knipscheer), and cultural barriers (Altergott, Knipscheer, and Andersson).

National Context and Daily Life:
Shaping Later Life

Demography and Limits of
Demographic Determinism

The populations of the nations included in this analysis are all mature or aging. The proportion of people 65 and older is currently highest in Sweden (17%) and United Kingdom (15%), moderate in the Netherlands, Hungary, and the United States, and lowest in Canada and Japan (10%) (U.S. Bureau of the Census, 1986). The life expectancy is highest in Sweden, Japan (77), and the Netherlands (76), a bit lower in the United States, Canada (75), and the United Kingdom (74), and considerably lower in Hungary (70) (U.S. Bureau of the Census, 1986). The proportion of older people in a society is the result of, mainly, longevity and fertility. Differences in the rank orders of longevity and the proportion of older people is likely to be due to fertility differences in the various nations.

In all nations considered, older women outnumber men. The sex ratio is most disbalanced in Hungary, but in every nation, women can anticipate spending a considerable length of time in widowhood. Each decade brings an increased feminization of one's peer group in each country.

The living environments of older people in the societies studied here are primarily nuclear family households. In Japan, there has been a significant decline in the proportion of older people living with their sons, as Wada points out, and in Hungary, there is a similar tendency for the generations to separate if they can. These two countries remain somewhat extended in ideal and actual family form, even though both ideals and actualities are changing. In Japan, 21% of households are extended and 18% of households contain just elderly members, but most older people still live with an offspring. In Hungary, 40% of older people live with a wage-earner, most often a child, according to Andorka. In the United States, where nuclear families are most valued and common, 12% of married and 17% of unmarried older people live with their offspring (Schorr, 1980). It should be noted that this represents approximately equal proportions of offspring with continued dependence on older parents and older parents joining the offspring's household. The figures from each country represent shifts toward greater independence in residence for older people. Nations are becoming more similar, then, in terms of multigenerational households.

Knipscheer points out another demographic trend rarely noted. In each country, the proportion of never-married, divorced older people is rising and these forms of singlehood as well as the relative proportions of widowed and married people may alter significantly the nature of old age in the future.

Observing the age distribution of a society, and more important perhaps, of the aged segment of the population, as well as the gender, marital status, labor force status, and living situations of the elderly provides a demographic baseline for comparing nations. There may be compositional differences between nations that help us understand differences among nations in the patterns of daily life. This is one reason the authors of this volume chose to control for gender, age, and other defining characteristics as they analyzed daily life in later life. Future studies could examine compositional differences in greater detail: examining marital status, urban/rural settings, health status, and economic resources as they relate to differences in the daily lives of older people.

While growing numbers and proportions of older people call our attention to their daily lives, these demographic trends are not sufficient to explain the nature of daily life in later life.

Economic Environments and
Age-Specific Resources

The economic environment of older people is determined by the income maintenance policies for retired people, the labor force structure, and the economic situation of the nation. Considering the rank order in per capita gross national product provides some comparative insight into the economic situation of nations. The United States, Sweden,

Canada, Japan, the Netherlands, United Kingdom, and Hungary, from highest to lowest GNP, provide different objective standards of living for older people (U.S. Bureau of the Census, 1986). Another measure of investment in government action may be reflected in the proportion of the GNP people pay in taxes. The 1977 tax rate was 4.3% of the GNP in the United States, 6% in the United Kingdom, 7% in Sweden, and 10% in the Netherlands, for example (Nusberg, 1984). Of course, each country allocates the amounts received through taxation in different ways. In the United States, for example, 22% of the federal budget is invested in defense and 41% is invested in social security or other entitlements (Senate Special Committee on Aging, 1984).

In Hungary, both individuals and policymakers are trying to enhance the level of living in later life, according to Andorka. The difficult work life followed by a fairly early retirement leads to a "stressed" life-style for Hungarian elders (Andorka). The legal age of pension is 60 for men and 55 for women. Retirees receive 50% of their previous income and some annual adjustment to pensions is made. Part-time employment is allowed and many (30%) do work on a part-time basis. In addition, many elderly Hungarians supplement their income with extra agricultural productivity. Nevertheless, retirees and their surviving family members are often among the poorest in Hungary.

This may be a more common pattern than was once recognized, because even in the nation with the highest per capita GNP—the United States—a substantial proportion of older people live in poverty (Villers Foundation, 1987). Supplementing pension income with income from paid work depends on abilities as well as opportunities that may or may not be available. In Japan and Hungary, some older people have found ways to market produce or locate part-time work. Not all older people in even these two countries are likely to be able to earn added income. In the other countries under consideration, opportunities for alternative or part-time employment are scarce.

A dramatic reduction of discretionary income accompanies the increase in discretionary time older people have. In general, households headed by those over the age of 65 have about half of the income of households with a nonelderly head. The amount of economic change varies from nation to nation. According to Nusberg (1984), a single worker will have from around one-third of his or her preretirement income replaced by a public pension in Canada and in the United Kingdom, about half in the United States and the Netherlands, and about 68% in Sweden. A married, retired couple is likely to have about half of their preretirement income replaced by a public pension in Canada and the United Kingdom, about two-thirds in the United States, Japan, and the Netherlands, and about 83% in Sweden (Nusberg, 1984).

Sweden provides social insurance to all and pensions begin at 65 whether or not retirement occurs. As of 1983, 1560 kroner for a single person and 2545 kroner for a couple are provided (about $188 and $341 in U.S. dollars) and is supplemented by an earnings-related pension or a standard amount for nonearners (U.S. Department of Health and Human Services, 1984). People are rewarded with increments in pension for deferring benefits until age 70. Canada has a dual-level pension system, with one level universally available and a second level available on an income-tested basis (U.S. Department of Health and Human Services, 1984). Likewise, the United Kingdom has a basic income benefit available to all residents plus supplements for dependents, those aged 80 or older, and increments for deferring retirement. Men may receive benefits at 65, women at 60. In the United Kingdom, retirement is necessary for receipt of a public pension (U.S. Department of Health and Human Services, 1984). In the United States, old age pensions are available to workers and their dependents at age 65, with reductions for early retirement, and means-tested supplements for low-income elders. The pension is earnings tested with $1 reduction in pension for each $2 earned. The automatic increment based on the cost of living has been slightly altered in recent years. Dependent spouses receive a 50% supplement. Delaying retirement beyond 65 results in small increments (U.S. Department of Health and Human Services, 1984).

Hungary and Japan, as stated above, have early retirement ages to qualify for public pensions, yet they have high levels of late-life employment. Pension benefits in Hungary amount to about 33% of average earnings during recent years to 75% of earnings for workers with long work histories. A small adjustment for spouses (about $46.80) and a small adjustment annually add to the value of the public pension. Yet, as Andorka pointed out, the amount received may not be sufficient to allow Hungarians truly to retire at the ages of 55 for women and 60 for men. Economic incentives are provided to those who stay in the labor force beyond these ages (U.S. Department of Health and Human Services, 1984). In Japan, the pension system is not yet mature (Maeda, 1980) resulting in many older people receiving limited pensions. Recent reforms in Japan create a universal benefit for all residents and a second earnings-related benefit for insured retirees (Ricketts, 1986). Many elders live with their offspring; among those that do, about half receive financial support from their offspring (Maeda, 1980).

In the Netherlands, the basic pension equals the minimum wage and is indexed to rising prices. It is paid regardless of work status. A spouse supplement is included.

According to Ricketts's (1986) review of social security programs throughout the world, many nations are modifying programs to assure that the most disadvantaged receive sufficient benefits from the programs. The United States now taxes social security benefits for recipients who have incomes over $25,000 for an individual or $32,000 for a couple. Many other countries have modified benefits: creating universal coverage and lowering benefit levels (Japan); decreasing employer contributions (Netherlands); adding value to certain pensions (United Kingdom) or reducing them (the Netherlands, for disability); equalizing men's and women's age of retirement (Japan); and other changes.

Sweden has provided the most economic security for older citizens and no other country considered in this volume approaches the age equality in income their replacement level implies. In Sweden, paid and unpaid labor are less dominant and a variety of leisure and sociable activities are more common.

The economic resources provided to older citizens sets the stage for many aspects of daily life. At what level of living are older people maintained, based on public action? What opportunities for individual variation on the level set by public policy exist, based on labor force structure, cultural acceptance of older workers, and individual abilities and propensities? These conditions, more than any demographic reality, exert considerable influence over the nature of daily life in later life.

The Care System: Self, Family, Society

The variations in direct economic resources and opportunities to enhance one's quality of life observed are coupled with a variation in the other social resources allocated to older people. Cantor and Little (1985, p. 747) define social care as meeting three needs:

need for help in carrying out tasks of daily living;
need for personal assistance during times of illness or other crisis; and,
need for socialization and personal development.

Each society under consideration has a different care system to meet the needs of older people. The type and effectiveness of the care system determine a great deal about daily life.

(1) Tasks of daily living. A major difference among nations concerns the relative proportion of care provided by the formal versus the informal care system. Family is central to the care system in every nation. In Sweden, where the formal system is most highly developed, half of all "people 80 and above receive help from relatives, friends and acquaintances at least once a week" (Smyer, 1984). Volunteers play an important role in the care system of many nations. In the United Kingdom, volunteers and voluntary organizations deliver meals at home, and in Hungary, most home help to older people is provided through a system of volunteers (Nusberg, 1984, p. 116).

Most countries also have systems of formal service provision with varying amounts of public expenditure for care to older people. In countries like Sweden, the United Kingdom, and the Netherlands, social care is considered a citizen's right and is not stigmatized (Nusberg, 1984, p. 116). Formal services provided in the home, referred to by Little (1982) and others as open care and by others as home help, are much more common in the Netherlands, where 16% of older people receive them, and Sweden, where 25% of older people receive them, than in the United States, where home-based services are less developed. For example, only about 1% of older Americans receive home-delivered meals (Nusberg, 1984). Ironically, Japan has adopted the home-help system as a result of the U.S. model, but like the United States, Japan provides this formal resource to relatively few older people.

Rates of availability of home help for all citizens can be ranked for most of the nations considered in this volume: Sweden (923 home helps per 100,000 population), the Netherlands (599), Great Britain (265), the United States (29), Canada (15), and Japan (8) (Nusberg, 1984, p. 118). According to Andersson, for those elderly people receiving home help in Sweden, 205 hours of help is received in a year. In the United States, and in other countries with little home help available, the barrier may be funding decisions, a lack of emphasis on quality of community care, or a lack of public, nonprofit services, according to Ellen Winston, Chair of the U.S. Committee on World Aging (Nusberg, 1984). A naive reliance on family resources may explain the neglect of community-living elders. The extent of misery and suffering is rare in countries with extensive formal care systems, according to Nusberg (1984, p. 130).

Housing is a societal resource. The Netherlands may have the longest history and the most intensive support for housing for the elderly. According to Van Zonneveld (1980), sheltered housing for the elderly has existed since the fifteenth century. These environments, called *hobjes*, were provided by private employers, charitable organizations, or churches. Now, though local organizations still oversee and take responsibility for the variety of housing environments for the aged, the national government subsidizes the organizations providing low-cost housing to the elderly (C. Knipscheer, personal conversation, 1985). Public funding for private, nonprofit initiatives seems to be the model. Very few older people (5%-10%) live with their offspring in the Netherlands (Van Zonneveld, 1980).

In Sweden, housing policy stresses the right of older people to remain in the community and to retain autonomy. More age-integrated living is found, therefore. Sheltered housing with services, systems of checking on the resident, medical care, and home-centered caring are increasing (Kane and Kane, 1976). These services are often delivered to the older Swede in his or her housing environment, whether rural or urban, through a network of care-providers that includes home helps, nurses, and even postal delivery people. This contributes to the high percentage of older people who remain in ordinary housing (88%, according to Andersson).

In the United Kingdom, there has been an increase in the number of homes and sheltered living environments for older people, but there have also been programs to facilitate remaining in one's long-term home. Services delivered to the home are an important part of this program. This includes visitors, home helps, fostering older people, and other support (Bytheway, 1980). Local authorities have responsibility for administering programs (Kane and Kane, 1976).

In the United States, about 28% of the older population lives in apartments, boarding houses, or hotels. Some rent subsidies are available and special housing for the aged was built in the 1970s. Homeowners, constituting the majority of older people, have received some tax relief. Generally, the adequacy of older individual's housing depends on income (Olsen, 1982).

Living arrangements, the way tasks are accomplished, and the social resources available modify daily life. More or less socialization and solitude, self-care or receiving services, maintaining equality or learning new frugalities and humility result from variations in the care systems across the nations considered.

(2) Assistance during illness and crisis. In Canada, Hungary, and the United Kingdom, care during illness is handled through a universal

medical insurance program and is not age restricted. Also, in Sweden, 90% of medical expenses are reimbursed through national insurance covering all ages (Kane and Kane, 1976). In the Netherlands, all older people are covered by health insurance and the elderly contribute to the fund if they are able. Long-term care is funded by a separate act and nursing homes are administered by nonprofit voluntary organizations or by municipalities (Kane and Kane, 1976). This same act (Exceptional Medical Expenses Compensation Act) provides protection for people of all ages. The patient shares in the cost of long-term care, if he or she can afford to (U.S. Department of Health and Human Services, 1984). In Japan, medical care is available to all over 70 for either partial or no cost (Maeda, 1980). The United States has had, since 1965, a system of health care for those 65 and older, supplemented by a system of health care benefits for the medically indigent, regardless of age. Recent efforts have been made to reduce the cost of medical care to the aged through limiting reimbursement for service and time spent in the hospital.

Though countries provide help during illness, it is provided to different degrees and through different mechanisms in the countries observed here. The abundance of medical technology and services in the modern world is not fully available in some countries, not equally available within some countries, and equally and readily available in a few countries. The impact of health care on daily life operates by affecting older person's abilities, self-determination, living environments, and the extent to which informal care must be provided for themselves and for others.

The management of chronic conditions, however, perhaps the most significant aspect of health and aging, is not well addressed by the medical system in any of the societies considered. The chronic health problems, like cancer, arthritis, diabetes, paralysis, and other conditions, influence the daily lives of people. Frail elders constitute about 15%-20% of all older people in the industrialized countries (Neugarten, 1982). The various limits they endure could be modified by various types of medical help: rehabilitative treatment, health education to assist them in living well even with chronic problems, differential diagnosis to discern treatable conditions, research into the nature of diseases and discomforts that affect the aged, and prevention.

The mission of the National Institute on Aging in the United States is to differentiate normal aging from the disease states that all too frequently accompany aging. Living with chronic conditions is often considered a necessary by-product of growing old. As our forefathers suffered stoically with gout, toothlessness, and other pains of age, older people now are unnecessarily suffering from treatable and preventable conditions. According to T. Franklin Williams (personal communication), there are many physical decrements that are now known to be due to environment and illness but that were once thought to be part of normal aging.

In addition, modern societies have the capacity to produce illnesses and more needs to be done for children, young, and midlife adults in order to enhance good health in later life. For example, smoking is well known as a health hazard that may have its deleterious results in later life. Environmental pollutants, malnutrition or obesity, work-related risks, and other influences early in life produce a less-healthful later life. Prevention of health problems among adults is underdeveloped in the modern world and is not as well supported by policymakers or medical establishments as treatment and high-technology solutions.

Whether older people are healthy or not, whether they are dependent or interdependent, caring or cared for—all of these modify daily life. Each of these personal conditions is influenced by national context.

(3) Socialization and personal development. Neugarten (1982, p. 118) asserts:

> Competent older people seek meaningful ways to use their time. Some stay at work, some undertake second careers, some retire, and some seek self-fulfillment through education or various forms of leisure activities. Many are serving their communities in remunerated or non-remunerated ways. They represent a great pool of expertise and talent in the society, much of it underutilized.

While she offers this appealing image, she remains vague about the numbers and, therefore, cannot be refuted. Some do seek, but how many find? Many are serving, but most are not. Much of their talent, however that is defined, is underutilized; this is true of other age groups as well.

The vision of happy and helpful older people finding new and expanded paths to a high quality of life in later life is not reflected in the national reports provided here, and cannot be considered the modal experience in later life, though most older people are indeed competent. There was little evidence of new activities and opportunities for personal development in later life in the societies considered. Rather, most of the activities of midlife absorbed just a little more time for the older adults in each nation. The major time obligation of paid work was reduced. Given freedom from paid work, self-care, and obligatory activities like eating, meeting physiological needs and sleep take more time. Domestic work time increases, generally, and women remain highly involved in home-care tasks to benefit themselves and other household members. Helping others outside of the household is variable, with the highest levels documented in the United States and low levels in the Netherlands. But informal help is exchanged between older people and others. This is not a one-way dependency of old on young by any means. Whether helping a son to build a home, as in Hungary, or caring for grandchildren, as in Japan, or providing care to other older people, the older citizens in the modern societies engage in unpaid productivity. Compared to other uses of time, however, this form of activity is not a major portion of the day in any country.

Rather, the tendency in each of the countries was for older people to engage in more home-bound and passive leisure than younger counterparts. While home is a place that draws most of us for many hours a day, older people are more likely to be at home than people of younger ages. While television and other passive pursuits dominate the leisure time of all ages, the older people in each country devote more of their time to these activities. This passivity and home-boundness does not seem to conform to their wishes; rather, it represents a compromise with reality.

The style of life observed depends, in part, upon the cultural context present for all ages and the unique constraints of later life. Robinson (1977) has referred to the postindustrious society in his analysis of change over historical time in the ways people use daily time. Over the decades, an increasing amount of time has been devoted to television and other passive leisure and less time to family care and active leisure, according to his analysis. Other theorists have noticed the privatization that emerges in many modern societies (Brittan, 1977; Zaretsky, 1976). How then can older people escape the general patterns of activity in their context? The absence of paid work allows the restructuring of the daily life for an age stratum. But transformation of daily life for older people, or for any of us, requires cultural innovation. In none of the societies under consideration do we find evidence of cultural innovation to encompass the new stages of life that emerge out of this century's demographic revolution—the aging of populations.

In short, creating meaningful roles after work careers end is required because of the new life we have gained during the twentieth century. Older people may be the pioneers on the frontier of free time, but the settlement has just begun and the new social roles, expectations, and structures have not yet developed. If the labor forces of the world absorb fewer people, we may all look to the retired as role models as more of us are freed from paid labor. If, on the other hand, we continue to compete for scarce positions, we are going to want to be sure that the retired are satisfied with their lives and their livelihoods, lest they rejoin the competition for positions that pay and that provide, through their cultural value, a meaningful role.

Why is Neugarten's ideal so far from the daily lives of most older people? Cultural and societal constraints and the lack of social invention to match demographic successes offer powerful explanations. Economic resources, policy, environment, role structures, and norms differentially constrain the growing older population.

Far from a criticism of older individuals, this analysis indicates a critical lack in the modern societies. Where in the culture, where in the role structure, is the social innovation going to come from?

Economics are an often-ignored and more widespread source of limits on daily life. The evidence that older people do what they must to eke out a livelihood and don't do many things because of limited material resources is clear in many of the analyses presented in this book. These limits are set, in large part, by a network of policies that influence the fate of older people. Those in retirement, as well as the unemployed and disabled of any age, depend on a mixture of public and private resources. They must live within their limits and those limits are defined through political actions in large part. These political actions, in turn, are influenced by culture. In particular, the beliefs and attitudes about older people and about work, worthiness, and the role of the state in sustaining the society are central to the decisions made in the political arena. Some societies studied are more generous in social resources allocated to the public good, and within the public resource pool, more or less is allocated to the aged citizens.

Culture and economic resources operate together to define and delimit the life-styles of the elderly and especially of the old and unemployed. Policy is an intervening social construction that is influenced by cultural patterns as well as by political considerations. Life-style in later life is hardly the individualistic pattern of choices of activities in any given day. But some constraints do operate at the individual level. The constraints of age are illustrated by the drop in time devoted to many activities that occurs at age 75. While most people reaching old age are able and unrestricted in activities into their eighties, the prevalence of limiting health conditions increases dramatically during later life.

Daily Life in Later Life: A Multilevel Model

F. Stuart Chapin, Jr. (1974) provides a model useful for constructing an explanation of daily life in later life. Using his framework, we can construct a final summary of this volume. In Chapin's model, opportunities and propensities are central.

First, activity patterns of an aggregate are affected by individual propensities to engage in certain activities. These propensities are, in turn, affected by internal motivations and enjoyments as well as by social roles and relevant personal characteristics. The activities engaged in are either satisfying or not. Individuals change their motivations in response to the outcome of activities.

Second, the activity patterns of an aggregate are affected by the opportunities to act and interact. The availability of places, time, people, and circumstances as well as the lack of external barriers to participation affect the opportunities available. Chapin suggests that private and public sectors act to change opportunity structures for activity in response to actual activity patterns. Through organized activity, the environment and availability of facilities or circumstances to engage in activities can change.

Daily life in later life can be understood using this multilevel model. Propensities to engage in action and interaction are shaped by long-term socialization and current motivations and enjoyments. Personal characteristics and roles that influence propensities include health, work roles, age, gender, and marital status. Propensities are not clearly understood in social gerontology. Although we know how much people engage in certain activities, we need further study of what they would ideally choose to do and what the subjective process of activity selection entails.

On the other hand, it is clear from this volume that the analysis of opportunities has been central to explaining the nature of daily life of older people. The national context represents a complex set of opportunities to participate in social activities, affected by the schedules, practices, and facilities of the entire nation as well as the resource allocation, barriers, and circumstances established for older people in particular. There is no invisible hand creating the opportunity to engage in activities, rather the public and private sectors shape the community and circumstances in which people act. One theme of the volume is that older people, constrained by work and income transfer policies, are, therefore, more affected by other policy and private sector activities as well.

Theorists stress the importance of social change in modifying the opportunities for people to engage in activities (Chapin, 1974) and the socialization and allocation processes that prepare people to participate in activities (Riley et al., 1972). The need to understand the social structure as it affects aging is reinforced by extant theoretical frameworks as well as by the cross-national analyses presented here. This comparative analysis provides an initial view of activity patterns of older people in several modern nations, a basis for further research, and an invitation to consider alternative life-styles for the aged of the future.

Gerontology developed a unique comparative base of knowledge fairly early (e.g., Shanas et al., 1968; Cowgill and Holmes, 1972). Comparative inquiry continues to be valuable in the quest for understanding of aging and old age. According to Dieck (1985), cross-national research allows us to understand the nature of aging in different social environments, to transcend our own cultural biases about aging, to advance theories of social aging, and to provide practical information to policymakers. It is also, we would maintain, necessary for clear vision regarding the opportunities and constraints within the role structures of modern nations and for clearly defined action to enable older people to act and interact in ways that reflect their propensities, motivations, and abilities to participate in society fully.

This volume is only the beginning of the task of discovery: How do nations shape personal conditions for those in old age? Only continuing comparative inquiry into the cultures, structures, policies, and people of the contemporary societies can help us understand the likely life-styles for our futures. We can begin future efforts with a discovery produced by this volume. However important modernization is in shaping individual's lives, other national conditions operate to produce different ways of aging within the modernized world. We continue the search for the structures and processes that shape old age.

REFERENCES

Brittan, A. 1977. *The Privatized World.* London: Routledge & Kegan Paul.

Bytheway, W. R. 1980. "United Kingdom." Pp. 418-33 in *International Handbook on Aging,* edited by E. Palmore. Westport, CT: Greenwood.

Cantor, M. and V. Little. 1985. "Aging and Social Care." In *Handbook of Aging and the Social Sciences,* edited by R. Binstock and E. Shanas. 2nd ed. New York: Van Nostrand Reinhold.

Chapin, F. S., Jr. 1974. *Human Activity Patterns in the City.* New York: John Wiley.

Cowgill, D. O. 1986. *Aging Around the World.* Belmont, CA: Wadsworth.

————. and L. Holmes, eds. 1972. *Aging and Modernization.* New York: Appleton-Century-Crofts.

Dieck, M. 1985. "Cross-National Research in Gerontology: A Critical Review of Methodology, Theory and Results." Paper presented at the 13th International Congress of Gerontology, New York.

Kane, R. and R. Kane. 1976. *Longterm Care in Six Countries: Implications for the United States.* Washington, DC: John C. Fogarty International Center for Advanced Study in the Health Sciences.

Little, V. 1982. *Open Care for the Aging: Comparative International Approaches.* New York: Springer.

Maeda, D. 1980. "Japan." Pp. 253-70 in *International Handbook on Aging,* edited by E. Palmore. Westport, CT: Greenwood.

Neugarten, B. 1982. "Aging: Policy Issues for the Developed Countries of the World." Pp. 115-126 in *New Perspectives on Old Age: A Message to Decision Makers,* edited by H. Thomae and G. Maddox. New York: Springer.

Nusberg, C., with M. J. Gibson and S. Peace. 1984. *Innovative Aging Programs Abroad: Implications for the United States.* Westport, CT: Greenwood.

Olsen, L. 1982. *The Political Economy of Aging: The State, Private Power, and Social Welfare.* Irvington, NY: Columbia University Press.

Ricketts, J. M. 1986. "Worldwide Trends and Developments in Social Security, 1983-1985." *Social Security Bulletin* 49(4):5-11.

Riley, M. W., M. Johnson, and A. Foner. 1972. *Aging and Society: A Sociology of Age Stratification.* Vol. 3. New York: Russell Sage.

Robinson, J. 1977. *How Americans Use Time.* New York: Praeger.

Schorr, A. 1980. *"Thy Father and Thy Mother": A Second Look at Filial Responsibility and Family Policy.* Social Security Publication No. 13-11953. Washington, DC: Department of Health and Human Services.

Senate Special Committee on Aging. 1984. *Older Americans and the Federal Budget: Past, Present and Future.* Washington, DC: Government Printing Office.

Shanas, E., P. Townsend, D. Wedderburn, H. Friis, P. Milhoj, and J. Stehouwer. 1968. *Old People in Three Industrial Societies.* New York: Atherton.

Smyer, M. 1984. "Aging and Social Policy: Contrasting Western Europe and the United States." *Journal of Family Issues* 5:239-53.

U.S. Bureau of the Census. 1986. *World Population Sheet.* Washington, DC: Government Printing Office.

U.S. Department of Health and Human Services. 1984. *Social Security Programs Throughout the World: 1983.* Research Report No. 59. Washington, DC: Government Printing Office.

van Zonneveld, R. J. 1980. "The Netherlands." Pp. 278-309 in *International Handbook on Aging*, edited by E. Palmore. Westport, CT: Greenwood.
Villers Foundation. 1987. *The Other Side of Easy Street*. Washington, DC: Author.
Zaretsky, E. 1976. *Capitalism, the Family, and Personal Life*. New York: Harper & Row.

About the Contributors

Mark Abrams (Ph.D., London School of Economics) is Research Associate at the Institute of Gerontology, King's College, London University. He is currently writing a history of Britain's elderly population in the twentieth century. His recent publications include *People in Their Late Sixties: A Longitudinal Survey*; *Changes in the Life-styles of Elderly British People, 1959-1982*; *The Elderly Shopper: Behaviour, Constraints and Attitudes*; and his coedited *Social Change and Social Values in Modern Britain*.

Karen Altergott, Ph.D., is currently Assistant Professor of Family Studies at Purdue University, West Lafayette, IN 47907. She has been affiliated with the Midwest Council for Social Research on Aging, first as fellow, now as Associate Director, for 13 years. Her interests in comparative gerontology, social networks, family life, and time use have resulted in publications on marital companionship across the life course; interdependence of the aged, their families, and the state; and the structural position of the aged in society.

Lars Andersson is Researcher at the Psychosocial Environmental Medicine section of the Karolinska Institute in Stockholm. His doctoral dissertation was on aging and loneliness. His publications are on psychosocial aspects of health, retirement, and intervention to prevent loneliness.

Rudolf Andorka, who was born in 1931, worked first as a manual laborer. He received a degree in law in 1963 and his Ph.D. in sociological science in 1976. He worked from 1962 to 1984 in the Central Statistical Office, as the first Researcher in the Demographic Research Institute, as Statistician in the Department of Social Statistics, and as Head of the Division of Social Stratification. Since 1984, he has been Professor and

Head of the Department of Sociology at the Karl Marx University of Economics in Budapest. His research includes projects on the determinants of fertility in advanced societies, social mobility, time budgets, and deviant behavior.

Sheila J. Box is a graduate student at the University of Waterloo. She has interests in leisure and recreation across the life course.

L. Claessens studies sociology at the Catholic University of Nijmegen. Her specialization is sociology of the family and social welfare. Within this area, she pays special attention to gerontology and to methods of social research. In spring 1987, she finished her master's thesis, which is focused on a gerontological issue.

Stephen Duncan recently completed his doctorate in Family Studies at Purdue University. His dissertation is on never-married older men, and his recent publications are on family stress and intergenerational relations. He is now in the Department of Family and Child Development at Auburn University, Alabama.

C.P.M. Knipscheer completed his graduate studies at the University of Tilburg (the Netherlands). He recently joined the faculty at Vrije University in Amsterdam. Prior to that, he had a position at the Catholic University in Nijmegen. He has published on social networks of older people, family relationships in old age, and social support of impaired parents. In 1985-1986, he was a fellow of the Andrew Norman Institute for Advanced Studies in Gerontology and Geriatrics of the Andrus Gerontology Center at the University of Southern California.

K. Victor Ujimoto, Ph.D., is Professor of Sociology and Research Associate, Gerontology Research Center, University of Guelph, Guelph, Ontario, Canada. He has coedited, with Gordon Hirabayashi, the book *Visible Minorities and Multiculturalism: Asians in Canada*. He has published numerous articles on Japanese Canadians, multiculturalism, and aging ethnic minorities. At present, he is engaged in a national research project titled "Comparative Aspects of Aging Asian Canadians: Social Networks and Time Budgets."

Shuichi Wada is Associate Professor of Sociology at Waseda University, Tokyo, Japan. He is a sociologist who has studied the retirement process and social conditions for the adjustment to later life from the perspective of occupational career and social stratification. He coauthored *Retire-*

ment and Occupational Life in the Middle and Later Life Stages (in Japanese). His current research interests are in the sociological approach to later life, and the mathematical and statistical approach to social phenomena such as status inconsistency, social mobility, and mental health.

M.F.H.G. Wimmers graduated in clinical psychology in 1969. He has worked at the Department of Developmental Psychology and the Department of Social Gerontology. He received postgraduate training as a Rogerian therapist. Much of his educational and research activities are devoted to research methodology and clinical psychogerontology. He has published in national and international journals, is a member of diverse professional committees, and Chairman of the Social Gerontological Section of the Dutch Institute for Psychologists.

Jiri Zuzanek is Chairman of the Research Group on Leisure and Cultural Development, University of Waterloo, Canada. He has written a number of articles and books in the area of time budget and leisure studies, including *Work and Leisure in the Soviet Union: A Time-Budget Analysis* for Praeger Special Studies. He directed two studies of the uses of time among elderly Canadians in 1981 and in 1983. Recently, he published an article, "Being Alone Versus Being With People: Disengagement in the Daily Experience of Older Adults," in the *Journal of Gerontology* with R. Larsen and R. Mannell.

NOTES

NOTES

NOTES

NOTES